D1471356

Christopher Sinclair-Stevenson

Inglorious Rebellion

The Jacobite Risings of
1708, 1715 and 1719

Panther

Granada Publishing Limited
Published in 1973 by Panther Books Ltd
Park Street, St Albans, Herts

First published in Great Britain by
Hamish Hamilton 1971
Copyright © Christopher Sinclair-Stevenson 1971
Made and printed in Great Britain by
C. Nicholls & Company Ltd
The Philips Park Press, Manchester
Set in Intertype Times

For Dar

'Happy is the land that needs no heroes'

Brecht's
Life of Galileo

Contents

EPILOGUE
REBELLION 1745

LIST OF ILLUSTRATIONS

Acknowledgments

I would like to thank the following: the Duchess of Alba and Berwick for allowing me to see the many fascinating Jacobite relics in the Palacio de Liria, Madrid; the Marquess of Huntly for his hospitality and for piloting me through the countryside around Braemar; Sir Charles Petrie for his encouragement in historical territory which he knows so expertly; Mr. R. E. Hutchison, Keeper of the Scottish National Portrait Gallery, for his great patience in going over possible illustrations for this book; Mr. Patrick Leeson for his meticulously drawn maps; the staff of the London Library and the British Museum for their invaluable help; Mr. Hamish Hamilton and Mr. Roger Machell for reading the script of the book with such care; the Duke of Buccleuch and Queensberry, K.T., G.C.V.O., the Earl of Mar and Kellie, the National Portrait Gallery, the National Maritime Museum, Greenwich, the Scottish National Portrait Gallery, the Trustees of Blairs College, Aberdeen, the Edinburgh Central Public Library, and the Mansell Collection, for permission to reproduce the illustrations in this book; and, above all, my wife who has given me continual encouragement, sympathy and strength of purpose.

C. S.-S.

Introduction

BOOKS about the Jacobites are likely to fall into one or more of a number of inviting traps. There is, first and foremost, the danger of over-romanticising a dynasty and a cause which have never lacked their apologists. Not every Highland clansman was a brave, selfless warrior, *sans peur et sans reproche*, ready to sacrifice his life for the Stuarts – although Sir Walter Scott, pioneering a virtual crusade of the pen, and his less remarkable disciples would have us believe such a splendid travesty. Even so, a mysterious halo has settled round the heads of the Stuart kings and princes (although James I is conveniently excluded from this gallery of paragons). Charles I's obstinacy and his intense disloyalty to his friends vanish before the dignified courage he displayed on the bitter cold morning of his execution. Charles II's wit and humanity conceal his diplomatic double-dealing and immorality. James II's long years in exile and all the pathos surrounding them seem more noteworthy than his bigotry and indiscriminate whoring. And his grandson, Charles Edward, the Young Pretender, Bonnie Prince Charlie – depending on the individual's attitude – has sometimes appeared almost sanctified. But, like a painted plaster saint, his nature is concealed by art.

Not every Highlander was a hero, and not every Government supporter was a renegade traitor to his legitimate monarch. The annals of Jacobite hagiography have their remarkable and glamorous men – Montrose, Graham of Claverhouse, Berwick, Marischal – whom the Hanoverians cannot match; but adversity very often throws up outstanding figures who would not flourish against a background of orthodoxy.

The second danger is that of over-emphasising the importance of the various Jacobite rebellions, both to England and to the European political scene. They are hedged about with talk of "if" and "what might have happened", but the truth is that they affected hardly at all the European balance of power. No thrones toppled as a consequence, few politicians of real significance fell from office. Bolingbroke, it is true, was forced to flee the country, but he returned in due course. Oxford found himself in the Tower, but his days of supremacy were already at an end. Alberoni did indeed fall dramatically from his virtual dictatorship in Spain, but the failure of the 1719 enterprise contributed no more than a particle to his disgrace. Only in Scotland was any marked effect felt, and it could be argued that the recurrent Jacobite threat held back the progress of that country for a century and a half. Not everyone in London shared Dr. Johnson's profound contempt for all things Scottish, but it cannot be denied that the great mass of the English population at best ignored, and at worst violently mistrusted, that barbaric race continually fomenting trouble north of the Border. If the new spirit of the Union had been allowed to flourish, economic, political and agricultural development would have advanced rapidly. The Highland Clearances would not have taken place. Even that modern, fashionable upsurge of Scottish Nationalism would have been unnecessary. This is an "if" of major proportions, but it is still a valid hypothesis. James Stuart and his son Charles Edward, by their repeated attempts to regain the crown of a united Britain, ensured that that very unity would be nothing more than a geographical term. The dividing line had been erased from a map, but not from men's minds.

Finally, any writer who approaches the beginning of the eighteenth century must avoid judging those times by modern standards. By our reckoning they were cruel times, of horrifying public executions and murderous floggings, of religious intolerance and wholesale drunkenness, of superstition and bitter political satire. But it was also the age of Handel and Wren, of Defoe and Swift, of Addison and Pope. It should perhaps not surprise us that a lady of fashion could extract equal enjoyment from the spectacle of a man being drawn and quartered and from the mellifluous sounds of Handel's Water Music or one of his stately operas. There were, in any case, compassionate men, as well as bloodthirsty mobs. And any age can only be judged by its own criteria, not by those of hindsight or posterity.

An attempt has been made in this book to give a brief summary of half a century of Jacobitism; the narrative ceases deliberately at the very start of the '45, since that campaign has been analysed almost to excess. Much material has necessarily been omitted, and the intricacies of day-to-day politics have not always been dealt with as fully as they no doubt deserve. There are no startling revelations, forgotten manuscripts gathering the dust of centuries in obscure muniment rooms and locked chests do not contribute to the story. There is, in short, little or nothing for the delectation of the professional historian. It is hoped, though, that a pattern emerges, that some vestige of the atmosphere of those desperate years has been caught, that the sound of artillery and musket-fire and the skirl of the pipes and the groans of dying men come down over the centuries, that the dust has been momentarily swept away from old history. Inglorious rebellions the risings of 1708, 1715 and 1719 may have been, both in their execution and in their results, but the many incidental glories which they fashioned in ordinary men on both sides should be recorded.

A continual confusion to readers of books written during or about the first half of the eighteenth century is presented by the two alternative methods of dating then in operation. Until 1752 the English when in their own country always used the Old Style; after 1700 this was eleven days behind the New Style formulated in the Gregorian Calendar and in use throughout the Continent with the sole exception of Russia. Sometimes, however, it is impossible to be certain which style is being utilised, as diplomats abroad usually, but not invariably, kept to the New Style; soldiers fighting in Marlborough's campaigns also used the New Style; but sailors generally adhered to the Old Style. As will be seen, mistakes or disagreements can easily arise. And matters are not helped by the fact that before the Gregorian Calendar was finally adopted in this country, thus leading to violent riots by people demanding the return of their eleven days, the New Year was deemed to begin on March 25 and not on January 1, March 24 belonging to the old year and March 25 ushering in the new.

In this book, wherever possible, events in Britain are dated by the Old Style, and those abroad by the New.

Part One

The Seeds of Rebellion

Chapter One

Saint-Germain

Over the mansion and the domain brooded a constant
gloom, the effect, partly of bitter regrets and deferred
hopes, but chiefly of the abject superstition which had
taken complete possession of James's own mind, and
which was affected by all those who aspired to his
favour. His palace wore the aspect of a monastery.

MACAULAY's *History of England*

DURING the first days of September 1701, the heat wave
which had forced Louis XIV to remain indoors, until
the comparative cool of the late afternoon, gave way to
thunder and torrential rain. The Marquis de Dangeau,
that inveterate purveyor of insignificant scandal and one-
man court circular, found other topics besides the
weather on which to dilate, and he began to intersperse
his dutiful accounts of hunting expeditions, deaths and
military appointments with news from Holland and from
Saint-Germain. On Friday the 2nd, writing to Meudon,
he passed blandly on from some snippet of information
concerning the improved health of the Comte de Tessé's
son, to a report that William III, King of England since
his father-in-law's precipitate departure into exile thirteen years previously, was sinking rapidly. He had never

been strong, and the acute asthma from which he had suffered all his life appeared to be snapping the last ves-
tiges of resistance.

But Dangeau was premature; the French court's less
than pious hopes for the removal of the Dutch usurper
from the complex European scene were not to be satisfied
for a further six months. On the 3rd, however, the persistent diarist's entry, penned on his return to Versailles,
was more accurate: "King James is sinking; it is not
thought that he will recover; he is no longer in a fit condition to contemplate the journey to Fontainebleau ...
The king is dying like a saint, and the poor queen is in-
consolable." There was scant satisfaction to be gained
from Dangeau's piece of somewhat spicier gossip: that
William, obviously quaking at the thought of death, had
gone so far as to write under the guise of a simple country curé to Louis's personal physician, Fagon, in order
to consult him about possible remedies. He received short
shrift. Fagon was considered by Saint-Simon "an expert
surgeon, an excellent doctor", and even Madame, the
king's sister-in-law, who never hesitated to lampoon him
for his excessive ugliness, so far forgot her normal cen-
soriousness to grant that he was "really extremely clever
and tactful". In this case, however, tact was not noticeably apparent. The standards of the day were admittedly
low – contemporary accounts of diagnoses and surgery
chill the blood of the least squeamish – but Fagon seems
more than usually callous in his answer to the supposed
Dutch priest: he merely replied that the patient could do
nothing better than prepare himself for imminent death.
This long-distance diagnosis was inaccurate. But the doctors at Saint-Germain could not possibly escape the inevitable conclusion that James II of England and still
considered James VII of Scotland, the monarch in exile,
had only a few days to live.

The odour of sanctity which had impregnated the fab-
ric of Saint-Germain since the arrival of the Stuart court

at the climax of the Glorious Revolution certainly provided the ideal atmosphere for a royal death. Indeed a
sense of mourning had hung over the château for many
decades already, and Louis had perhaps shown rather
less than his customary sensitivity for the feelings of his
guests when presenting them with such a home. Unless
sheer forgetfulness or a touch of unkind malice had
played a part, he must have been aware that James's
mother, Henrietta Maria, had received at Saint-Germain
the news of her husband's execution in the courtyard of
Whitehall. It was not a lucky place for the Stuarts.
Charles II and his brother James, when still nominally
Duke of York, had experienced its doubtful pleasures in
their youth; so too had their paternal great-grandmother,
Mary Stuart, before the end of her brief marriage to the
boy-king François II and her return to Scotland.

The French monarchy, on the other hand, had always
had a fondness for Saint-Germain throughout its distinctly chequered existence, ever since Saint-Louis had
added a chapel to the original convent and twelfth-
century fortress. François I, seized with the Renaissance
building mania, was much struck with the fineness of the
site and decided to raze the mediaeval buildings and replace them on a much more grandiose scale fitting to his
personal ideas of royal splendour. Henri IV added the
Pavillon and a series of terraced gardens descending towards the Seine; and Louis XIII loved to retire there,
dabbling in music, painting and cookery, hunting, and
temporarily forgetting his homosexual inclinations in
such a passionate pursuit of the reluctant Mlle de La
Fayette that she was forced to enter a convent. Louis
XIV was born at Saint-Germain, and his father died
there. Then, for a short period, the château was deserted,
increasingly decaying and dilapidated, offering the most
meagre lodging to Henrietta Maria. When the Fronde,
the rebellion of the nobles, broke out like an elegant,
dangerous display of fireworks, the widowed Anne of

Austria, her court and the young Louis XIV were obliged to take refuge there and, according to Mme de Motteville, found it empty of beds, furniture, linen, servants or any necessaries. Much to their disgust, the courtiers had to sleep on straw, and the price of this bizarre precious commodity rose so sharply within a few hours that it exceeded the means of even the richest.

After the departure of Charles II, Louis, determined never to set foot in Paris again, established his court at Saint-Germain, not in Henri IV's Pavillon, which had become uninhabitable, but in the Vieux Château; and it was during this greatest and gayest period in its history that so much ingenuity and artifice were lavished on what had been raised to the status of a palace. The site was, of course, superb. Andrew Lang and his co-author Miss Shield describe it in reverential terms, coloured by a rosy romanticism for the Stuart cause: "The ancient hunting palace of the Valois kings, destined to be the seat of English royalty for a quarter of a century, stands upon a promontory made by a sweeping bend of the Seine, surrounded by a forest twenty-one miles in circumference – a bleak situation in spite of park and gay parterres. The noble terrace, a mile and a half long, commands a view over the plain of Paris, 'and all the dim rich city' towered and domed, including that distant glimpse of Saint-Denis,* which had so depressed Louis XIV, with its perpetual intimation of mortality as to drive him away to the splendid cheerfulness of his own new Versailles."

By the time that Lang was writing, the seventeenth-century aspect of Saint-Germain was virtually invisible. Edwin and Marion Sharpe Grew, also looking back in nostalgia, were shocked by the changes wrought by the two intervening centuries: "The Jacobite pilgrim of today, seeking to sentimentalise over the haunts of the last of the Stuarts, will meet with nothing but disappointment . . . In the two hundred years that have passed away since

*The French kings were buried in the church of Saint-Denis.

the Queen of England, worn out with fatigue and anxiety, alighted at the hospitable doors of the ancient Château of Saint-Germain-en-Laye, it has been so completely restored and renovated that the first sight of the brand new pink brick dispels any historical associations, and all images from the past that the imagination has conjured up fade into the light of common day." Even the interior was not sacred, and, according to the Grews, "further disillusionment" was in store for the latter-day Jacobite. He might hope to walk through the empty rooms and "people them in imagination with the faded liveries of the past", but "the uniformed custodian (all unwitting that the walls beneath which he is standing are weighted with august memories), puzzled but indulgent, waves him towards an open door beyond which he finds only neat galleries laden with Franco-Roman antiquities". The exclamation mark is implicit.

But nothing could alter the shape of the countryside. The situation might be bleak but the panorama stretching away to Paris was undeniably magnificent: "The broadly winding Seine was at their feet, and beyond the fertile spreading countryside, girdled with hills, sprinkled with villages and spires among its trees, broods distant Paris and the rising ground of Montmartre." It was the "noble terrace", alluded to by Lang, from which Paris could best be seen, and it was at the time of James's arrival in France and still is the chief remaining glory of Saint-Germain. It is also one of the best memorials to the genius of Le Nôtre, the greatest of Louis XIV's designers. His predecessors, the elder Barauderie and the Mollets, lacking his ability to conceive on the grand scale, simply pandered to current fashion and to the whims of Mlle de La Vallière, the young king's first influential mistress. She had romantic leanings and delighted to walk in the moonlight. To please her, terraces and hidden grottoes were created; and to accommodate the rather peurile fondness for practical jokes, these grottoes were fitted with elaborate surprise-waters which, at the touch of a lever, would drench the unsuspecting victim. La Vallière's successor, the much more formidable Mme de Montespan, had no time for such frivolities, preferring her creature comforts, and commissioned lavish plans for the redecoration of the château's interior. But none of these improvements was of great consequence, and it was not until Le Nôtre's tenure of office that the ambience of Saint-Germaine was radically altered.

He was presented with a series of daunting problems, the chief one being the presence of two châteaux in differing architectural styles; but he resolved each difficulty with consummate distinction. Commencing in 1668, he laid out two parterres, one so vast that it could only be seen end to end from the second-floor windows. Immensely striking it undoubtedly was, but the courtiers were less than complimentary, referring to the great stretches as Senegal in the summer and Siberia in the winter, because of the lack of trees to ward off the sun or the wind. But if the parterre in front of the new château was huge, it was nothing in comparison to the Grande Terrasse. As Helen Fox, Le Nôtre's biographer, says, "it was another of his great conquests over nature". Superbly proportioned, it runs parallel to the Seine for one and a half miles of straight avenue. The trees line the side away from the river, and separate divisions are laid out for carriages and for pedestrians. It is hardly surprising that the cost and the upkeep of these gigantically ambitious alterations should have proved such a strain on Louis's exchequer that he decided to spend infinitely vaster sums on the building of Versailles. The novelty of his new architectural plaything had worn off, he had become bored with the faint provincialism of the court, perhaps he was even influenced by that famous view of Saint-Denis. Saint-Simon, for one, greatly deprecated his king's decision and always compared the marshy, low-lying surroundings of Versailles highly unfavourably with the superior siting of Saint-Germain. But, to Louis, Versailles was synonymous with the prestige and glory of the French Crown, and Saint-Germain languished, untenanted.

This was the position until the arrival of the exiled Stuarts. And, after the first two bouts of enthusiasm and excitement, those who hoped for a return to some of the old atmosphere of the château were disappointed. James had greatly altered since his earlier days of flagrant infidelity – his more selective brother had commented acidly on the ugliness of his mistresses – and was now blessed or burdened with a saintly wife and a pack of priests. Almost everyone approved of the ex-queen, Mary of Modena, dignified and kindly; but both James and his religious advisers reaped contempt and often abuse. Mme de Sévigné considered that he possessed courage but "a common mind, and he recounts all that happened in England with an insensibility that makes him look a fool". Mme de La Fayette remarked that the more the French saw of the exiled Stuart the less they sympathised with him over the loss of his kingdom. And what seemed far more reprehensible – he was continually surrounded by Jesuits, and there was a rumour that he even belonged to the highly suspect Society.

There was certainly no doubt about his piety; the Archbishop of Rheims said sarcastically as he watched him coming away from church: "There is a very good man; he has given up three kingdoms for a mass." To the worldly French clergy compromise was more sensible than blind faith. Mme de La Fayette was shocked by this unarchiepiscopal criticism, but was not reluctant to relay any gossip to the detriment of James. "The appearance of the King of England," she noted, "has not at all impressed the Court, and still less his conversation." He stammered and lacked those social graces by which the French set so much store; failure to adapt to the strict ceremonial of the Court and at the same time to dazzle with wit and repartee was surely the cardinal sin. The honeymoon period was over hardly before it had begun. The initial outrage which the French felt over James's treatment at the hands of his rebellious, and Protestant, subjects, and above all over the monstrous behaviour by his daughter Mary, subsided rapidly and was replaced by a certain apprehension over the sums of money being lavished by Louis on the court at Saint-Germain.

The régime there was not, however, devised for the pleasure of the young or the unconventional. Hunting, the ritual exchange of visits between Versailles and Saint-Germain with all their attendant and irritatingly obligatory ceremonies, an occasional military review, plays of an improving nature at Saint-Cyr, and endless masses, confessions, fasts and ubiquitous devotion to God and His not always estimable flames of fire: these were the events in a dreary calendar. Life was a continual penance for past and future sins. Middleton, a Protestant among Catholics, called the court at Saint-Germain "the dreadfullest place in France next to the Bastille", and the acidulous Matthew Prior dismissed the inmates of this royal penitentiary as "a great many chaplains and servants below stairs".

But perhaps the most vivid description was given by Anthony Hamilton, one of the wittiest men of the age, in his preface to *Zeneyde*: "The Château has so little accommodation that with the exception of thirty or forty priests and Jesuits the rest of us have to find lodging outside. It is true that the view is enchanting, the works wonderful, and the air so exhilarating that one could make four meals a day, though we have not the wherewithal to provide half that amount, and we should really be better off in some marshy place, where our senses and appetites were subdued by being always enveloped in a thick fog. As for the men here, we hardly muster enough merit to furnish the Prince of Wales's household; for the rest, those whom example has not brought to play the hypocrite, they are thought little of here whatever their reputation elsewhere.

"Our occupations have all the air of being very serious and this is no place for those who do not either spend half the day in prayer, or pretend to do so. Common misfortune, which usually brings its victims together, seems only to have sown discord and bitterness among us; the friendship which we profess for one another is always simulated, the hatred and envy that we conceal is always sincere. Agreeable flirtation, even love-making is severely proscribed in this melancholy Court, though in the whole of Cupid's realm there is nought more beautiful, more dangerous, more inspiring than are to be found here."

It is a depressing indictment, creating an image of life as led under the puritanical Protectorate rather than by the Stuarts; Charles II would have been scandalised. The fact that there were a number of remarkably pretty girls at the Court compounded boredom with temptation. Hamilton wrote on another occasion: "The most difficult taste would be gratified among our ladies, in whose small circle beauty, charm, wit and wisdom shine in all their brilliancy"; and he referred, in a letter to the Duke of Berwick, to "the adorable troupe of nymphs at Saint-Germain". But even he was one day seized upon by a half-crazed old woman, for ever hoping to present a petition to the king, and escaped only by leaping over a wall with a considerable drop on the other side. And, in any case, the charms of the women were small compensation for the sheer monochromatic tedium of everyday life, the prevalence of the *faux dévots*, and the backbiting and jealousy among the courtiers.

This was the background against which the Prince of Wales, James Francis Edward, grew up. It was very far from being ideal. As Shield and Lang put it: "The atmosphere of hope deferred and bitter disappointment, of penances and austerities, must have oppressed a young spirit cabined in a body which from the first was so very frail. The keen bracing air of Saint-Germain, exposed as it stands to the bitter blasts that sweep the plains of Paris, was cruel to his weak lungs, and he was often brought by fever to the very gates of death." Always liable to fall ill at the most critical moment; possessing that fatal Stuart flaw of being congenitally incapable of choosing good advisers or generals; fastened on by the flock of priests as if he were a piece of royal carrion; with the knowledge that even his legitimacy and consequently his rank had been under suspicion ever since the rumours of a baby being smuggled into the queen's bed in a warming-pan had run through a London vehemently determined against a Catholic succession, the Prince of Wales from his first day on earth failed to command more than token obedience and minimal love. There were no fairy godparents at his christening, the Pope and the queen-mother Catherine of Braganza being poor substitutes. Modern psychologists would hint at traumas set up by the circumstances of his birth, his abrupt departure from England, the uncertainty of life at Saint-Germain, his father's doctrine of the divine right of kings conflicting so obviously against the will of the people. And they would no doubt be correct. James Francis Edward was a born loser.

And yet he had many more attractive characteristics than his father. Dangeau called him "a very pretty prince, who made himself much beloved". And there is a rather charming description of his behaviour when encountering a number of Scottish gentlemen deprived of their estates after Killiecrankie and forced into exile in France. He met them at the gates of Saint-Germain, commiserated with them, and gave them his purse containing the princely sum of twelve pistoles. He was six years old at the time.

His early life was controlled by the most rigid set of rules, laid down by James II on July 19, 1696, when his son was a mere eight years old. The choice of Governor

was an inauspicious start, the appointment going to the
Earl of Perth, a man almost universally disliked but
hated particularly in Scotland, where his arrogance had
not endeared him to his fellow peers or to the ordinary
people. Macky, during a series of acid pen-portraits of
the English and Scottish nobility drawn up for the edi-
fication of the Electress Sophia, dismisses Perth with
sharp effect: "He was always violent for the party he
espoused, and is passionately proud; tells a story very
prettily; is capricious, a thorough bigot, and hath been
in each religion, while he professed it." He was the last
man who should have been picked to govern the prince's
daily life during such a formative period, although in
fairness to Perth not even the most likeable and admirable man could have breathed much vigour into such a
dusty set of rules as he was presented with.

Drafted scrupulously and unequivocally in twenty-
eight paragraphs, they seem determined to exclude any
freedom or chance of individuality. The Governor or one
of the Under-Governors has to be constantly with the
boy, even when he is asleep at night or when he is at table
(James may here have been guarding against possible
chances of assassination). No one is allowed to talk pri-
vately to him, let alone whisper in his ear, and he can
accept no presents – "flowers, perfumes or sweet waters"
are considered especially pernicious. All his reading
material must be carefully vetted, and he can never be
allowed to play with more than a couple of other children at any one time, and then only at specific hours of
the day. He is not permitted to go out of doors unac-
companied or to dress and undress himself. Every
minute of his day is carefully allocated for some improving activity. He should rise at half past seven and in the
next hour and a half be dressed, complete his morning
prayers, pay his respects to his parents and, as an after-
thought, eat his breakfast. For the next three hours mass
and lessons dominate, after which thirty minutes at the

most can be given over to dancing-lessons or writing.
The afternoon is again devoted to lessons, although an
hour is provided for play. He is allowed to receive company at certain times, "but orders must be given not to
let in all sorts of people without distinction, and care
must be taken that those who are admitted may not talk
with the Prince too familiarly without observing that distance which ought to be kept". Finally, it comes as no
surprise that Sundays and Holy Days are exclusively the
province of the "Preceptor in Catechisme", and contain
nothing more than the "reading of good books, Christian
doctrine, and the like".

It is always unwise to judge long-past educational sys-
tems by modern or even nineteenth-century standards,
and many contemporaries would have considered the
rules conceived by James both benevolent and beneficial;
there is no mention of punishments, although these were
no doubt not absent, and the soul of the boy was catered
for with all-embracing fervour. One should also make
allowance for James's well-founded fears for the safety
of his son. France abounded with dubious adventurers
only too eager to sell their swords for a reasonable fee.
Saint-Germain was far from impregnable, and it would
be a simple matter for an assassin to approach the prince,
if he were quite alone. His life must be preserved at all
costs. He was an only son, and the clear successor to the
English throne when James, as he inevitably must, re-
gained it. He was a prince of the blood royal, and he was
also a valuable pawn in the game, potentially vital.

Yet there is a coldness, an exclusiveness, a lack of humanity about the twenty-eight sections which repels far
more than the rough-and-ready, often brutal educational
system then current at Eton or Winchester. It seems the
perfect preparation for a saint, or a prig, or a bigot, or a
combination of all three by no means separate vocations.
What it emphatically was not was a grounding for a
future king, no longer exiled, whose life is being moulded

with the express end in view of recapturing his patri-
mony. There is little provision for either strength of
character or compassion, the grasp of diplomacy or
charm of manners, the understanding of tactics and stra-
tegy, or the ability to profit by the mistakes of Stuart
predecessors, clear examples to all but the purblind.

It is, therefore, all the more strange that James Francis
Edward should have reached adulthood with as definite
a character as he did. Certainly he lacked the devious
diplomacy of James I, reprehensible but successful, the
curious magnetism of Charles I, the intense charm and
practicality of Charles II, and the single-mindedness of
his own father; but he also remained untainted by some
of the more pronounced Stuart failings, and many observers, at the time and with hindsight, have considered
with some measure of justification that he would have
made a very good king of the passive variety – provided
only that he did not choose his own advisers, and that he
became less inflexible on matters of religion. One traveller to Saint-Germain, writing in the October after the
death of James II, summed up the general feeling when
he reported that the royal family's "sorrows are allayed
by the hopefulness and good qualities of the young master. He charms everybody who sees him, and seems designed to be a useful man in his generation."

*

Seven months earlier, on March 4, James II was at mass
on the Friday in Lent in the chapel at Saint-Germain. He
was observed to be pale and patently unwell, and he
suddenly fell forward in a dead faint, just as the choris-
ters were singing an anthem set to the appropriate words:
'Remember, O Lord, what is come upon us; consider
and behold our reproach. Our inheritance is turned to
strangers, our house to aliens; the crown is fallen from
our head. Wherefore dost thou forget us for ever?''
His health had been bad for some time past. Matthew

Prior had noticed the deterioration in his usual pointed way: "I faced old James the other day at Saint-Cloud. *Vive Guillaume!* You never saw such a strange figure as the old bully is, lean, worn and rivelled." But his attack on March 4 was more serious, and a week later he had a seizure followed by haemorrhaging. Paralysis set in down his right side, but this promised to be only temporary. Louis XIV immediately sent Fagon to diagnose and treat, and it was decided that the thermal waters at Bourbon, so fashionable and curative that even marshals of France drank there before beginning a campaign, were the obvious solution. Financed through Louis's generosity, a sizeable part of the Saint-Germain court supplemented by the Marquis d'Urfé and the hunchback Fagon himself, set off for the centre of France, to what is now the *département* of Allier. The pace was leisurely and the journey frequently interrupted by civic receptions and religious demonstrations. At Chaillot, the royal couple's favourite retreat, the Superior observed the improvement in James's health; at Nevers there was a presentation of pears, and a royal inspection of nuns, lined up outside the cathedral by a zealous bishop. What had become almost a progress lasted fifteen days, four more than had been estimated.

Bourbon was both attractive and peaceful. "It had a ruined castle with red-roofed turrets shaped like witches' hats, mirrored in a lake, and a tiny grey church, very early, and a little terrace belonging to the Capuchin friars, on which the king could walk." James duly bathed and drank the waters, and his paralysed right arm was douched, but he refused to set aside the composition of his memoirs and continued to work on them with a feverish haste indicative of his own certainty that death was imminent. A faint improvement in his condition was chimerical. More haemorrhages occurred, and the journey back to Saint-Germain in the heat of one of the best summers on record was enlivened only by Mary of

Modena's optimism. She wrote on June 3: "Here we are within three days of Paris and all well, God be thanked. The king gains strength every day." But Lord Manchester, the English ambassador, was nearer the truth when he reported to London that "he is far from being well, and is very much broke of late, so that none think he can last long ... His senses and his memory are very much decayed, and I believe a few months will carry him off."

Five weeks after James's return to Saint-Germain, he suffered a second paralytic seizure, and on September 2 had yet another stroke while in his chapel. He could not last, and Madame, when she went to visit him, was shocked at his condition: "I found King James in a piteous state. His voice, it is true, was still as strong as usual, and he recognised people; but he looks very bad, and has a beard like a Capuchin. Last Sunday, after having received the sacraments, he summoned his children and household, gave them his blessing – after which he preached a long sermon to the Prince of Wales and the servants." Louis XIV also visited him, on three occasions, and it was on the last of these that the King of France took a step which was applauded emotionally at the time but later criticised for its lack of statesmanship. Speaking in front of the whole court and the servants, he launched into a speech to the dying man: "I am come, sir, to acquaint you, that whenever it shall please God to call your Majesty out of this world, I will take your family into my protection, and will treat your son the Prince of Wales in the same manner I have treated you, and acknowledge him as he then will be King of England."

It was a magnanimous gesture but it destroyed any hope of peace in Europe. As Saint-Simon commented: "No action of the King's would have done more to falsify his position or belie the promise solemnly given at the Peace of Ryswick to accept William of Orange as the English king ... The announcement touched King William at his most tender spot and all England with him, not to mention the Dutch. It demonstrated how little trust could be put in the treaty and made it easy for them to muster all the princes of the former alliance to break openly with France." Louis's chief minister, Torcy, had been firmly against such a recognition, and it was only an impassioned knight-errant's speech by the Grand Dauphin which had finally swayed the king.

The relations and the prelates descended on Saint-Germain. James's natural son by Arabella Churchill, the Duke of Berwick, was much impressed by his father's behaviour on bidding farewell to the queen for the last time: "He took leave of the queen with extraordinary firmness, and the tears of that disconsolate princess made no impression upon him, though he loved her tenderly." The Prince de Conti was there; so too was Gualterio, the Papal nuncio. In one of his last lucid moments, James sent for his son, reminded him of all Louis XIV's generosity, and impressed upon him that he should always rate spiritual matters over the temporal.

On the afternoon of September 16, he died. Mary of Modena told the Abbess of Chaillot: "Yes, we now have a great saint in Heaven." A French cynic thought otherwise: "Everyone granted him to be a saint, but they looked in vain for his aureole." Nevertheless, the official autopsy carried out on his body, passing on from more germane considerations of stomach ulcers, liquids on the brain, haemorrhages and the state of the heart, dilated on the saintliness of the king which was considered so great that, the moment his body was opened, bystanders hastened to dip their handkerchiefs in the blood, and the guards even made use of their cravats for this pious purpose. And, later, twenty-three instances of miraculous cures effected by contact with the royal coffin, including rheumatism, paralysis, canker, asthma, epilepsy and stomach-ache, were reported. The Bishop of Autun thought that his *"fistule lacrymale"* had been cured through the late king's intercession and wasted no time in informing the widowed queen, Louis XIV and Mme de Maintenon, all of whom were suitably impressed. Unfortunately the *fistule* promptly reappeared a few days later, and the bishop, covered in confusion and a new scepticism, departed speedily for the peace and quiet of his diocese.

Saint or no, James was mourned surprisingly deeply, and it should be remembered that he had many devoted friends and servants. One, John Caryll, a man of intelligence and discrimination, wrote the following character sketch, which does something to redress the balance, normally weighted heavily against perhaps the least attractive of the Stuart kings:

"He was something above the middle stature, well-shaped, very nervous and strong; his face was rather long, his complexion fair and his countenance engaging; his outward carriage was a little stiff and constrained, which made it not so gracious, as it was courteous and obliging. He was affable and easy of access, for he affected not formalitie ... and having something of a hesitation in his speech his discourse was not so gracious as it was judicious and solid ... He was a great lover of exercise, especially walking and hunting ... He was a kind husband, notwithstanding his infirmities during his youth, but especially in his later days, when he repair'd his former infidelities by a most tender affection, mixed with a respect and deference to the incomparable merit and virtue of the Queen."

The portrait may be over-kind, as memorial eulogies are inclined to be, but at least here is the man behind the rather sad, rather dreary automaton of the last years at Saint-Germain. And it certainly cannot be disputed that he awoke feelings of great devotion and love in Mary of Modena, who was prepared to forgive him what Caryll so euphemistically termed his "infirmities during his youth". She was stricken with grief at his death and withdrew immediately to the spiritual comfort of Chaillot, where she remained for three days. By her return, the body of James II had been divided, according to the singularly repellent custom of the time, part of his entrails going to the church at Saint-Germain and part being forwarded to the English College at Saint-Omer; his heart to Chaillot; the "brains and fleshy part of the head" to the Scotch College in Paris; and his body, until it could eventually be interred in Henry VIII's chapel at Westminster Abbey, to the church of the English Benedictines in the Rue Faubourg Saint-Jacques in Paris.

There is a curious postscript to the burial of James. During the French Revolution, virtually all traces of his remains vanished in the general holocaust of church-burning. George IV, however, with his mania for anything Scottish and for the Stuarts in particular, pressed on with enquiries and excavations, besides commissioning Canova to design a monument to the Stuart family in the Vatican. The excavations in the church at Saint-Germain bore fruit when three lead boxes were uncovered, the first of which bore the words: "Here lies a part of the body and the noble portions", with the royal arms superimposed; the other two boxes were thought to contain parts of the bodies of Mary of Modena and of Princess Mary Louise, James's daughter and his "consolation". The relics were solemnly transferred to the crypt of Sainte-Anne on September 12, 1824; and, according to the *Quotidienne*, "the gentlemen of the body-guard rendered to the remains of James II the honours due to royalty". But the search for the body itself produced a still stranger result, in the form of a deposition sworn by a certain Fitzsimmons, an eighty-year-old Irishman:

"I was a prisoner in Paris in the convent of the English Benedictines in the Rue Faubourg Saint-Jacques, at the time of the Revolution, with the Prior of the Benedictines, Mr. Parker. It was 1793 or 1794. In one of the chapels of the church, the body of King James had been laid, in expectation of one day being transported to Westminster Abbey. He had never been buried, and was placed in a wooden coffin enclosed in a lead one, the latter in a third one made of wood and covered in black velvet. The sans-culottes broke open the coffins so as to remove the lead and make bullets from it. The body lay exposed the whole day. Tied up with bandages, he resembled a mummy. When the sans-culottes lifted it, it gave off a strong smell of vinegar and camphor, having been well embalmed. The state of preservation was perfect, the hands and finger-nails very fine. I moved and bent each finger. I have never seen such fine teeth. A young lady, like me a prisoner, desirous of possessing one, I attempted to pull it out, but I could not succeed, they were so firm. The feet also were very fine. The face and the cheeks had not altered at all. I attempted to make the eyes roll, but the pupils were firm beneath my finger.

"The French and English prisoners, desirous of seeing the body, gave money to the sans-culottes; these said that James had been a good sans-culotte and that they were going to place him in a pit in the public cemetery like the other sans-culottes. Thus the body was carried off; where was it thrown? I do not know. King George [IV] has done everything to find out, but his researches have proved fruitless. A wax mask very similar to the King's face was hanging on one of the walls in the chapel."

It is ironic to think that such a perfervid protector of the divine right of kings could be transformed so unexpectedly into a sans-culotte. No one deserved more to turn in his grave.

*

James Francis Edward was proclaimed without delay after his father's death. His titles of James III, King of England, Scotland, France (the old Plantaganet claims died hard and appear to have been overlooked by Louis), and Ireland, by the Grace of God, Defender of the Faith,

were read to a stirring background of trumpets at the
gates of Saint-Germain and elsewhere in the town by
James Terry, herald-at-arms of the kingdom of Ireland;
and the Pope and the King of Spain immediately recognised him.

But the young king had no kingdom beyond the walls
of Saint-Germain, and had to content himself with a
queen-regent, a council of variable competence, his
father's will, and his final instructions to his son. These
last were exceedingly detailed and generally beyond reproach. Besides the inevitable entreaties to serve God,
uphold the Catholic religion, and to govern his people
kindly and paternally, they dilate more surprisingly on
the need to avoid war and to establish new laws of
conscience; to balance the exchequer and to root out op-
pressive ministers; to study diligently the British Constitution, and "above all things, endeavour to be and to
remain superior at sea without which England cannot be
secure [the navy was one of James II's few genuine and
useful interests and, even in exile, he could audibly admire the bravery of the English sailors at the battle off
Cape La Hogue, much to the astonishment of French
onlookers]".

A separate section of these instructions is devoted to
Scotland, and here James shows considerable perception
and foresight:

"Take all care to let no alterations be made in the Government of that Kingdom, they will stand by the Crown,
and the Crown must stand by them, for though there has
been Rebellions and Revolutions, as well as in other
Countries, the body of the Nobility and Gentry, and the
Gentry of the Commons are very Loyal and Monarchical
especially the Commons by North Forth and all the Highlanders, except the Campbells; the rest of Scotland being
the only place where there are numbers amongst the
Commons of ridged Presbyterians, and Enthusiasts and
field Conventiclers, the first of which are the most dan-

gerous, and will be always bitter enemies of the Monarchy and so ought to be observed, and kept out of any
share of the Government; the others, though now and
then troublesome, are less to be feared, hardly a Gentleman amongst them, and of so extravagant principles as
they can never agree amongst themselves ... This the
true interest of the Crown to keep that Kingdom separate
from England, and to be governed by their own Laws
and constitutions. Look on any who should propose
though under some specious pretence, the uniting of
the two Kingdoms, to be weak men, bribed by some private concern, or as enemies to the Monarchy."

Needless to say, such wise advice on matters of statecraft is intermingled with more moral concerns: his son
must beware in particular of women. James spoke with
"a dear-bought experience", but on one point he had no
fears, the temptations of the bottle. "It was not necessary to enlarge upon that point, since few princes among
the civilised nations are addicted to so foul a vice."

Mary of Modena, left to implement these instructions,
was to prove a by no means dictatorial regent, allowing
her children their own confessors and doctors when they
were old enough, and generally relaxing the stiff rules
insisted upon by her late husband. The advisers who surrounded the new king were, however, a less satisfactory
collection. Perth, now elevated to a dukedom, had not
changed for the better, and his brother, the Earl of Melfort, tall, dark, thin and stooping, was equally unreliable.
Macky said that "he is very ambitious, hath abundance
of lively sense, will stick at nothing to gain his end ...
nor is he much to be trusted himself, but where his am-
bition can be fed".

Fortunately, the queen-regent relied far more heavily
on Secretary Caryll and on Lord Middleton. Both had
their detractors, Ailesbury dismissing Caryll as "an old
bigot"; and Saint-Simon suspecting Middleton of all
manner of villainies, calling him "fiendishly spiteful and

scheming", "thoroughly worthless", and "a professed
and practising atheist". Caryll may have been pompous
and reactionary, but he was also loyal and hard-working.
And Middleton appears as possibly the most admirable
man in the entire court at Saint-Germain. Continually
loyal to James II, both before the rebellion and in exile,
he nevertheless greatly deprecated his royal master's bigotry in religous affairs and his senseless interference in
politics, and was not afraid to say so. A lover of the
classics and of Samuel Butler's *Hudibras*, witty and excellent company, as even Saint-Simon admitted, a moderate in all things years before Harley was to bring the
golden means of statecraft to perfection, Middleton
stands out with the intensity of one brilliant ray of sun-
light through banked thunder-clouds. According to
Macky, who dubbed him "one of the pleasantest companions in the world", "he had so mean an opinion of
converts, that he used to say, 'A new light never comes
into the house, but by a crack in the tiling'." Even so,
having remained a Protestant when such behaviour was
considered not only rare and perverse but deserving
anathema, he suddenly became a convert early in 1702,
after dreaming that he had seen James II, who had so
often urged him to change his religion, standing at the
foot of his bed. Inevitably, this *volte-face* was attacked
as vociferously as his former Protestantism and slan-
dered as merely a political ruse.

Shocked and exhausted by the continual bickering and
recrimination, he offered his resignation to Mary of
Modena with these words: "Converts are loaded with
all reproach, which wit, malice, indignation, and zeal
can devise ... it would be a mighty prejudice to the
Queen to have one about her so universally obnoxious.
I have heard the Queen say that the King, her son, would
do anything he could in conscience to please his Protestant subjects ... and here is now an opportunity of giving
a cheap proof of this by dismissing an useless Servant."

Mary, greatly to her credit, refused to accept this offer of resignation, and Middleton remained in office, no doubt much to the fury of Saint-Simon and his other enemies.

There was one further influence of the utmost importance at court, the Duke of Berwick. One of the greatest soldiers of his day, this illegitimate son of James II by a sister of the Duke of Marlborough, was almost unanimously liked, indeed loved, for his qualities of bravery, loyalty and distinction. Bolingbroke, no easy admirer of other men, wrote this eulogy, which though exaggerated offers an inkling into a fine character: "his faults were so few, so slight, so fugitive, as to be almost invisible and not worth mentioning. Like his royal grandfather he was the most docile of sons, the best of fathers, the most tender of husbands, the most sincere of friends, the most considerate of masters, the most faithful of subjects, the best great man who ever existed." He overshadowed his half-brother and he should have been a king. Not for the first time, the mixture of royal and less exalted blood produced something of a phenomenon.

These were the men of power and stature at the beginning of the new reign at Saint-Germain. In Whitehall, the news of James's death and the recognition of his son by Louis XIV was received with mixed feelings of decently muted joy and unabashed outrage. William III, suffering increasingly from his asthmatic attacks, had been at Loo in Holland when Lord Manchester arrived from Versailles to announce the bare facts. According to Saint-Simon, "he flushed scarlet and pulled down his hat over his eyes, for he could not control his emotions". Without any doubt, and quite justifiably, he was very angry indeed. He ordered Poussin, the French chargé d'affaires, to be recalled from London, and set about forming an offensive and defensive alliance consisting of England, Holland and the Empire.

Back in London, he hypocritically donned purple

mourning for his father-in-law, ordered five of his
coaches into black, and displayed all the outer trappings
of filial sorrow. In the meantime, he not only organised
the publication of yet another pamphlet which endeavoured to disprove James Francis Edward's legitimacy
in contradiction to innumerable eyewitnesses; but also,
and far more significantly, drew up a bill of attainder,
declaring James guilty of high treason and liable to execution without trial in the event of his falling into the
hands of any succeeding reigning sovereign.

The bill passed through the Lords easily enough, but
the Commons were more reluctant and delayed it with
various suggestions for modification. But William was
impatient, and Parliament was not prepared to take a
stand against his authority. They were just in time. "On
February 20," Macaulay says, "William was ambling on
a favourite horse, named Sorrel, through the park of
Hampton Court. He urged his horse to strike into a gal-
lop just at the spot where a mole had been at work. Sorrel
stumbled on the mole-hill, and went down on his knees.
The King fell off, and broke his collar-bone. The bone
was set; and he returned to Kensington in his coach. The
jolting of the rough roads of that time made it necessary
to reduce the fracture again. To a young and vigorous
man, such an accident would have been a trifle. But the
frame of William was not in a condition to bear even the
slightest shock." He might have recovered, but after falling asleep before an open window at Kensington Palace
he contracted pneumonia, and his doctors were agreed
that he only had hours to live.

Before his death, however, William sent a message to
the Commons, expressing his desire to see the two kingdoms of England and Scotland united by Act of Parliament. He was barely able to give the royal assent to the
Abjuration Bill, a facsimile of his signature being affixed
to the document, for on March 8 he died. England and
Scotland were still divided.

Chapter Two

The Union

A Day to be forgot in Scotland, a day in which the
Scots were stripped of what their Predecessors had
gallantly maintained for many Hundred Years.

LOCKHART'S *Memoirs*

RELATIONS between England and Scotland have probably never been more strained than in the years preceding
the ratification of the Act of Union. The lack of understanding and indeed the refusal to attempt such an understanding are extraordinary to contemplate even when the
long history of mutual enmity is taken into account. It
is conceivable that the Scots have sharper memories than
the English; certainly thoughts of Flodden, humiliation
at the hands of Cromwell at Dunbar and Worcester, and
the collapse of the first Jacobite insurrection in 1689
after Graham of Claverhouse's death at the moment of
victory in the Pass of Killiecrankie festered. But then the
English had no love for their northern so-called breth-
ren. They remembered the freebooting raids over the
border in the sixteenth century, and the constant threats
offered by the existence of Mary Stuart. They recalled
the highly equivocal behaviour of the Scots during the

Civil War and the Protectorate. They viewed them with a mixture of derision and dislike.

William III's attitude to his northern subjects had been uncompromising: a series of strong forts, strung across the country and presenting a psychological and very real threat to the existence of the clans; red-coated soldiers with no love for an apparently primitive and evidently arctic region; and government by Whitehall and, worse, by Edinburgh. The massacre of the Macdonalds by the Campbells at Glencoe, genocide in miniature, for which William must shoulder a major part of the responsibility, was the system at its most brutal and horrifying. But the Darien Scheme was undoubtedly the ultimate catastrophe, in economic and spiritual terms.

Following an appalling succession of bad harvests, any project which combined the chance of enrichment with patriotism was bound to be popular, and William Paterson's scheme for a "Company for trading with Africa and the Indies" was inundated with money. It seemed as if every man in the country, from the Duke of Hamilton to the least exalted Edinburgh citizen, had invested a few pounds in the new colony of the Isthmus of Darien designed to sit conveniently at the narrowest point between the Atlantic and the Pacific, and to command the trade of both. On paper the site was admirable; in reality none more unsuitable could have been chosen. Two successive expeditions set out, together with a number of relief ships, but the majority of these were sunk in the Caribbean. Even those which reached their destination faced the most appalling odds. The Darien territory belonged to Spain, who was hardly likely to look with approval on such an encroachment. And, to make matters worse, the country was terribly disease-ridden. The wretched settlers had no answer to the ubiquitous mosquito, and those who did not succumb to malaria and the other tropical diseases died on the blades of Spanish swords. There were few survivors of the "noble undertaking". The English traders, who had bitterly opposed the scheme, were the sole gainers. In Scotland, there were only mourners, and debtors, and men eager for revenge.

Curiously, some good would emerge from the tragedy, as it became increasingly obvious to the few enlightened north of the border that either total separation or the total union of the two countries were the only solutions, with the majority opinion favouring the former. But these men were rare, and the general consensus turned its face resolutely away from England.

Not that the English had any desire to be forced into a closer association with their neighbours. Urged on by the High Tories, insistent on maintaining the separation of countries and parliaments, the London pamphleteers kept up a stream of vituperation against the barbarities of the Scots. This climate of opinion owed much to sheer ignorance. Not more than a dozen people visited Scotland for pleasure in a year, and trade was practically nonexistent. Certainly, the conditions likely to be encountered in the inns were revolting, in spite of the abundance of fine French wines denied to the English in their own homes; and, in the years before the Romantic Revival, the beauties of the countryside went quite unappreciated. The Highlands, in particular, appalled the English traveller and were denounced as "frightful" and "most of all disagreeable when the heath is in bloom". And the country-people reaped their share of slander. One distinctly biased observer called them "proverbially clownish . . . their women ugly, stupid, immodest, etc."; and another declared that they were "proud, arrogant, vainglorious, boasters, bloody, barbarous and inhuman butchers. Couzenance and theft is in perfection among them."

The Scots, very naturally, retaliated with such inspired efforts of versification as *A Pill for Pork-eaters, or a Scots lancet for an English swelling*:

For England, insolent and proud like hell,
Whose saucie boldness nought but blows can quell,
... let another Bannockburn redress
Too long endured affront and grievances.

But what the lampoonists and diarists refused to contemplate, the politicians could no longer avoid. The
great nobles ranged themselves according to future expectations and present conditions, while it was left to
such out-of-the-ordinary men as Andrew Fletcher of
Saltoun, "full of fire, with a stern, sour look", to speak
for Scotland. The man entrusted with the unenviable task
of promoting Anglo-Scottish co-operation was the Duke
of Queensberry, suave and devious but with a far more
determined side to his character than his enemies gave
him credit for. Lockhart of Carnwath, a fervent patriot,
disliked him heartily, recording that he had been the first
Scotsman "that deserted over to the Prince of Orange,
and from thence acquired the epithet (amongst honest
men) of 'Proto-rebel'". Sir John Clerk was more charitable in his assessment: "His Grace was a compleat cour-
tier, and partly by art, and partly by nature, he had
brought himself into a habite of saying very obledging
things to everybody. I knew his character, and therefore
was not much elated by his promises. However, I found
afterwards that there was nothing he had promised to do
but what he made good."

But it was the Duke of Hamilton who hated him most
avidly, and for the best reasons. Perhaps the most crucial
personality of his era, semi-royal and himself a secret
claimant to the throne, Hamilton was firmly opposed to
William III, his sister-in-law and successor Anne, and
their servant and Commissioner Queensberry. He was
far from being a statesman to admire, yet Lockhart called
him "a great and extraordinary man", and his contemporaries were in general agreement in this verdict.
According to Macky, he was "of middle stature, well-
made, of a black, coarse complexion, a brisk look". He

was an incisive debater and "had so nervous, majestick, and pathetick a method of speaking, and applying what he spoke, that it was always valued and regarded". Haughty and bantering he could certainly be, however, and even Lockhart admitted that "his greatest failing lay in his being too selfish and revengeful, which he carried along with him in all his designs". Hamilton and Queensberry had been in bitter conflict over the Darien Scheme, and they were not likely to sink their differences when such an immensely more vital concern as union between England and Scotland was mooted.

These were the two main opponents as the Scottish Parliament met on June 9, 1702, in the first of a protracted series of verbal contests which were to last nearly five years and were to be concerned with what Daniel Defoe very properly dubbed "the greatest and nicest concern" of the age. But there was one further statesman who was to perform an even more important rôle and who stands out by the unusual reasonableness of his behaviour. The Earl of Seafield, who succeeded Marchmont as Lord Chancellor, was the perfect civil servant of his day and was loaded with opprobrium for such outlandish conduct. Few people could understand a man who could be so devoid of strong feelings that he was prepared to serve a succession of totally disparate masters, and serve them efficiently. Rarely out of office, however the current administration might alter its policies, he was the go-between *par excellence;* many of his countrymen denounced him as a traitor to Scotland, but he was never content to pay lip-service to the English ministers and could press his point of view unswervingly. Macky, as always incapable of avoiding the sting in the tail, described him as "very beautiful in his person, with a graceful behaviour, a smiling countenance, and a soft tongue"; and even Lockhart, who despised his political pirouettes, admitted that he was "finely accomplished, a learned lawyer, a just judge: courteous and good-

natured". Without the moderation of Seafield, it is safe
to say that the Act of Union would have taken far longer
to come into being, and might indeed never have been
ratified in its final form.

Without any doubt at all, Seafield and Queensberry
were faced with daunting problems. The Scottish Parliament was in no mood to be cajoled with sweet words,
and Hume of Crossrig vividly described how "we were
often in the form of a Polish diet with our swords in our
hands, or at least our hands at our swords". They proceeded to discuss the Act of Security, which set out to
establish England's right to impose a successor to the
Scottish Crown. The Act indeed passed through the Estates in spite of the desertion of Cromarty, the Secretary
of State, Atholl and even Seafield from the side of
Queensberry; but Queen Anne's Commissioner refused
to give the Royal Assent, as many of the original clauses
had been modified. In the midst of this constitutional
crisis the scandal of what came to be known as the Scots
Plot broke.

Simon Fraser of Lovat was a peculiarly surreptitious
visitor from France in the month of August 1703, but
there was nothing surreptitious about his words of warning to the embattled Queensberry. What he outlined concerned clear treason: a plot was being hatched under
the chief aegis of Atholl, with the object of organising
a rising of the Highland clans in favour of James Francis
Edward. Fraser was an out-and-out rogue, a charlatan,
a maverick of Jacobite intrigues. Hogarth caught him
for posterity in the superb, grotesque caricature which he
drew before Lord Lovat, as he styled himself, walked to
meet the executioner on Tower Hill in the final dead moments of the '45. There he sits, almost sprawls, obscene,
gross, faintly satanic, still bursting with life, awaiting the
axe with cynical amusement, an intemperate toad immor-
talised on the engraver's stone.

In his youth, he had not acquired those features which

demanded Hogarth's attention. But the air of conspiracy shrouded him from an early age. Time and time again, he appeared to flit briefly through the conspiracy and counter-plot which enveloped the Jacobite cause in the first half of the eighteenth century, managing, like an inefficient chameleon, to end up almost invariably on the wrong side. His returns to his native land were always clandestine, always cloaked and daggered, for the authorities regarded him with more than suspicion. He had been forced to flee from Scotland after he had, somewhat precipitately, proclaimed James Francis Edward at Inverness. But this was perhaps the least of his crimes. The affair of the Dowager Lady Lovat was too scandalous to escape the notice of statesmen not over-nice in their attitude towards sexual peccadilloes; and it touched one particular grandee who was emphatically not prepared to forgive and forget.

Simon Fraser's claim to the Lovat barony was never more than exceedingly dubious, and his method of, literally, consummating it was ingenious if bizarre. He thought – and the plan seemed beautifully simple – that if he married the Dowager, he would be in a position to control also her daughter, heiress to the Fraser lands and to the Lovat barony. Unfortunately, he forgot that old Lady Lovat happened to be the sister of Lord Tullibardine, High Commissioner for Scotland at the time, and later to become first Marquis and subsequently Duke of Atholl. Fraser's means of persuasion owed nothing to the courtesy and long-winded delicacy favoured in France; abduction and rape were more in his line – they were, after all, speedier and more effective. Tullibardine disagreed, and letters of fire and sword were promptly issued. Simon Fraser was lucky to escape to the Continent with his head intact. His stupid lapse of memory had made him a common outlaw, but he was not to forget that it was Atholl who had virtually caused his enforced exile at the court of Saint-Germain.

He had been greeted with some enthusiasm; his version of recent events no doubt was a trifle bowdlerized. Now he reappeared in Edinburgh, and later in London, with a story which implicated Atholl to the highest degree. Queensberry was no fool, and he was at first deeply suspicious of the tale which Simon Fraser unravelled in the presence of Lord Leven with such a wealth of circumstantial evidence and innuendo, and which Leven duly forwarded to Edinburgh. Atholl, Hamilton, Seafield, Cromarty, so many men of influence seemed to be involved. Queensberry was on the horns of a dilemma. Was it simply a matter of revenge? Was it a subtle Jacobite plot to bring about the Commissioner's downfall? Or could there be some truth in the accusations? The evidence was very thin taken in isolation and uncorroborated, but Queensberry decided to wait no longer. He was well aware that the tide of Jacobite enthusiasm was daily swelling, and that the pathetically small army and naval contingents based in and around Scotland would be quite inadequate to cope with any rebellion. So, he did not linger on, hoping for some piece of conclusive intelligence, but instead rashly informed Lord Nottingham, the Secretary of State.

Whitehall was only too ready to act on the merest whisper of Scottish treason. An enquiry was instigated by the House of Lords and its findings infuriated the Scottish Parliament, who were not prepared to tolerate such foreign meddling and insolence. Atholl presented a personal memorial to Queen Anne in full Council, defending himself successfully and taking the classic line of accusing his accuser, challenging Queensberry to explain his own relationship with Fraser. The latter, as usual escaping arrest by the skin of his teeth, had sailed for Holland on November 16. Much to his chagrin, on his return to Saint-Germain he was immediately taken into custody on the orders of Lord Middleton. He eventually managed to escape from his prison, before re-

emerging in an unexpected guise during the '15. The
uproar duly died down. The chief loser was Queensberry
himself. Any popularity he had possessed vanished, as
his opponents and erstwhile supporters formed an un-
beatable alliance against him. In March 1704 he resigned,
and the New Party took office. It was led by Tweeddale,
Roxburgh and Secretary James Johnstone. They were
light-weight men with light-weight policies and ideals,
and even the presence of Seafield in what came to be
known contemptuously as the Squadrone Volante could
not disguise the fact that these were not the statesmen to
steer Scotland towards Union. The case of Captain
Green demonstrated this with vicious clarity.

It was in July that Captain Thomas Green, the twenty-
six-year-old captain of the English trading vessel the
Worcester, put into Leith harbour. The North Sea was
a notorious hunting ground for French privateers out of
Dunkirk, and Green prepared to wait for a proper convoy on its way south rather than brave the open sea by
himself. It was an ill-fated decision. Relations between
England and Scotland were now at rock bottom, and
Green must have been aware of this. What he could not
have realised was that the atmosphere had been still
further exacerbated by the seizing, earlier in the year,
of a ship acting for the disastrous Darien Company.
The English East India Company, which had never forgiven the Scots for their attempt at breaking a virtual
trading monopoly, had impounded the *Annandale*; and
the mere thought of an English merchant or trading ship
to the Scots was like the quick fuse to a barrel of gunpowder. It was Captain Green who, in all innocence,
found himself strapped to the barrel.

Roderick Mackenzie, Secretary of the Darien Company and acting with all the force of revenge and patriotic bigotry, promptly seized the *Worcester*, and at
Burntisland she stayed. At this stage in the affair, there
seemed to be no indication of bloodshed, and the crew

of the *Worcester* loitered in Edinburgh and Leith in complete freedom. But this did not satisfy Mackenzie, and he
saw a heaven-sent opportunity to further his campaign
of vengeance when a rumour concerning the *Worcester*'s
recent activities began to spread through the harbour
bothies and brothels. It was the *Worcester*, so the news
spread, which had attacked and carried off the *Speedy
Return*, a Scottish ship which had in reality been captured by a pirate called John Bowen off Madagascar and
burned on the Malabar coast; ironically, members of the
Speedy Return's crew were already back in England as
the witch-hunt commenced. Green and his men were arrested and, after a mockery of a trial based wholly on
perjured and contradictory evidence, condemned to be
hanged on Leith sands, as was the custom for all executions relating to crimes at sea. They would be disposed
of in three batches over the course of three weeks.

The Edinburgh crowd was jubilant. Not surprisingly,
however, there was an outburst of rage in England. The
Duke of Argyle, Queen Anne's new Commissioner for
Scotland, was determined not only to avoid a tragic mis-
carriage of justice but also to oust the incompetents of
the Squadrone Volante and replace them with himself
and Queensberry. The Squadrone itself seemed incapable
of exertion. Secretary Johnstone, writing from London,
complained feebly that "this business of Green is the
devil and all. It has spoiled all business"; and Baillie of
Jerviswood warned that if "the Queen shall grant them
remissions, it will spoil the business of Parliament, and I
am afraid will so exasperate the nation as may render it
difficult for them to join with England on any terms
whatever".

Scotland was indeed exasperated by the idea that
London could order a reprieve. Seafield, much to his
credit, was far from convinced of Green's guilt and summoned a meeting of the Privy Council for April 10, the
day before the first executions which had already been

postponed a week. Only approximately half the Council bothered, or dared, to attend. Tweeddale suddenly had urgent matters to deal with on his estates. Roxburgh was suffering from a sprained ankle which would not even allow him to walk downstairs. The Lord Justice Clerk, Cockburn of Ormiston, sent a message explaining that his son had departed for the west of Scotland taking all his father's horses. Only eleven of the full thirty members of the Privy Council could find no excuse for not attending and for not braving the procession from Holyroodhouse up the Royal Mile to the Parliament House.

The discussion was no more than a face-saving formality. As the mob shouted "No Reprieve!" outside the door of the Parliament House, eleven frightened men came to the conclusion, as Seafield himself later wrote, "that there was no possibility of preserving the public peace without allowing some that were thought most guilty to be executed". Seafield announced the decision from the threshold of Parliament House, and it was greeted with a wave of delight. Even then a rumour began to spread that it was all a trick, and that the seamen would be reprieved. Seafield was set upon by the mob and only escaped with his life by displaying total coolness and walking slowly and with great dignity between the jeering faces. As G. M. Trevelyan says, "If he had announced a reprieve he would have been torn limb from limb". The authority of the Privy Council and of Parliament had been bludgeoned down by the menaces of some 80,000 armed rioters (this probably exaggerated number was estimated by Captain Robinson, in command of the Town Guard). "The prisoners were left to the course of justice upon expiring of the former reprieve." Sensible men remained indoors.

The scene out on Leith sands, where the gallows had been set up, was blood-curdling. The crowd, so vast that "one might have walked on their heads from Edinburgh", "huzza'd, in triumph as it were, and insulted with the sharpest and most bitter invectives". There were three victims: Green himself, Simpson, and the Scot Madder. Even now, Green seemed convinced that a horseman would soon be galloping up bearing the reprieve. But at last the realisation dawned that there would be no reprieve. All three behaved calmly and resignedly, "like innocent men, English men and Christians, and made no other returns than by forgiving them, and desiring their charity and prayers".

"The tragedy was completed," wrote the author of *A Letter from Scotland*, "and from many points of hilly Edinburgh the bodies of the victims might be seen swinging on the sands of Leith." The three deaths acted as an assuagement, and as so frequently happens when the rule of the temporarily aroused majority is in the ascendant the change from blood-lust to pity, from fierce patriotism to belated sentiment, came almost as the legs of the murdered men ceased twitching. Duncan Forbes of Culloden, then only twenty, recalled the chilling events a generation later: "I was so struck with the horror of the fact that I put myself in deep mourning and with the danger of my life attended the innocent but unfortunate men to the scaffold, where they died with the most affecting protestations of their innocence. I did not stop here, for I carried the head of Captain Green to the grave."

Darien had been avenged, and the other seamen did not hang. Curiously, this ritualistic slaying made the possibilities of Union more feasible. In the course of nine months, feelings had run the gamut between outraged passion and post-orgiastic calm. Now the Duke of Argyle seized his moment. The futile Squadrone rendered up their staffs of office. Queensberry, Seafield and Argyle were the new triumvirate.

Argyle was young, he was more than a trifle arrogant, and he was a Campbell; the last being the most serious defect. His great-grandfather had been executed at the Restoration of Charles II, and his grandfather had suffered the same fate after the collapse of the Monmouth insurrection. His father had been more cautious, and had preferred to tread a wary path towards a dukedom rather than mount the steps of the Maiden, the Scottish machine of execution which pre-dated by centuries Dr. Guillotin's humane invention. True to the acts of his life, he died in bed in his mistress's arms. John Campbell, second Duke of Argyle, was made of different stuff. He had fought against the French at Ramillies and faced the bitter enmity of his own countrymen during the Green affair. Macky approved strongly: "His family will not lose in his person the great figure they have made for so many ages in that kingdom; having all the free spirit, and good sense natural to the family; being always able to bring eight thousand armed men into the field; and hath the power of trying and executing within his own territories ... Few of his years hath a better understanding, nor a more manly behaviour." And Lord Chesterfield, normally so censorious, recalled that Argyle "though the weakest reasoner, was the most pleasing speaker I ever heard in my life. He charmed, he warmed, he forcibly ravished the audience, not by his matter certainly, but by his manner of delivering it. A most genteel figure, a graceful, noble air, an harmonious voice, an elegance of style and a strength of emphasis, conspired to make him the most affecting, persuasive, and applauded speaker I ever saw."

Even Lockhart said that his word was so sacred "that one might assuredly depend upon it". But Argyle was a soldier, a chieftain, a great noble, not a politician. His temper must have unnerved his pacific colleague Seafield, and his imperiousness infuriated Queensberry. With Lord Stair, working away indefatigably in the background and still tarred with the black pitch of Glencoe, these three very disparate men were to see the great Union debate through its final stages.

The Scottish Parliament was still reluctant to exchange

truculence for complaisance. Hamilton and Atholl had
not altered their views, and Lockhart and Fletcher of
Saltoun continued to fight their lone struggle based on
disinterest. Even stupid, ageing Lord Belhaven – "a
rough, fat, black, noisy man, more like a butcher than a
lord", according to Macky – was moved, by a mixture of
patriotic rushes of blood and disappointment at being
without office, to launch into a flood of bathetic rhetoric
of which he was so proud that he had it specially printed
and widely distributed. "I think I see," he thundered,
"our ancient mother Caledonia, like Caesar, sitting in the
midst of our senate, ruefully looking round about her,
covering herself with her royal garment, and breathing
out her last with an *Et tu, mi fili*." This was too much
for Lord Marchmont, who dealt with such nonsense
trenchantly: "Behold he dreamed, but lo! when he
awoke, he found it was a dream."

For all Belhaven's blustering and Saltoun's clinical
reasoning, both London and Edinburgh were intent on
Union. Godolphin underlined the feeling of urgency
when he wrote from Whitehall to Seafield: "We are now
in so critical a position that all Europe must in some
measure be affected by the good or ill ending of the Parliament of Scotland." The two Commissions, set up to
discuss the minutiae of the treaty, had gathered for the
first time on April 16, 1706, in separate rooms in the
Cockpit in Whitehall. Lockhart watched sourly from the
wings, but he was in an obvious minority; Seafield had
chosen the commissioners fairly but selectively. There
were ritual demands for various petty compromises from
the Scottish contingent, but they counted as so many
phrases in a vacuum. The twenty-five articles of the treaty
were duly agreed, and Seafield and Stair had merely to
carry them through the Scottish Parliament virtually un-
altered.

The final session of the Scottish Parliament began
against a background of last-ditch antagonism. Queens-

berry's glass coach had to be protected from the stones of the angry mob by a tight phalanx of servants; there were riots in Glasgow; everywhere throughout the country people forgot personal problems and concentrated on the fate of their nation being decided in Edinburgh. Baillie of Jerviswood noted pessimistically: "I'm afraid this nation will run into blood, whether the Union or Succession be settled." But Seafield cajoled and blandished, and on January 16, 1707 the Treaty of Union was passed by the Scottish Parliament. It was its final act. Like an insect dying after its essential act of sexual consummation, it promptly ceased to exist. Eight days earlier, Stair, perhaps the final architect of the treaty, had died, exhausted. Enemies – and there were many – said that he had hanged himself through remorse over his part in the Glencoe massacre.

The State of Union was decreed to commence on May 1. In England there was no doubt about the general reaction. Seafield and Queensberry, travelling south for the celebrations, were greeted with wild enthusiasm. Queen Anne, setting the seal on the Act with a show of splendour, processed to St. Paul's with four hundred coaches. Everyone seemed to have forgotten their feelings of apathy or outright antagonism. There had been nothing like it since the news of Marlborough's great victory at Blenheim. A new age was dawning.

In Scotland, however, optimism and rejoicing were noticeably absent. The elders of the Kirk decided that May 1 should be a day of fasting, to atone for the country's humiliation. One of the Earl of Mar's correspondents reported that no less than thirty-one huge whales had been washed ashore on the Firth of Forth; and it was also remarked that the very first tune to be pealed out by the bells of St. Giles's was "Why should I be sad on my wedding-day?" Lockhart, true to the last, mourned the supposed passing of Scotland and reminded his readers of a number of ominous coincidences. The first article of the Union had been agreed on "the Birth-day of our Dutch ironical saviour, King William, being the day preparatory to Gunpowder-Treason"; the peerage had been renounced on the anniversary of the warrant "for the Religious Murder of Glencoe"; the ratification of the articles was "upon the sixteenth of the Date of the Sentence of the Royal Martyr, King Charles the First"; the dissolution of the Scottish Parliament was on "the first of the Year in England, and a handsome New Year's gift to that Kingdom", and so on.

Lockhart also had harsh words for the sudden inrush of civil servants from the south, and for their lack of calibre: "Immediately two Commissioners were appointed, one for managing the Customs, the other the Excise of Scotland, which consisted partly of English, partly of Scotsmen (though these latter had no pretensions to entitle them to that Name, save their being born in that Country; they and all that were employed afterwards as Commissioners for managing the equivalent, or advanced to any of the new Posts, being down right Renegadoes, and rewarded on no other account than the Assistance they gave in selling their Country); at the same time vast Numbers of Surveyors, Collectors, Waiters, and in short, all or most of the Officers of the Customs and Excise were sent down from England, and these, generally speaking, the very Scum and Canalia of that Country, which remembers me of a very good story: Sometime thereafter a Scots Merchant Travelling in England, and shewing some apprehension of being Robbed, his Landlady told him he was in no hazard, for all the Highway-men were gone, and upon his enquiring how that came about; why truly, replied she, they are all gone to your Country to get Places."

Lockhart may have chuckled wryly to himself over this chestnut, but he waxed sarcastic about the so-called Equivalent, or as he put it "alias Price of Scotland", which Seafield had considered one of his chief gains from England. This sum of money, nearly £400,000, had been granted to Scotland as compensation for what she had sacrificed in the past and what she might lose in the future; and more than half the total had been allocated to paying off the debts of the company that had launched the tragic Darien expedition.

To men like Lockhart it appeared nothing more or less than an out-and-out bribe, but to the majority it seemed to guarantee a refund of life savings. However, May 1 arrived and the Equivalent did not accompany it. Godolphin had made no arrangements, there had been a prototype Whitehall blunder. Mar received another letter from Edinburgh. "The Equivalent is so much despaired of here," noted the sender, "that among the vulgar the greatest part believe it is gone to Spain, and some believe that the bridge of Berwick is fallen with the weight of it, and all is lost."

Not until August 5 did a dozen waggons, guarded by a contingent of dragoons, trundle into Edinburgh. Predictably, the mob greeted the convoy with stones rather than huzzas. And even then no one was satisfied when it was discovered that three-quarters of the money had been paid in suspect Exchequer bills, and only a quarter in good, honest bullion. Where a modicum of thought and diplomacy could have worked wonders with the fickle Edinburgh townspeople, the chicanery surrounding the Equivalent was to rankle and lend fuel to rising Scottish exasperation and disillusionment. The processes of law were everywhere ignored and, contrary to the articles of the Act of Union, smuggling between Scotland and France reached unprecedented levels, eight hundred tons of brandy arriving illicitly at the port of Glasgow within the space of two months. The excise-men could not contend with this tide of lawlessness, the military had more serious threats to consider. For invasion was in the air.

Part Two

Rebellion 1708

Chapter Three

The Expedition

> That very night a gale of wind put the whole fleet in peril. The King, young as he was, faced the danger with a courage and coolness beyond his years; but his suite was thoroughly frightened.
>
> *Mémoires du Comte de Forbin*

ALL through February 1708, contingents of troops could be seen arriving at the Channel ports of Dunkirk and Saint-Omer. Six French regiments, those of Bernay, Auxerre, Agen, Luxembourg, Beaufermé, and Boulogne, marched in; and the Irish corps, with its d'Oringtons, de Galmoys and de Fitzgeralds lending a polyglot air to the enterprise, prepared to go on board. The Comte de Forbin, an outspoken buccaneer, regarded the matter in hand with sarcasm. He had already burst forth during an interview with Pontchartrain, the French Minister of Marine. Admittedly, the Union between England and Scotland was unpopular, and those opposed to it might be expected to rise; but a rebellion organised by a handful of dissident noblemen and a full-scale revolution were two very different propositions. "And besides, the Minister did not mention any Port which was in a condition to receive us, and I could not refrain from telling him ...

that the project of invasion was entirely without grounds
of encouragement; that Scotland was calm and tranquil;
that not a single district had risen in arms; that we could
not count on any port where our fleet might anchor, or
where the King of England and his troops could disembark in safety; and finally, that to land six thousand
men without an assured means of retreat was, in fact, to
sacrifice them and to send them to certain destruction."

Pontchartrain, faced with this onslaught of criticism
about anchorages and lines of supply and retreat, was
understandably testy in his rejoinder. "You are too ready
to raise objections; it should suffice you that such are the
King's wishes. His Ministers, no doubt, are better informed than yourself." But Forbin remained adamant.
The six thousand men would be better employed elsewhere than on a hare-brained and doomed expedition.

What Forbin, no subtle statesman, did not realise was
the existence of one very valid reason for French support
of an invasion attempt. In the Low Countries, the flood-
tide of Blenheim and Ramillies was over, and local sympathies were veering away from Marlborough. Faced
with a rising in Scotland, the Government at Whitehall
might very well feel obliged to recall a sizeable body of
troops from the European theatre of war, thus affording
Vendôme, the French commander in the field, an opportunity to re-conquer Belgium. In other words, a diversion
was needed, even an unsuccessful one.

Besides, there were reports from the treacherous John
Ker of Kersland and from the somewhat mysterious
Colonel Hooke to add weight to the French scheme. Ker,
in reality a Government spy, spoke for the Presbyterians,
that religious sect which James II had so mistrusted. He
composed a special memorial, a fifth-column piece of
moonshine, in which he set out the intentions of his
fellow Presbyterians: "[They] are resolved never to
agree to the Union, because it hurts their consciences,
and because they are persuaded that it will bring an in-

finite number of calamities upon this nation, and will render the Scots slaves to the English. They are ready to declare unanimously for King James ... Those among the Presbyterians who are called Cameronians will raise 5,000 men of the best soldiers in the country; and the other Presbyterians will assemble 8,000 more ... Provided powder be sent to them, they engage to defend themselves in their country with their own forces alone against all the strength of England for a year, till the arrival of the king and the succours that he shall bring with him ... They have a correspondence with the north of Ireland, and they are certain that the Scots who inhabit that province will declare for them ..."

All this was very plausible but even if Ker's opinions were discounted, Colonel Hooke provided considerable evidence in support; and Hooke's credentials were impeccable. He was actually employed by the French Government as their agent in any negotiations with Stuart sympathisers in Scotland, and he had long experience in his stormy career of the tricks of secret diplomacy. An Irishman in his early forties, he had been chaplain to the Duke of Monmouth and accompanied him during the disastrous rebellion which ended at Sedgemoor. After two years spent in hiding, he had thrown himself on the mercy of James II and, on receiving a full pardon, showed his gratitude by becoming a Catholic convert and going into exile with him. He fought at the Boyne and later joined the Irish corps in France.

Hooke had been in Scotland in 1705 and he returned there in 1707. No less a person than the Constable of Scotland, the Earl of Erroll, had entertained the Colonel lavishly at Slains Castle, and he had been able to sound out the general climate of opinion from his advantageous base. His mission appeared successful. Certainly the most influential noblemen showed considerable reluctance to commit themselves on paper, but Hooke returned to Versailles with a great many splendid, if nebulous, promises; he also carried with him a document setting out "the present state of this nation, and the things we stand in need of".

Bearing ten signatures, headed by those of Erroll and the Earl of Panmure, and of Lords Stormont and Kinnaird, this memorial of the Scottish lords stated unequivocally that "the whole nation will rise upon the arrival of its king". They anticipated being able to muster a force of 25,000 foot and an additional 5,000 horse and dragoons. But there were the inevitable drawbacks: the few cannon and mortars were all in Government hands; the number of experienced officers was sadly low; the clansmen were only "pretty well armed"; above all, after five years of famine, the failure of the Darien scheme, and the neglect of their estates by the absent landlords down in London, any financial contribution to the cost of the rising would be minimal. His Most Christian Majesty at Versailles should provide 8,000 men, weapons for the entire Scottish army, the sum of 100,000 pistoles, artillery, ammunition and grenades, and "majors, lieutenants and serjeants to discipline" the Scottish commanders.

What, however, Colonel Hooke did not provide for Louis XIV's chief ministers Torcy and Chamillart, was anything more than the vaguest hints of encouragement from such crucial grandees as Hamilton, Gordon and Atholl. On the other hand, if Lockhart can be believed, Hooke had the ear of Louis; and in addition, Simon Fraser, before his untimely incarceration in the Bastille, claimed to have persuaded an impressive galaxy of chiefs to bring out their clans in support of the projected invasion: Macdonald of Sleat, the Captain of Clanranald, Lochiel, Keppoch, Glengarry and Appin were all apparently ready and eager. Sir Winston Churchill was no doubt exaggerating when he said that "Highland clansmen, Lowland Jacobites, Whig noblemen, Covenanters, Catholics, and Presbyterians, were all ripe for rebellion, though with different objects. Now, if ever, was the hour for the rightful heir to Scotland's ancient crown to set foot upon Scottish soil"; but undoubtedly the evidence in favour of an immediate expedition must have seemed virtually conclusive to the French king and his advisers. The armies in Flanders would be relieved of pressure, and it was known that only a bare minimum of Government troops were under arms in Scotland. An almost euphoric sense of adventure was in the air, as a fleet of fifteen transport ships and five men o'war under Forbin's command, and an army of 6,000 to be led by the Comte de Gacé, were duly assembled.

Forbin continued to grumble to the last. The Intendant of Dunkirk had been summoned to Versailles and, much to his annoyance, Forbin was excluded from the ensuing discussions. But the Chief Commissioner suggested that he should at least be consulted, since he was to be responsible for the naval contingent, and Forbin seized upon the opportunity to speak his mind. "The entire scheme appeared to me so ridiculous, that forgetting to whom I was speaking, and giving full rein to the vivacity of a typical Provençal, I asked, 'Who is the ignoramus responsible for this arrangement?'" The Minister of Marine, showing admirable patience, enquired why he found it so defective. Forbin proceeded to criticise the choice of Dunkirk as the starting point, vulnerable as it was to attack by the English fleet operating between the east coast and Holland; and also the cumbersome nature of the transport ships which would be quite incapable of running to safety in an emergency. Instead, he recommended that privateers should be assembled at Dunkirk. "Though they will carry fewer soldiers than the transports, we can take more of them with us. With such vessels we shall sail much quicker, and if we encounter contrary winds, we can bring-to without drifting from our course; while, if the enemy come up with us in superior numbers, we shall be in a better position to escape." Pontchartrain agreed with this suggestion and asked Forbin to arrange the details with the Chief Commissioner.

Even then he was not content, and he decided to voice his fears to the king himself. When Forbin arrived to take leave before setting out for Dunkirk, Louis was in no mood to tolerate a lecture. "Monsieur le Comte," he said, "you realise the importance of your Commission; I hope that you will acquit yourself worthily in it." The interview was over, but Forbin pressed on. "Sire, you do me a great honour; but if your Majesty would vouchsafe to me a few minutes, I would venture to represent certain matters in regard to the Commission with which I am charged." The atmosphere was by now glacial, and Louis dealt sharply with his talkative admiral. "Monsieur de Forbin, I wish you a successful voyage; I am busy and cannot listen to you now." The king, hauteur and open irritation overcoming his proverbial good manners, turned away. The following morning, Forbin departed for the coast. He remained quite convinced that the expedition was doomed to failure.

Chaos reigned at Dunkirk. Forbin and Gacé cordially disliked one another, and both men's tempers were further aroused by continual inter-departmental squabbles; Gacé, being a protégé of Chamillart's, was naturally suspicious of the entire naval ministry, and refused to stir himself on his colleague's behalf. Forbin had the utmost difficulty in equipping his fleet which now consisted of thirty privateers and five men o'war, and in concealing the real reason for so much fierce activity from the eyes and ears of any casual onlookers who might be in the pay of the English.

The army was encamped at Saint-Omer, a day's march away, but the sailors had not yet arrived. The sudden appearance of 6,000 men and the presence of a sizeable flotilla could only signify one thing to a spy; and in addition there suddenly seemed to be an unusual number of gentlemen speaking with English and Irish accents who had clearly not posted from all over France to the Chan-

nel simply for the sake of their health. General Cadogan
at Ostend had already received news of the expedition,
and the intelligence was passed speedily on to Whitehall.
It was not long before thirty-eight English men o'war
were anchored off Gravelines, a scant two leagues from
Dunkirk.

It was in the middle of this confusion that James arrived. He had left Saint-Germain at the beginning of
March, accompanied by Perth and Middleton, and
shortly followed by Lord Griffin, determined in spite of
his age to join the expedition. There had already been
too many delays, and a further complication was added
when James, as always throughout his life hounded by
bad luck, caught measles and lay critically ill. The equi-
noctial gales were raging in the Channel and the soldiers
were disembarked from the privateers. Forbin viewed
the situation with a certain grim satisfaction and suggested that the expedition should be indefinitely postponed. Admiral Leake's ships were waiting to sweep
down, and an order was dispatched from Versailles can-
celling the whole enterprise. But Forbin had many
enemies, and Mary of Modena, desperately anxious that
her son should set sail, extracted a promise from Louis
that the plan should be put into action.

At last the wind veered round, driving Leake's watch-
dog fleet back towards the Downs. Sir George Byng's
ships had not come up from Ostend, and at the right
moment the fog lifted. James, still weak, was carried on
board Forbin's flagship, the *Mars*, and at six o'clock
on the evening of March 6 the French fleet set sail. Forbin was still opposed to any such precipitate move, and
later attributed the decision to sail before a favourable
wind had sprung up to Gacé's desire to earn the marshal's
baton which he had been promised as soon as James had
left French waters.

James himself sided with Gacé and as he now had
authority over the fleet and the army, Forbin at last gave

way and prepared himself for the worst. His chief pleasure would now be to taunt Gacé beyond endurance, and he proceeded to paint the gloomiest picture of what would happen if his opinion were set aside: "Monsieur, you are anxious to induce the King of England to embark before the proper time. Be very careful what you do, and rest assured that you deceive neither the Minister of Marine nor myself. The king ought to embark only when Wind and Tide are favourable. If you persist, I must obey. But mark this, you will all certainly be drowned." He added smugly: "As for me, I risk nothing. I can swim, and shall come to no harm."

Forbin could not conceal his delight when the weather changed yet again and they were forced to alter course to the comparative shelter of the Ostend dunes. Gacé and his staff were all suffering acutely from sea-sickness, and the intolerable admiral did not hesitate to point out how right he had been. "I can do nothing," he gloated, "the wine's drawn and you must drink it. Suffer, feel as uncomfortable as you please; I'm quite content, and don't pity you at all. You have your wish. Why are you so dissatisfied?" Only James behaved well; the Chevalier de St. George, as he now styled himself for the first time, was about to experience the first in a long succession of disappointments.

The gale continued to rage, and three of the best-fitted ships, the *Proteus*, *Guerrier* and *Barrentin*, broke their cables and were nearly lost. This was a serious matter, as they carried 600 troops, although the *Proteus* at least was able to sail on the 9th.

At last, two days later, the wind veered once more and the battered fleet set sail at eleven o'clock at night on Monday, March 8. The confusion surrounding the expedition remained; it was only at the last minute that the harbour of Burntisland was fixed on as the landing place. Charles Fleming, Lord Wigtoun's brother, had crossed over to Scotland some time earlier in order to herald the arrival of the expeditionary force and was at this very moment supposed to be arranging and coordinating the signals which would pass between the Jacobites on the shore and the French fleet as soon as it was sighted. His journey was to prove futile.

Fleming later put down on paper his impressions of the general mood in Scotland: "Never was seen so universal a joy at Edinburgh as that which appeared in everybody's countenance for three or four days before the king's arrival. The loyal subjects thronged together, and those of the government durst not appear in public. They had no confidence in the regular troops, knowing that the best part, both of the officers and soldiers, were well affected to the king. Besides, there was neither powder nor ammunition in the castle of Edinburgh, nor in that of Stirling; and they knew that all the gentry would revolt from the government the moment the king landed: So that it was believed, that on the king's arrival, those who adhered to the government would retire towards Berwick."

James was not yet completely recovered from his attack of measles. He wrote to his mother on March 9: "Here I am on board at last. My body is very weak, but my spirit is so strong that it will make up for the weakness of the body. I hope not to write to you again until I do so from the palace of Edinburgh, where I expect to arrive on Saturday." Land was indeed sighted three days out, and the sails of the French fleet did not go unnoticed. Lord Leven, the English commander at Edinburgh, was in a high state of nerves and echoed Charles Fleming's reading of the situation when he wrote anxiously to the Earl of Mar in London: "Here I am. Not one farthing of money to provide provisions. None of the Commission yet sent down. Few troops and naked. It vexes me sadly to think I must retire to Berwick if the French land this side of Forth." He need not have worried; things had gone awry again. The pilots had miscalculated, and Forbin was obliged to alter course eventually dropping anchor near the Isle of May, north-east of the Bass Rock and North Berwick.

Forbin takes up the story. "In vain we made Signals, lit Fires, and fired our Cannon; nobody appeared." He sent a frigate with orders to fire five shots, the pre-arranged signal, and a landing was made at Pittenweem, once famous for its witch-hunts; but there was no welcoming army, only a few Jacobite gentlemen. "On the stroke of midnight I was informed that five Cannon-shot had been heard from the South. I had not taken off my clothes since we sailed from Dunkirk, and rising hastily, I concluded that the five Cannon-shot must be the signal of the Enemy, who had followed our Fleet."

His guess was correct. "At daybreak we discovered the English fleet anchored at four leagues distance from us. The sight of them caused me considerable uneasiness. We were shut in a sort of a bay, with a cape to be doubled before we could gain the open sea." They were caught in a trap, with Byng's fleet beating fast up the Firth of Forth.

Forbin, in his own self-congratulatory words, saw that "considerable coolness was necessary if we were to extricate ourselves from our critical position. So, rapidly making all sail, I bore down on the enemy as though I designed to attack him." The ruse was effective. Byng was convinced that Forbin was on the point of attacking, ordered his ships into battle order, and so lost the initiative. Forbin's fleet clapped on all sail and outran the slower English vessels; but he could not avoid a fight. One of his ships, the *Salisbury*, with Lord Griffin and Middleton's two sons on board, was captured, but Byng seemed strangely reluctant to press home his advantage, allowing the French to sail northwards and to re-gather off the Aberdeenshire coast.

But, in the meantime, one English frigate had continued the pursuit, and James's advisers panicked. They had already accused Forbin of cowardice, when Byng's fleet

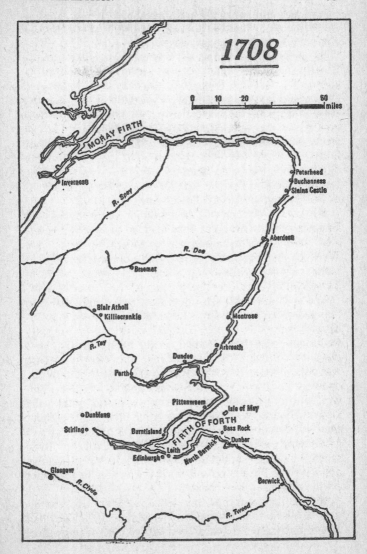

first hove into view, maintaining that they were nothing
more dangerous than Danish ships putting in at Edinburgh to take on a cargo of coal (or Dutch East-
Indiamen according to an alternative account); now he
turned on them sarcastically. The nervous tension is,
however, understandable. The frigate managed to fire a
broadside into the next French ship in line, the *Auguste*,
and one of Forbin's ships which he had sent to reconnoitre the enemy's strength returned with the alarming
news that they numbered thirty-eight men o'war, more
than ten of which were three-deckers. It was proposed
that James should go on board the fast frigate which had
just returned from its reconnoitring, and sail for the
Scottish coast; he could then take refuge at Slains Castle
under the protection of Lord Erroll, who was known to
be loyal. James relayed this suggestion to Forbin, who
reacted predictably. "Sire," he said, "you are quite safe
here and your enemies can do you no harm. That vessel
which is pursuing us, to the alarm of all these gentlemen,
is not formidable, and, were your Majesty not on board,
would soon be sent to the right-about. But I will take
all necessary measures, and soon we shall be far away
from all pursuit."

James appeared satisfied with this, but his advisers
hammered away at him about his, and presumably their,
safety. The arguments went on, with Forbin asking for a
private interview with James in his cabin, James chang-
ing his mind yet again, and Forbin at last agreeing to have
a boat prepared if a quick getaway really proved essential. Forbin continued to speechify: "I am charged with
your safety, and my head will answer for any harm that
may befall you. I beg you, therefore, to trust me impli-
citly and to listen to no one else. Those who venture to
give you other advice than this are either traitors or
cowards."

At last, though, Byng's fleet hove to off Buchanness
and then returned to Leith, bearing the captured *Salis-*

bury as its only prize. James was safe, but the whole enterprise was now clearly seen to be a fiasco. There were thoughts of landing James and his retinue at Inverness, but the weather was against such an attempt and Forbin decided to cut his losses and sail back to Dunkirk. After a nightmarish journey, beset in turn by calms and contrary winds, the expeditionary force struggled in at the end of March. Some English prisoners watched from the quayside: "We saw the person called the Pretender land on the shore, being a tall, slight young man, pale smooth face, with a blue feather in his hat, and a star on his cloak; at his first going off they mightily huzzaed him with *Vive le Roi*, but were very mute at his coming back."

The inevitable recriminations commenced. James blamed his own sickness, the pilots' mistakes, violent contrary winds, the dispersal of the fleet, ignorance of the coastline and lack of provisions. Gacé, secure in the French king's favour as the newly created Maréchal de Matignon, simply blamed Forbin, who returned the compliment. Berwick was convinced that the planned disembarkation on the shore of the Firth of Forth should have been pushed through regardless of the danger to the ships; although, in his opinion, the whole enterprise was misconceived and should have been directed towards the west coast of Scotland. Lockhart and his fellow Jacobites in Scotland suspected that Forbin had been ordered never to land at all.

There was deep gloom at Versailles and Marly, and rumours of treachery spread. Saint-Simon, observing the melancholy meeting between James and Louis at Marly, had no hesitation in pointing an accusing finger at Middleton. In Scotland, according to Charles Fleming, "the consternation was so great, that everybody appeared distracted". But it is doubtful whether a sufficiently large number of Scots to present a real threat to the Government would have risen in any case. Defoe was probably

nearest the mark when he wrote: "It began to be said at
the time of the invasion, 'It lay between the English
and the French; let them fight it out.' There was nothing
for the honest people, as they called themselves, to do in
it." No expedition could succeed without large-scale indi-
genous support.

In England, the Whigs breathed again. Only prompt
action by Godolphin in transferring the Treasury's complete holding of gold to the Bank of England had saved
that august body of financiers and the Tories. Now, that
ingenious politician, with a general election imminent,
was wary of antagonising the Scots and decided on a
policy of reasonable leniency. The hangman went un-
employed, but even so the Habeas Corpus Act was suspended and Lord Leven given full powers to arrest all
persons suspected of treachery. Aided and abetted by
Mar, he launched a campaign directed mainly against
Catholics and those who had not voted in favour of
the Act of Union, but also embracing an impressive
number of Scottish noblemen.

Lockhart was scandalised: "Orders came from London to send them up thither, which was accordingly done
... led in Triumph under a strong Guard, and exposed
to the Raillery and Impertinence of the English Mob;
and now it appeared to what a fine Market Scotland had
brought her Hogs, her Nobility and Gentry being led in
Chains from one end of the Island to the other, merely
on account of Suspition and without any Accusation of
Proof against them." The Duke of Gordon travelled
south to London on a dragoon's horse provided by the
Government, in order to stand trial. Even the Duke of
Hamilton was put under arrest, although he managed to
wriggle out of any complicity in the affair. Breadalbane,
Erroll, Nithsdale, Aberdeen, Strathmore, Marischal,
Stormont and Saltoun were ordered to deposit bonds to
the value of between three and five thousand pounds as
surety for their future good behaviour. A number of

castles were appropriated, and Atholl's seat at Blair Atholl was provided with an unwelcome garrison. That pathetic old buffoon, Lord Belhaven, tarred with his vociferous attacks on the Union, was arrested and soon afterwards died of a broken heart. Only the aged Lord Griffin was condemned to death, but he was reprieved and died in the Tower two years later. Queen Anne herself, although outwardly furious about the abortive invasion, was no doubt highly relieved that the prisoners did not include her half-brother. She contented herself with ordering a special medal to be struck, to commemorate the Pretender's insolence and his failure.

Godolphin's manoeuvres were, however, in vain. The country was weary of the European war and eager for a change of Government. At the general election, the first to be held since the Union of England and Scotland, the Whigs triumphed and Godolphin found himself saddled with an administration drawn almost exclusively from the Whig Junta. The war dragged on; but the rebellion was over.

Chapter Four

The Succession

> The thunder had long grumbled in the air; and yet when the bolt fell, most of our party appeared as much surprised as if they had had no reason to expect it. There was perfect calm and universal submission through the whole kingdom.
>
> Bolingbroke's Letter to Sir William Wyndham

THE eminent Leipzig philosopher Gottfried Wilhelm Leibnitz is perhaps best remembered for his celebrated dictum, "all is for the best in the best of all possible worlds". It aroused Voltaire's scorn and he satirised it memorably in *Candide*. But Leibnitz had other interests. He discovered the basis of differential calculus comtemporaneously with Newton, and he even undertook, with the assistance of Bossuet, the fusion of the Catholic and the Reformed Churches. He was also an inveterate genealogist.

Delving in the archives at Modena, whose ruling duke represented the Italian Guelphs, Leibnitz slowly pieced together the family tree of Ernest Augustus, first Elector of Hanover. His discoveries, which he made public over the space of the decade following 1707, might have been considered merely the gratification of a somewhat paro-

chial German ruling house's desire for lineage, for old
blood-royal. The statesmen at Versailles and London
might indeed have scoffed if Leibnitz's friend and pat-
roness had not been the Electress Sophia. And her son,
George, was the clear and acknowledged successor to
his cousin Anne on the English throne.

Sophia was the daughter of the tragically romantic
Winter Queen, Elizabeth of Bohemia, who had married
Frederick V, Elector of the Palatinate; as a consequence,
she was the granddaughter of James VI of Scotland and
I of England. Of her exalted descent there could be no
doubt. But, as Leibnitz demonstrated, by her marriage
to Ernest Augustus she had joined her Stuart blood to
the purest Teutonic strain in Europe, which reached back
through the Emperor Otho of Germany and his father
Henry the Lion, the husband of Henry II of England's
daughter Matilda, to Guelph, Prince of the Scyrri, one of
Attila the Hun's allies. The whole thing was highly complex and more than a trifle suspect. It was also unden-
iable that the blood of the Guelphs had thinned over the
centuries. And even Leibnitz had some difficulty in re-
vealing the immediate predecessors to Ernest Augustus's
great-grandfather, Ernest of Zell. Nevertheless, though
perhaps insignificant, they existed the right side of the
blanket.

Ernest of Zell's third son William, Duke of Lüneburg,
was a remarkable man. Extremely religious, his only
solace in old age, when he had lost both sight and reason,
was to listen to his favourite psalm-tunes; he also had
fifteen children in the true biblical tradition, eight
daughters and seven sons. The amassing of prolific
broods of unappealing boys and ill-favoured girls seems
to have been one of the few occupations indulged in by
the hordes of petty German princelings, and William of
Lüneburg was a typically industrious progenitor. But, as
so often happened, the territory over which he ruled was
far from sufficient to accommodate seven sons, let alone

their offspring. An ingenious solution was reached, if one
can believe Thackeray's tongue-in-the-cheek version,
which often reads like a parody of a Grimm fairy-story.
"They drew lots to determine which one of them should
marry, and continue the stout race of the Guelphs. The lot
fell on Duke George, the sixth brother. The others remained single, or contracted left-handed marriages after
the princely fashion of those days. It is a queer picture –
that of the old prince dying in his little wood-built capital,
and his seven sons tossing up which should inherit."

George toured Europe and returned to Germany in
1617, setting up a collective court with all his brothers in
Zell. "And presently," as Thackeray puts it, "in due
course, they all died – all the honest dukes; Ernest, and
Christian, and Augustus, and Magnus, and George, and
John – and they are buried in the brick church yonder, by
the sandy banks of the Aller." George, after a stormy
military career, died at Hildesheim in 1641, leaving four
sons, the youngest of whom was Ernest Augustus. The
eldest of the four died in 1665 without leaving any mark,
but the second and third were more memorable.
George William led a rackety life, continually rushing off
to the fleshpots of Venice and returning with troupes of
highly dubious Italian singers and dancers, and even
going so far as to marry a Frenchwoman of much less
than royal birth; their daughter, Sophia Dorothea,
would be Queen of England. John Frederick, the third
brother, was no less original, deserting his Brunswick
principles for those of Louis XIV, and holding fervently
to the Catholic faith in spite of the fact that his great-
grandfather had studied under Luther at Wittenberg.

But Ernest Augustus was all that might be expected of
a German prince with Lutheran antecedents. Like so
many of his contemporaries, he was hostile to the France
of Louis XIV, although not to that monarch's approach
to life at court. In 1692, a ninth Electorate was created
by the Emperor Leopold at the request of William III

of England and in recognition of Ernest Augustus's staunch adherence to the Protestant cause; but this new honour did not prevent the elaboration of the palace at Herrenhausen. As Thackeray tartly observed: "Every prince imitated the French king, and had his Versailles, his Wilhelmshöhe, or Ludwigslust; his court and its splendours; his gardens laid out with statues; his fountains, and waterworks, and Tritons." Here, though, the similarity ended. There was no place at Ernest Augustus's court for the diamond glitter of Versailles. Hunting was virtually the sole amusement, although the royal couple occasionally travelled abroad. The English consul at Amsterdam, who visited Herrenhausen in 1668, left with a distinctly favourable impression. Sophia was fluent in Italian, French, English, High and Low Dutch, and generally "a lady of extraordinary virtue and accomplishments". The Elector-to-be himself was civil, graceful, a good horseman and a valiant soldier, kind to his subjects. Although he was himself a Lutheran, he was tolerant enough to accompany his wife to her Calvinist church. And he had fifty-two teams of coach-horses in his private stables.

The picture is too good to be true, and Ernest, fostering the Hanoverian predilection for womanising which was to reach such scandalous proportions with Victoria's wicked uncles, was not the upright, rather suburban ruler portrayed by the English consul. He was certainly not averse to making what was euphemistically called the loan of nearly 7,000 of his subjects to aid Venice in the Morea campaign. Only 1,400 returned, but a substantial payment of ducats by the grateful Seigniory provided Ernest Augustus with the means of financing dazzling entertainments. Whether these were any compensation for Hanoverian widows and orphans is another matter. However, such an action was perhaps no more than a sign of the times, and there is no doubt about Ernest Augustus's ability as a schemer and unostentatious self-

aggrandiser. By introducing for the first time in his country the system of primogeniture, he made certain that his
lands would not be split up among his many offspring,
some of whom were understandably annoyed by such a
threat to their future.

Ernest Augustus died in 1698, and within months of
his funeral William III of England was conferring with
the widowed Electress Sophia and her son George. As
the years passed, and first the sickly Duke of Gloucester
and then William himself died, this solemn young German prince featured in every discussion of who should
succeed to the British crown. But for the time being he
was content to rule over Hanover. And life at Herrenhausen continued as a frail, warped shadow of Versailles.
Thackeray visited the palace, researching diligently for
his entertaining caricature of the four Georges, and
found it unchanged after a century. "You may see at Herrenhausen the very rustic theatre in which the Platens
danced and performed masques, and sang before the
Elector and his sons. There are the very fauns and dryads
of stone still glimmering through the branches, still grin-
ning and piping their ditties of no tone, as in the days
when painted nymphs hung garlands round them; guid-
ing rams with gilt horns; descended from 'machines' in
the guise of Diana or Minerva; and delivered immense
allegorical compliments to the princes returning home
from the campaign."

The sharp elegance of Versailles has been coarsened,
the water-works seem clumsier, the statues less distinguished, the theatrical displays lacking that elusive
French wit and polish. The food is undoubtedly more
rustic and the panoply of the hunt less flamboyant. One
cannot imagine George taking part in a ballet as Louis
XIV in his salad days so often did. Imitation is the sin-
cerest form of flattery, imitation without the effervescence
of the original is mere pastiche.

But William III, himself no arbiter of fashion, was not

influenced by the bourgeois raffishness of the Court at Herrenhausen. George could be a powerful ally in the struggle against Louis XIV which became the *raison d'être* of the cold, persevering Dutchman. Hanover, relatively constricted territorially, was crucially positioned near the Cockpit of Europe, the Low Countries, with easy access to the Elbe, Weser, Aller and Embs rivers. The Electorate also tapped the considerable mineral resources of the Hartz mountains, rich in silver, copper, iron, lead and zinc, while the wool and linen trades flourished throughout Brunswick. Its population was a mere half million but, true to the traditions of German militarism, the army – very much a standing force – was 15,000-strong. All these were potent reasons for William's advocacy of the Brunswick-Lüneburg dynasty as successors to his sister-in-law Anne. They were the natural Protestant claimants, and there was little danger of the line dying out as seemed the case with the unfilial daughters of James II. George had five brothers, and only the one sister who was to die in 1705 the first Queen of Prussia. Frederick Augustus and Charles Philip were both killed in 1685 fighting for the Emperor against the Turks, and a third was drowned in the Danube at the age of thirty-two, but there still remained Maximilian and Ernest Augustus.

There also remained the Electress Sophia. Possessed of infinitely greater charm and charity than her eldest son, she was never afraid to temper diplomacy with the truth. When William grasped the English throne, she wrote to congratulate him: "I believe you cannot doubt of the part which I take in everything that contributes to your elevation and your glory; yet," she added, almost wistfully, "I lament King James, who honoured me with his friendship." She certainly had no desire to reign at Whitehall. Writing to an English diplomat, Stepney, she was entirely frank: "If I were thirty years younger, I should have a sufficiently good opinion of my birth and of my religion to believe that I should be appreciated in England. But as there is little probability of my surviving two people much younger, although more subject to ordinary dangers than myself, it is to be feared that at my death my sons would be regarded as strangers, the eldest of whom is much more accustomed to claim a high prerogative as sovereign than the poor Prince of Wales [James], who is too young to profit by the example of the King of France, and who would apparently be so glad to recover that which the King, his father, has so inconsiderately lost, that they would be able to do with him just what they wished. I am not so philosophical nor so thoughtless that you should think I do not like to hear a crown spoken of, and that I do not give due consideration to the weighty judgment you have given on this subject. It seems to me that in England there are so many parties that one can be sure of nothing."

Through the long years during which the Hanoverian star gradually climbed into the ascendant, as the deaths of the Duke of Gloucester and of William III, the passing of the Act of Succession and the signing of the Treaty of Utrecht each contributed to the optimism of George's advisers, the Electress Sophia never intruded, always acted with tact and dignity. She would take part in the jollifications surrounding the Earl of Macclesfield's visit in 1701 to announce the implications of the Act of Succession; she would contribute to the exchange of elaborate civilities when Lord Halifax arrived to invest George with the Order of the Garter; but, basically, she was happier living in an atmosphere of muted intellectualism which allowed her to act as the patron of Leibnitz without really grasping the subtleties of his philosophy, following a régime which consisted of tapestry-weaving and wandering through the park at Herrenhausen. She would not or could not – probably a combination of the two – seriously consider the possibility of her inheriting the throne of England, and her sole fantasy was a desire

that "Sophia, Queen of Great Britain," should be in-
scribed on her tomb.

With the Electress turning aside from reality, and her
son more often on the battlefield than with his advisers
in the council-chamber or with his wife Sophia Dorothea
in the bedroom,* the reins of government and diplomatic intrigue fell increasingly into the hands of Robethon, the Elector's secretary. The beginning of the
eighteenth century was the great age of the secret politician, of the statesman who ruled by stealth, who preferred to cajole than to bludgeon, who was equally in his
element on the back stairs and at the centre of great state
occasions. Robert Harley was the prime exponent of the
art in England, just as Seafield was in Scotland, and
Heinsius at the Hague. Hanover was particularly rich in
the species and could always call on the services of Count
Bernsdorff, Baron Bothmar and Baron Schutz, besides
a number of interfering Hanoverian court ladies. But
Robethon was the arch-intriguer. Born of a French
émigré family, he had been private secretary to William
III and to the Duke of Zell before becoming confidential
secretary to George. He was considered by many to be
presumptuous and insolent, and had an unenviable reputation for venality, but of his diplomatic finesse there
was no doubt.

The man who was to reap the benefit of Robethon's
sureness of touch did not perhaps deserve the cornucopia
of plot and intrigue which was lavished on him and on
his future expectations. George Lewis, Elector of Hanover, future King of Great Britain and founder of the
dynasty which still rules there, has been over-exposed to
history and to posterity. The butt of Jacobite-inclined

*This is not the place for an elaboration of the tragi-comic-
romantic story of the lonely Sophia Dorothea, her entanglement
with the handsome Count Königsmarck, and her incarceration
in the castle of Ahlen. For an entertaining narrative of the *cause
célèbre*, see T. H. White's *The Age of Scandal*.

writers who draw lip-licking attention to his dubious morals, his treatment of his wife, the hideousness of his mistresses, and the position in his household of those two Turkish procurers Mustapha and Mahomet, preserved for ever in Kent's *trompe-l'oeil* mural at Kensington Palace; to staunch Whigs and Protestants, a St. George in shining armour, vanquishing the dragon of Rome and protecting British democracy against the assaults of Catholic believers in the divine right of kings – both these are caricatures rather than full-length portraits, both have elements of verisimilitude.

*

While the House of Brunswick-Lüneburg waited for the death of Queen Anne, James was not entirely idle. Both at Oudenarde and particularly at Malplaquet, he fought with distinction in the French army; and at the second battle was wounded in the arm as he charged with the Maison du Roi. His military prowess was well received both by his adopted country and, more surprisingly, by Marlborough's officers and men against whom he had taken up arms. Bravery was esteemed in an opponent, and his career was followed with admiration and his health frequently drunk.

The prospect of a Jacobite succession was greatly assisted by a change of Government in England in 1710. The Whig Junta tendered up their staffs of office and were replaced by Tories distinctly sympathetic towards James. Godolphin, exhausted by a year of impossible coalition, was dismissed in August and the Lord Treasurer's white staff was handed to Robert Harley, newly created Earl of Oxford, the following May. During the last years of Anne's reign, such men as Harley, Henry St. John, later Viscount Bolingbroke, the Duke of Ormonde, Lord Lansdowne, Sir William Wyndham, the Duke of Buckingham and the Earl of Mar all held high office in a succession of Tory re-shuffles. With a queen

who disliked her Brunswick cousins and desperately
wanted to atone to her half-brother, a predominantly
favourable Government, and a populace exploding with
enthusiasm whenever James's birthday came round on
June 10, the court in exile's star was suddenly climbing.

Two events altered any hope of a reversal of the Act
of Settlement: the death of the Duke of Hamilton, and
the signing of the peace at the Treaty of Utrecht. In the
autumn of 1712, the British Government decided to send
an ambassador extraordinary to Versailles. Matthew
Prior had been struggling diligently during the final negotiations for peace, but it was thought that a man of eminence and noble blood should be present to lend the
proceedings an air of grandeur. The choice fell on Hamilton, once so involved in the bitter opposition to the
Act of Union, and still considered the leader of the Jacobite faction in Scotland. The impression given by this
appointment was clear-cut. Hamilton was travelling to
Versailles, not only to hasten on the peace treaty, but
also to prepare the way for James's return on the death
of Anne.

One particular Whig took drastic action. Lord Mohun
detested Hamilton both for his politics and because they
had both recently been involved in a protracted and acrimonious law-suit. Mohun challenged Hamilton to a duel,
and a meeting was fixed for the day before the duke's
departure for France. Mohun chose as his second Gen-
ral Macartney, another man with a deep sense of
grievance against the Tories. He had been one of Marlborough's senior officers and was dismissed when the
Whig administration fell. He was also an inveterate gam-
bler with a reputation for violence. Hamilton's second
was a Colonel John Hamilton of the Scots Foot Guards.

The opponents met in Hyde Park in the cold early
morning of November 15. It was more of a scrimmage
than a duel. The two principals hurled themselves at each
other, "desperately like wild beasts, not fencing or parry-

ing". Hamilton killed Mohun outright, but was severely
wounded himself. In the meantime, the two seconds had
also been fighting and Colonel Hamilton had received a
slight leg-wound. Seeing what had occurred to Mohun
and Hamilton, however, they broke off and Colonel
Hamilton rushed over to the duke and held him in his
arms. Macartney, according to the colonel, then aimed
his sword at the duke's prostrate body. When the surgeon opened the duke's coat, he "found a wound upon
his left breast which never bled, though it was a large
orifice, which he took to be the wound given him by Macartney". But Colonel Hamilton's story was not cor-
roborated by the servants who had watched the entire
proceedings, and it seems strange that he took no action
against Macartney at the time. Whatever the real facts
of the case, however, Tory supporters were convinced
that it was a deep-laid Whig plot, and Macartney fled for
his life. He did not dare return to England until after
George I's accession, when the political climate had
shifted in his favour. He stood trial and was acquitted.
Lord Chesterfield, who sat in court during the case, considered him "very capable of the vilest actions" but in
this particular instance wholly innocent.

   Whether or not the Whigs were involved in this dramatic duel, they were certainly not distressed at its outcome.
The Duke of Shrewsbury, the only Whig in Oxford's
administration to hold high office, was selected as a replacement for Hamilton, and he duly oversaw the signing
of the peace settlement. When its terms were made public, they were seen to include one vital clause, which dras-
tically affected James's future. Louis XIV had at last
reneged on his promise to support the Jacobite court in
France. James departed from Saint-Germain, but found
asylum not too far distant at Bar-le-Duc in the lands of
the Duc de Lorraine. There he settled down to watch the
plot and counter-plot which would bubble in the political
cauldron for the next year and a half.

Oxford took the opportunity given by the popular end of hostilities to call an election, and the Tories were duly returned with an unchanged majority in September 1713. This was to be the last Parliament in Queen Anne's reign, and the majority of the Tories knew perfectly well that if the succession fell to the Brunswick-Lüneburg dynasty their days of power were over. Only Sir Thomas Hanmer's Hanoverian Tories, dubbed contemptuously "the Whimsicals", openly opposed the notion of James on the throne.

Many years later, after his quarrel with James, Bolingbroke disputed the fact that any plot to restore the Stuarts was being hatched: "there was no design on foot during the last four years of Queen Anne's reign to set aside the succession of the House of Hanover, and to place the crown on the head of the Pretender to it ... I deny the fact absolutely." But this was very far from the truth, as Bolingbroke was the first to know. He had been in close correspondence with James for some time, and wielded all possible influence on the moderate Oxford to pack his administration with avowed Jacobite sympathisers. He went still further when he engineered Oxford's dismissal on July 27, 1714. Already the Whig Duke of Argyle had been stripped of his appointments, and the notorious Schism Act, which removed any control Dissenters might have over the education of their children, had been pushed through. But, even now, complete power eluded Bolingbroke. Queen Anne, in great pain and nearing her end, still had enough strength to withstand his persistent bids for the Lord Treasurer's white staff. It was an office he never attained. Anne could not stomach his immorality; as Erasmus Lewis wrote to Swift, "his character is too bad to carry the great ensigns, for the man of Mercury's bottom is too narrow, his faults are of the first magnitude".

Bolingbroke enjoyed two days of power as Secretary of State with no Oxford as Lord Treasurer above him.

But he had alienated too many factions. The Whigs could not serve with him, nor would Hanmer's Hanoverian Tories. Oxford's friends never forgave him; the Dissenters looked to the Hanoverian succession as their only hope; the majority of ordinary English church-goers had been deeply shocked when James had, once and for all, declared that he would never alter his religion. On June 8, the Electress Sophia had collapsed while walking in the gardens at Herrenhausen and died, at the age of eighty-four. Her son George, the new Elector, waited patiently and drew up his list of Regents who would administer the Government between the death of Anne and his own arrival in England. Thirteen out of the eighteen were Whigs.

Bolingbroke pressed on with his designs. Harcourt, as Lord Chancellor, Wyndham, as Chancellor of the Exchequer, and Ormonde, as Commander-in-Chief, were ready; and it was agreed to make Bishop Atterbury Lord Privy Seal in the place of the pro-Hanoverian Lord Dartmouth. But Bolingbroke was not wholly sanguine and even at this late hour threw out feelers to the younger Whigs. London was amazed by the news of a dinner party given at his house in Golden Square to Stanhope, Pulteney and Craggs – a fourth guest, Walpole, was out of town and could not attend. What Bolingbroke hoped to gain by this extraordinary and quite transparent manoeuvre is hard to say, but he received very short shrift at the hands of his startled guests. They would have no truck with compromises. There were two courses open to Bolingbroke: either he should join the Whigs in bringing over the Elector, or he should accede to French pressure and bring over James. They left him in no doubt as to the course they recommended. The dinner party was not a success.

These younger Whigs, untainted by any breath of co-operation with James in marked contrast to some of their elders like Marlborough and Somers, had their own plans. According to Lord Chesterfield, a cousin of Stanhope's and therefore likely to be reliable, Cadogan was to seize the Tower and Stanhope would arrest the most prominent Jacobites; Hanoverian supporters would mass in the duelling fields behind Montagu House, and King George would be proclaimed in the City of London. Such measures were unnecessary. On the morning of July 30, Anne's illness took a turn for the worse, and the Privy Council was hastily summoned to Kensington Palace.

The Jacobites heavily outnumbered the Hanoverians, who contributed only three, the Duke of Shrewsbury, John Robinson, Bishop of London, and Lord Dartmouth. But the proceedings of the Council were rudely interrupted by two unexpected arrivals. The Dukes of Argyle and Somerset had been to see the Elector's emissary Bothmar, and had informed him of the Queen's imminent death. They then drove to Kensington Palace and, standing on their rights as Privy Councillors in spite of the fact that they had not been invited, joined the deliberations. Shrewsbury welcomed their arrival, as it must have strengthened his hand in the move to thwart Bolingbroke. He was presented with the Lord Treasurer's staff by a Queen who was past caring what might occur; and under his chairmanship the Council began to draw up the orders which would ensure the accession of the Elector. They worked on until midnight, and relays of messengers rode out of the gates of Kensington Palace on their way to Lords Lieutenant, Mayors and Governors, to the Tower and Edinburgh Castle, and to Bothmar. The news went forth that the Queen was dying and that the name of her successor was not James but George.

Bolingbroke appeared to agree wholeheartedly with every proposal, although his feelings must have been very different. He later wrote blithely to Swift: "The Earl of Oxford was removed on Tuesday, the Queen died on Sunday. What a world this is, and how does fortune ban-

ter us." He needed all his wit and devil-may-care in-
souciance in such a bitter situation.

On July 31, Bothmar was advised of every development
to date and a letter, signed by all the Privy Councillors,
carried across to Hanover. In the early hours of the following morning, Queen Anne, the last Stuart to grace
the throne of England, died at half past seven. The Duke
of Shrewsbury and a few other Councillors, who had
been hastily summoned, arrived too late. Dr. Arbuthnot
penned the truest epitaph: "My dear mistress's days
were numbered even in my imagination, and could not
exceed certain limits; but of that small number a great
deal was cut off by the last troublesome scene of this
contention among her servants. I believe sleep was never
more welcome to a weary traveller than death was to
her."

Kensington Palace went into deep mourning, and the
Council moved to St. James's. It was the very day that
the Schism Act should have come into force, and with
the death of the Queen it lapsed. Mr. Bradbury, the dis-
senting minister of Fetter Lane, had begun his sermon
when he saw a man drop a handkerchief from the gallery.
It was the signal agreed with Bishop Burnet, and as Bradbury announced the accession of George I a wave of joy
swept through the building. The Dissenters were saved
and would be the Hanoverians' most fervent supporters.

The Jacobites were somewhat less overcome with delight. Bishop Atterbury offered to proclaim James at
Charing Cross in his lawn sleeves. Indeed, according to
Carte, "the night before the Queen died, when the Council broke up the Duke of Buckingham came to the Duke
of Ormonde, clapped his hand on his shoulder and said,
My Lord, you have twenty-four hours' time to do our
business in and make yourself master of the kingdom".
But the twenty-four hours vanished, and with them any
chance of turning back the Hanoverian tide. The list of
Regents was opened and found to contain thirteen

Whigs, four Hanoverian Tories and the unattached Earl of Pembroke, besides the seven *ex officio* members. Only Harcourt and Buckingham could be said to represent the Jacobite interests. Bolingbroke himself was not on the list, nor, more curiously, was Marlborough, although he was soon to be rewarded with Ormonde's post of Captain General. The Proclamation was signed by 127 people, and was read to a great throng outside St. James's Palace, and in all the principal towns throughout the country.

The heralds, preceded by the sound of trumpet and kettle-drum, read out the resounding words: "We therefore, the Lords Spiritual and Temporal of the Realm, being here assisted with those of Her Late Majesty's Privy Council, with numbers of other principal gentlemen of quality, with the Lord Mayor, Aldermen and Citizens of London, do now hereby with one voice and consent of tongue and heart, publish and proclaim that the High and Mighty Prince George Elector of Brunswick-Lüneburg is now by the death of our late sovereign of Happy Memory, become our only lawful and rightful liege Lord, George, by the Grace of God King of Great Britain, France and Ireland. God save the King." An address was prepared by the Scottish chiefs, including Cameron of Lochiel, Glengarry, Macleod of Macleod, Macdonald of the Isles and Chisholm; and in Dublin the same ritual blossomed forth. In London great bonfires were lit outside noblemen's doors, and it was remarked that one of the most substantial illuminated the portal of Henry St. John, Viscount Bolingbroke's doorway.

Over in Hanover, the new king prepared to set out. The yacht *Peregrine* had been lying at anchor off the coast of Holland ready for its royal passenger, and at last George said farewell to Herrenhausen and reluctantly departed for the Hague. He arrived there on September 5 and moved on to board the *Peregrine* at Orange

Polder eleven days later. Escorted by a sizeable fleet, he set sail without delay and arrived off Greenwich at six o'clock in the evening of the 18th. He was greeted by a dense fog, a mass of dignitaries and officials, and some execrable verse. Mr. Eusden, soon to become Poet Laureate, produced a choice example:

> Hail, mighty GEORGE! Auspicious smiles thy Reign,
> Thee long we wish'd, Thee at last we gain.
> Thy hoary Prudence in green Years began,
> And the bold Infant stretch'd at once to Man.
> How oft, Transported, the great *Ernest* smil'd
> With the Presages of his greater Child.

And a great deal more in the same vein. It was a fine day for third-rate poets and they made the most of it.

George was also forced to endure the full pomp and panoply of a state entry into London, fixed for the following Monday. Suffolk, the Lord Marshal, had already issued intricate and lavish details of ceremony and precedence; and both the expectant crowds and the eager participants in the procession would not be disappointed. King George, with his son and the Duke of Northumberland commanding the Life Guards-in-Waiting, duly drove up to London, following great numbers of carriages crammed with approximately 2,000 noblemen and gentry. He was met by the Lord Mayor and Corporation in Southwark and endured a lengthy speech from the Recorder. It was the first of a vast succession of perorations, and only his ugly mistresses could console him.

He was certainly not impressed by his first view of his new residence at St. James's, particularly when he had to pay Lord Chetwynd, the Ranger of the Park, for the present of a brace of his own carp "out of my canal, in my own Park". But he showed some determination in his selective treatment of those he considered his enemies. He refused to receive Ormonde, was markedly cold towards Oxford, and snubbed Mar. Westminster Abbey

on Coronation Day, October 20, was, even so, full of
Jacobite as well as Hanoverian supporters. Among those
present was Bolingbroke who had also been refused an
interview by the king. Lady Cowper noted in her diary:
"One may easily conclude this was not a Day of real
Joy to the Jacobites. However they were all there, looking as cheerful as they could, but very peevish with
Everybody that spoke to them, My Lady Dorchester*
stood underneath me; and when the archbishop went
round the Throne, demanding the consent of the People,
she turned to me and said, 'Does the old Fool think that
Anybody here will say no to his Question, when there
are so many drawn swords?'" There is a record that
when the King's Champion rode into the Abbey and
shouted his challenge, one lady answered that James III
was the rightful ruler of England, but if so hers was the
only voice to be raised in objection.

King George I was crowned. It would need a well con-
certed and skilfully led rebellion to topple him from his
throne and put in his place the King over the Water.

*A former mistress of James II and an outspoken lady. When
she espied the Duchess of Portsmouth, a mistress to Charles
II, and Lady Orkney, who had fulfilled the same function for
William III, both in the congregation at the Coronation, she exclaimed, "Good God! Who would have thought we three whores
would have met together here."

Part Three

Rebellion 1715

Chapter Five

The Rising in England

You may soon have your wish to enjoy the gallant
sights of armies, encampments, standards waving over
your brother's cornfields, and the pretty windings of
the Thames stained with the blood of men.

ALEXANDER POPE

ON the anniversary of King George's birthday, May 8,
1715, the Foot Guards demonstrated noisily outside St.
James's and Marlborough House. They had an understandable grievance. Their uniforms were badly in need
of replacement, and they were liable for punishment
for a supposed crime they could do nothing to remedy.
Exasperated, they strung their tattered and patched shirts
up on poles and paraded them through the streets, shouting, "Look at our Hanover shirts!" A bonfire was lit in
Whitehall into which uniforms were thrown. And more
articles of military dress landed in the very gardens of
St. James's. The message was obvious, and the Duke of
Marlborough, reviewing the Guards, was compelled to
deliver a honeyed speech of persuasion. And the following day, which happened to be the anniversary of Charles
II's restoration, saw further pro-Jacobite activity.

It was all symptomatic of the times. The accession of

George had been engineered so smoothly that no one had an opportunity to protest. A few hotheads had proclaimed James in Devon, and there had been a Jacobite-inspired riot in Bristol the previous October, but the atmosphere had remained comparatively calm until the Whig-dominated Parliament met in March. From that moment, the more extreme Tories began to consider very seriously the Jacobite alternative, and none more so than James Butler, Duke of Ormonde.

Ormonde was an immensely popular man, substantially because of his generosity and affable nature, and he appears with great regularity in all Jacobite plots. He had been born in Dublin Castle in 1665, and he succeeded his father, the first duke, twenty-three years later. He had supported William of Orange, been present at the Boyne, and fought at Steinkerque and Landen. In Queen Anne's reign he had commanded the Vigo expedition and had twice served as Lord Lieutenant of Ireland. He attained his greatest power when he succeeded Marlborough as Captain General in 1712. An ardent Tory, he was deeply implicated in the plots to bring over James on Queen Anne's death, and with a modicum of courage and speed might have become a king-maker. But, as the Duke of Berwick put it, "such grand designs need a hero, and that was what the Duke of Ormonde was not". In Michael Dahl's portrait, he is seen in a conventional warrior's pose, armoured and holding his baton rather aggressively in a large fist. His face is fleshy, the determination of the mouth offset by the double chin. It is the picture, in essence, of a man whose personal bravery is cancelled out by a weakness and lack of decision.

James Keith, who knew Ormonde well during the years of exile, confirms this impression: "He was a man of a very easy temper, and of ordinary understanding, so diffident of himself that he often followed the advice of those who had a smaller share of sense than himself; he was as irresolute and timorous in affairs as he was

brave in his person, and was apt to lose good oppor-
tunities by waiting to remove difficulties which naturally
attend great designs, and of which a part must always be
left to fortune in the execution; he was a man of entire
honour, a good friend, and a strict observer of his word."

Ormonde and Bolingbroke were the chief organisers
of the projected rising in England, and neither was to remain on the scene for very long. Bolingbroke had retired
to the country a month after Anne's death, on relinquish-
ing his seals of office, and he did not return to London
until February or March. Almost at once, he committed
the most crass mistake of his stormy career. Afraid that
evidence of his negotiations with the Jacobite court
might be uncovered, he sought advice from one of the
men who had most cause to hate him, the Duke of Marlborough. The restored Captain General seized this
heaven-sent opportunity to settle accounts. There was
no evidence, but he hinted to the worried Bolingbroke
that indeed the Government were about to pounce and
that he might well find his head in danger.

On March 26, Bolingbroke was at Drury Lane Theatre,
apparently in excellent humour, talking to the actor
Booth, gossiping with his acquaintances, and giving the
general impression that he had not a care in the world.
It was noticed that he reserved seats for the following
night's performance, a fact which surprised no one as
he was known to be a great lover of the theatre. The
seats, though, were never taken up. Half an hour after
leaving Drury Lane, with his eyebrows darkened and
wearing a black wig, he slipped away to the coast. The
London Gazette recorded the details:

"This day William Morgan, late Captain in Major
Holt's Regiment of Marines, appeared before a Com-
mittee of the Lords of His Majesty's most honourable
Privy Council, and declared, that he having sent one
Andrew Galway before to Dover, to provide a vessel for
carrying him over to Calais on some private business

of his own, went post from London on Saturday last for
Dover; that on Sunday morning about six o'clock, he
the said Morgan being at the Dolphin Inn at Dover, saw
two men come into the said inn, whom he at first took to
be French carriers; that soon after one of them spoke to
him, and discovered himself to be the Lord Viscount
Bolingbroke, that his Lordship was in disguise, having
a black bob wig on, with a laced hat, and very ordinary
clothes; but he the said Morgan knew the said Lord very
well, having formerly received several favours from him;
that his Lordship proposed going over in the vessel
which he the said Morgan had hired, that accordingly
they went on board on Sunday about noon, together with
the French carrier called la Vigne; that they landed at
Calais the same evening about six o'clock; and that after
landing the Governor of the said town waited on the
Lord Bolingbroke and carried him to his house, where
his Lordship lay, and the said Morgan saw him there the
next morning, and that on Tuesday he the said Morgan
left that place."

London was in an uproar at the news. By his flight,
Bolingbroke had virtually admitted his guilt, and fallen
straight into the trap so cleverly baited by Marlborough.
Bolingbroke's somewhat murky past was dredged up and
the ballad-mongers had a field day selling scurrilous
pamphlets which dwelled heavily on the subject's sexual
appetite and fondness for the bottle. Even his defenders
could only put up a weak case to explain away his sudden departure: "My Lord had too elegant a taste for
life to part with it, to gratify only the resentments of his
enemies! If he was a rake, it was his nature that was to
be blamed; if he was a villain, no one could charge
him with hypocritically attempting to hide it ... As to
personal frailties, his Lordship had his share, and never
strove to hide them by the sanctified cover which men
of high station generally affect ... His faults and levities
were owing to his complexion, and that life and humour

with which he enlivened them, made them so pleasing that those who condemned the action could not but approve the person." It was an unconvincing plea of mitigation, and the Whigs were not impressed. It is true that Bolingbroke did not make up his mind irrevocably for some months after he reached France – besides dallying with the seductive Mme de Tencin, he also approached Stair, the English ambassador, who would have none of him – but by July he had been appointed James's Secretary of State and at last received the earldom which he had coveted for so long.

Bolingbroke's fellow-conspirator, Ormonde, stayed on for a few months more. His impeachment was carried on June 17, but even then he moved no further than his White House at Richmond, where he planned a rising in the West Country. He would post down to Devon, using relays of fast horses already prepared, and strike at Exeter, Plymouth and Bristol. If he had carried out this plan, he might have presented a very severe threat to the Government; and there is a Jacobite memorandum in existence which suggests that if he had raised the standard of rebellion, the army might have mutinied in his favour, and George I would have departed speedily for Holland. But Ormonde lost his head. On hearing the news that there was a warrant out for his arrest, and that troops were already on their way to Richmond, he abandoned the plans without any thought of passing them on to a deputy, rode post-haste to Shoreham and was in France on July 21. Five days earlier, Robert Harley, Earl of Oxford, refusing to fly and so admit a guilt which he did not possess, had been conveyed to the Tower. The Government's nerves were at breaking point.

Throughout May, tension had been rising, and there had been one particularly violent outburst in Oxford, always a centre of Stuart sympathies since the days when Charles I had set up his headquarters there during the Civil War. The trouble started when a Whig club de-

cided to celebrate George's birthday by burning on a
bonfire effigies of Queen Anne, Ormonde, and Sachever-
ell, the High Tory divine. But the Oxford Jacobites went
one better by hiring the room above their opponents and
by bribing the crowd which gathered, to destroy the bonfire. There was much drinking, and uproar, and the proc-
tors were called out. The authorities, however, Jacobites
almost to a man, took very little action. Thomas Hearne,
for one, did not rejoice at King George's birthday: "This
being the Duke of Brunswick, commonly called King
George's birthday, some of the bells were jambled in
Oxford by the care of the Whiggish fanatical crew; but
as I did not observe the day in the least myself, so it was
little taken notice of (unless by way of ridicule) by other
honest people, who are for King James III, who is the
undoubted King of these kingdoms."

On June 10, James's birthday, on the other hand, there
were great demonstrations throughout the North and
West. In Manchester, a Presbyterian meeting-place was
razed to the ground. There were riots in Leeds, and in
Somerset James's health was drunk openly. In Gloucester there were disgraceful happenings. A correspondent
to the *Flying-Post* described them. Various Jacobites
were getting progressively drunker as toast followed
toast in the Swan Inn, and the singing of "tumultuous
songs" was well under way, much to the annoyance of
a neighbouring alderman, "a pious and very ancient
gentleman", who presumably carried things too far by
being also a confirmed Whig. The alderman, piously but
foolishly, complained. But "such was the villainy of the
cowardly faction, notwithstanding his age and magis-
tratical authority, they abused and beat him in such a
manner that he is now in a weak and dangerous position".

The Government took action, even if the local authorities were either too disloyal or too frightened to follow
their example. The whole situation was debated in the

Commons on July 15, and trenchant orders were sent out to magistrates and justices of the peace throughout the country. The Riot Act was renewed, and the impeachments of Tory leaders were moved. But the disturbances continued to spread, and only in the Home Counties and traditionally Puritan East Anglia did peace reign. In London, a camp was established in Hyde Park and artillery trundled down from the Tower. The Horse Guards were purged of possible Jacobite sympathisers, and at the beginning of September Colonel Paul of the First Regiment of Foot Guards, later the Grenadiers and the Duke of Marlborough's own cherished regiment, was arrested after one of his sergeants had laid evidence against him. According to the sergeant, Paul already had the Pretender's commission as colonel of a cavalry regiment and was busy enlisting men to serve James in the event of a rising. And on August 1, there had been further outrages in Oxford, on the anniversary of George's accession. Thomas Hearne, needless to say, did not join any rejoicings. Shop windows were smashed, and a few weeks later a recruiting officer looking for likely dragoons was stoned by undergraduates from Balliol and was forced to beat an ignominious retreat.

With Ormonde and Bolingbroke fled abroad, the general direction of the Jacobite cause in England fell to four men: Ormonde's brother Arran, a complete nonentity; Lansdowne, who hoped to control the West from his house at Longleat near Bath; Mar, smarting under George's snub, who was given Scotland as his concern; and Sir William Wyndham, the most energetic and influential of the quartet. Wyndham had held a number of high Government posts, including those of Secretary at War and Chancellor of the Exchequer. His plan was to make the rising in the West Country the salient feature of the country-wide rebellion, with activities in Scotland and the North only of secondary importance. Plymouth and Bristol would be seized, and James himself would

land in Devon. Sir Richard Vyvyan would raise Cornwall, and Lansdowne would take Bath. It was a reasonable plan on paper, but it was never put into operation.

On October 8, a month after Mar had slipped away to
Scotland, Vyvyan was arrested and brought up to London. On the 21st, Lansdowne and Lord Dupplin,
Oxford's son-in-law, shared his fate. And on the same
day, the House of Commons agreed to the arrest of six
members of Parliament, Sir William Wyndham, Sir John
Packington, Thomas Forster, Corbet Kynaston, Edward
Harvey and John Anstis. Packington was almost immediately released, and Anstis promptly cleared. Kynaston
escaped abroad, and Harvey attempted suicide. Thomas
Forster was safe up in Northumberland, and preparing
to take over the command of the northern rising.

Sir William Wyndham was the most important quarry.
He had already left London for his Somerset seat at
Orchard Wyndham, and his arrival was greeted with
much ringing of church bells. But an officer of the Foot
Guards, Colonel Husk, was even then on his way to
Minehead to arrest him. The colonel reached his desti-
nation in the early hours of the 22nd and was greeted by
Wyndham in his night-gown. The slighty farcical scene
is detailed by a contemporary writer:

"Sir William Wyndham presently leaped out of bed,
and came in his gown to the colonel, who told him he
was his prisoner; the messenger at the same time showing the badge of his office. Sir William told him that he
readily submitted but desired no noise might be made to
frighten his lady, who was with child."* Wyndham was a
little too quick in handing over his keys to Husk, and the
suspicious colonel found the papers he was looking for
in a coat lying on a chair. As he extracted them from
their hiding-place, he could see from Wyndham's expres-

*Husk had been given strict instructions to disturb Lady
Wyndham as little as possible, since she was the daughter of the
influential Duke of Somerset.

sion that he had struck lucky. Sir William tried a last trick. "He then desired the colonel that he would stay until seven o'clock, and he would order his own coach and his horses to be got ready, which would carry them all; telling the colonel he would only go in and put on his clothes, and take leave of his lady, and then he would wait on him." The colonel agreed to this request, "but he soon found himself mistaken in the person whose honour he had trusted to, for though the colonel had caused two doors of Sir William's bed-chamber to be secured, yet there being a third, he made his escape through it".

A reward of £1,000 was offered for Wyndham's capture, but he had got clean away, disguised as a clergyman. He reached Surrey without mishap, and at once sent a letter to a friend asking for shelter. At this point his luck ran out. The letter was opened by the man's wife and she, terrified that her husband might be involved in a case of high treason, reported the contents of the letter to the local authorities. Wyndham, receiving no answer to his plea for help, took fright and rode off to see his father-in-law at Syon House. Together, they decided it would be best for him to give himself up, and he immediately surrendered to his brother-in-law Lord Hertford. Wyndham was removed to the Tower, and Somerset resigned his post as Master of the Horse.

The ringleaders had now all either fled or been placed under lock and key, and the Government moved further on to the offensive. Bath and Bristol were strengthened by loyal forces, and Oxford was subdued at bayonet point by Handasyde's Regiment. In London, a number of suspected traitors were arrested, and three of Colonel Paul's men were put on trial for high treason; they were executed on October 28.

The rising in England, with the exception of Forster's insurrection in the far North, was over before it had begun, but even now attempts were made to rekindle it from the safety of the Continent. Bolingbroke, ignorant of

Wyndham's arrest, sent agents to Devon and Cornwall, to announce James's imminent arrival at Plymouth. Ormonde would follow shortly, and James himself four days later. But the weather once more played a decisive part. The agents could not sail, and Ormonde was still in Paris. When he did eventually reach the coast, he was met by grave news. Not only had Wyndham and Lansdowne been taken, but Ormonde's own secretary, Sir John Maclean, had betrayed the whole plot to the Government at Whitehall. Ormonde, in spite of these disastrous reports, set sail for Cornwall but was forced to return to Brittany when it was made abundantly clear to him that there would be no rising in the South-West.

Both James and his advisers and the British Government now turned their attention to Scotland. It was there that the 1715 rebellion would triumph or be crushed.

Chapter Six

The Rising in Scotland

The Earl of Mar, then at London, not finding how to form his own interest at court, had resolved on those wicked and traitorous measures he afterwards followed.

REA'S *History of the Late Rebellion*

THE small town of Braemar lies on rising ground between the Cairngorms and the main range of the Grampians away towards the sea. Past it swirls the river Dee, cascading down from the narrow, gloomy gorge at the Linn o' Dee. In the cold of winter, enveloped in snow-drifts, it takes on a desolate air, matched by the huge firs and pines, relics of the great Caledonian forests, and by the grey castle of Braemar, machicolated and turreted in the Gothic style. Here the bitterness of the wind complements the memories of murder and savage revenge which haunt the granite-dark walls. In summer, though, the Dee maintains a calmer flow and the Brae itself is a sweeping stretch of grass, shaded at its perimeter by fine trees. The mountains are no longer caught in mist and the peaks of Ben Macdhui and even Ben Nevis emerge from their wintry opacity.

It was during the month of August that the Earls of Mar traditionally organised a great hunt which often lasted for six weeks. It was an important annual event which attracted the nobles and their retainers from all over Scotland; for the Erskine family dispensed lavish hospitality, and the occasion afforded ample opportunity to hatch new plots and contemplate old feuds. Nearly a century before John, Earl of Mar's precipitate and somewhat undignified arrival at his neighbour Farquharson of Invercauld's castle, another curious individual had journeyed to the Brae of Mar from London. This was John Taylor, who held the bizarre post of the King's Majesties Water-Poet and felt that it might well be diplomatic to allow his sovereign James I's own country to inspire a new collection of sonnets.

His poetic exercises were hardly distinguished – "I must relate to my great Master James,/The Caledonian annual peaceful war;/How noble minds do eternize their flames,/By martial meeting in the Brae of Mar" is a fair example – but as a mere diarist, relating events on his "Penniless Pilgrimage", he was able to describe for the startled *littérateurs* of London the intricacies of Highland sport and society. He was much impressed by what he saw. Braemar itself he spoke of as "a large county, all composed of such mountains, that Shooter's Hill, Gad's Hill, Highgate Hill, Hampstead Hill, Birdlip Hill, or Malvern's Hills, are but mole-hills in comparison, or like a river, or a gizard under a capon's wings, in respect of the altitude of their tops, or perpendicularity of their bottoms".

The hunt had assembled – Murrays, Gordons, Stuarts, Buchans, and Erskines, all under the aegis of Mar. Taylor was struck by the clothes they wore: tartan short hose, shoes with only one sole apiece (double soles were normal in London), garters made up of wisps of straw, a jerkin but no breeches, a plaid "of divers colours", a blue flat cap on the head and a knotted handkerchief tied round the neck. And everyone, nobleman or servant, wore the same. The weapons of the chase were equally outlandish, long bows, dirks and Lochaber axes joining the more conventional muskets, swords and arquebuses. The quarry consisted exclusively of fine fat deer, although Taylor noted the presence of wolves and wild horses.

Commissariat arrangements were highly efficient and on the grandest scale; with a camp consisting of fifteen hundred men they had to be. The movable kitchen was permanently full of turning spits and boiling pots and kettles, and Taylor was open-mouthed at the variety of the food on offer: "venison baked, sodden, roast, and stewed beef, mutton, goats, kid, hares, fresh salmon, pigeons, hens, capons, chickens, partridge, moor-coots, heath-cocks, capercailzies, and termagants [ptarmigans]; good ale, sack, white, and claret, tent (or Alicante), with much potent Aquavitae." For a penniless pilgrim this was luxury indeed.

The ritual of the hunt had not radically altered in the decades which separated John Taylor's Highland visit from the gathering in 1715 which launched the rising. Sir Walter Scott, judiciously mixing research with imagination, describes the probable scene: "The lords attended to the head of their vassals, all, even Lowland guests, attired in the Highland garb, and the sport was carried on upon a scale of rude magnificence. A circuit of many miles was formed around the wild, desolate forests and wildernesses, which are inhabited by the red deer, and is called the tinchel. Upon a signal given, the hunters who compose the tinchel begin to move inwards, closing the circle and driving the terrified deer before them ... Being in this manner concentrated and crowded together, they are driven down a defile, where the principal hunters lie in wait for them, and show their dexterity by marking out and shooting those bucks which are in season."

Mar had left London abruptly, either on the evening of August 1, having just emerged from King George's

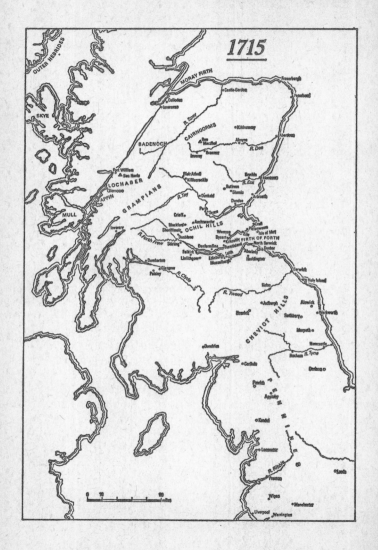

levée, or on the following day. He wasted no time in going on board a collier lying in the Thames and bound for Newcastle. He was accompanied only by Major-General Hamilton and by Colonel John Hay, the titular Earl of Inverness, besides a couple of servants. Together they hired a Newcastle boat which landed them on the Fife coast. Mar crossed the Tay on the 18th and on the following day sent out a number of letters announcing the Braemar gathering. He himself arrived there on the 20th, and took up temporary lodging with his reluctant vassal Farquharson of Invercauld, since his own castle of Kildrummy was in a bad state of repair.

The invitations had been issued to all the most influential Jacobite nobles and chiefs, although the Lowland lords, such as Kenmure, Nithsdale and Wintoun, did not attend. Those who did come, however, included the Marquesses of Huntly and Tullibardine representing their fathers (Gordon had been imprisoned in Edinburgh Castle, and Atholl, although offered the leadership of the Jacobite army, was to stick to his Whig principles and took no part in the rebellion); George Keith, Earl Marischal, and the Earls of Erroll, Southesk, Carnwath, Seaforth, and Linlithgow; Viscount Kilsyth, and Lords Rollo, Duffus, Drummond and Ogilvy; and General Hamilton, Gordon of Auchintoul, Campbell of Glendaruel, who represented the ancient and devious Lord Breadalbane, Glengarry, Lyon of Auchterhouse, and Auldbar, the nephew of the great Claverhouse.*

The sport on Saturday, August 27 was good, and the chase took the hunters round by Glen Cluny and back to Glen of Quoich, where, according to the legend, punch was brewed in a hollowed-out rock and the success of the rising drunk in a mixture of whisky, honey and boiling water. Mar then made a stirring speech – he was

*This is the traditional list, although it is by no means certain that all these people in fact attended. Such an impressive catalogue is more likely to be sheer propaganda.

always a persuasive orator. Rae gives his own idea of
what happened: "Having thus got his Friends together,
he address'd himself to them in a publick Speech, full of
Invectives against the Protestant Succession in General,
and against King George in particular; wherein, to gloss
his Actions with a seeming Reflection as of Sorrow for
what was past, he told them, That tho' he had been Instrumental in forwarding the Union of the two Kingdoms
in the Reign of Queen Anne, yet now his Eyes were
open'd and he could see his Error, would therefore do
what lay in his Power to make them again a Free People,
and that they should enjoy their ancient Liberties, which
were by that cursed Union (as he call'd it) delivered up
into the Hands of the English ... and to establish upon
the Throne of these Realms the Chevalier St. George
(the Pretender), who, he said, had the only undoubted
Right to the Crown, had promis'd to hear their Grievances, and would redress their Wrongs."

It was all very eloquent and convincing. There would
be a simultaneous rising in England, there would be
powerful assistance from France, funds of £100,000 were
announced, and Mar's commission from James as major-
general of the army in Scotland was displayed; although,
almost certainly, this document was only a draft drawn
up by Mar himself in anticipation of the real commission
which was not dated until September 7. After the hunt,
the majority of the participants departed to their homes
to gather their own contingents, while a few, like Lord
Erroll, took no further part in the rising. Mar himself, deserted by Farquharson and another near-neighbour Gordon of Abergeldie, moved on to Kildrummy, after first
ill-treating the Invercauld servants in a fit of petty revenge.

A week after the Braemar hunt, a further meeting was
held at Huntly's castle of Aboyne. This, though, was a
very different affair, consisting of eleven men, an inner
circle of Jacobites. Huntly, Mar, Tullibardine, Marischal,
Southesk, Glengarry, Glendaruel, Auchterhouse, Auld-

bar, Hamilton and Gordon of Auchintoul, these were the men who intended to lead the rising. Finally, on September 6, the standard was raised at Braemar. Lord Justice Clerk Adam Cockburn was informed that as many as 600 people were present, although other estimates go as low as sixty. There is equal confusion over the nature of the standard itself. Mar's own valet records merely that it had the initials J. R. and the figures 3 and 8 (James III of England and VIII of Scotland), whereas other authorities give a detailed description of a blue silk banner bearing the arms of Scotland in gold on one side, and the motto *"Nemo me impune lacessit"* over the words "No union" on the reverse, with in addition two white pendants declaring "for our wronged king and oppressed country" and "for ourselves and liberties". There are also eye-witness accounts of the golden ball on top of the standard having fallen to the ground, an event which gave full scope to the superstitious. What is undisputed is that Mar made another of his eloquent addresses, emphasising his own personal sorrow at having furthered negotiations at the time of the Union and inveighing against the iniquities of Hanoverian rule. Everyone present was handed a copy of the famous commission and sent off to raise the tenants and the clans. After so many pious hopes and fruitless deliberations the Rising was at last a fact.

*

In Edinburgh, there was a marked lack of surprise or panic. On the very day before the hunt at Braemar, the Lord Provost, George Warrender, wrote to Secretary of State Stanhope in London that news had been coming in of a gathering of dissidents in Aberdeenshire, and that all possible precautions were being taken by the city magistrates. He added, however, that reinforcements for the castle garrison would be needed if the rising showed signs of spreading. Whitehall did indeed take action. The

Habeas Corpus Act was suspended, a request was sent
to the Dutch for the 6,000 men promised by the Government at the Hague in the event of a threat to the Protestant succession, an act to legalise the suppression of
rioting was passed rapidly through both Houses of Parliament, and summonses were made out for a large
number of known Jacobites to present themselves at
Edinburgh. Only two, Murray of Auchtertyre and Lord
Lyon, obeyed, although the wily old John Campbell of
Glenorchy, Lord Breadalbane, one of the chief participants in the Glencoe atrocity, took the trouble to send a
letter pleading his age, together with a certificate signed
by a doctor and a minister listing an astounding number
of ailments from which he was supposed to be suffering,
"coughs, rheums, gravels, stitches, defluxions and disease
of the kidneys". By September 20, however, the patient
had clearly made a remarkable recovery, as he was able
to join the Jacobite camp at Perth; not for nothing did
Macky call him "as cunning as a fox, wise as a serpent,
and slippery as an eel". In addition, a certain number of
suspects, including Lockhart and Lord Home, were imprisoned. The ears of the Edinburgh authorities, or rather
of their informers, were remarkably acute, as the activities of such as Huntly, Marischal, Southesk and Brigadier Macintosh of Borlum were common knowledge
from the beginning of August onwards.

   Life in Edinburgh at the time was far from luxurious
or even particularly appealing. Built and maintained on
the model of a French fortified town, there were no fine,
detached houses for the noblemen when they assembled
for the sittings of Parliament, only mediocre apartments
in the High Street. The days of the superb Georgian
squares and terraces beyond Princes Street were still in
the future, and all that lay to the north of the smoke-
begrimed city was the Nor' Loch. The inhabitants, unable to spread themselves beyond the old gates, were
obliged to build upwards, and the tall tenement houses

with their exterior staircases in Canongate, the High Street and Cowgate were overcrowded and unhygienic. Indeed the entire sanitary system of Edinburgh was laughable – except that it was so appalling. Filth of every imaginable description was flung into the street, and passers-by were lucky if they first received the traditional warning of "gardy-loo", a corruption of *gardez l'eau*. The mingled refuse and excrement lay in the alleys and deep wynds until, early in the morning, the ludicrous City Guard with their Lochabar axes made a show of collecting it. And on the Sabbath even this makeshift service went undone. Joseph Taylor (no relation to the water-poet), who visited Edinburgh in 1705 and witnessed the affair of Captain Green, held his nose with disgust at these barbarous practices, and recorded that "we were forced to take care where we trod for fear of disobliging our shoes, and to walk in the middle at night, for fear of an accident on our heads".

Taylor had other criticisms. "The lodgings are as nasty as the streets, and washed so seldom, that the dirt is thick enough to be pared off with a shovel. Every room is well scented with a close stool, and the master, mistress and servants lie all on a floor, like so many swine in a hogsty; this with the rest of their sluttishness," he continues ominously, "is no doubt the occasion of the Itch, which is so common amongst them." The dreaded Itch, it appears, "is occasioned by a minute little creature, in shape resembling a tortoise, of whitish colour, a little dark upon the back, with some thin long hairs, of nimble motion, with six feet, a sharp head, with two little horns at the end of the snout". Fortunately, the fastidious Mr. Taylor and his companions were able to avoid this monster through a judicious use of white thread stockings and gloves. All in all, the Scots seemed to him nasty, profane and vicious, their inability or refusal to provide any entertainment extraordinary, the arable land around Edinburgh shockingly farmed, and

even the splendours of Holyroodhouse disappointing,
He was in definite agreement with the English captain
who, when asked whether he liked Scotland, replied that
he did not because the inhabitants were less religious
than those of other countries. His audience, bred on a
healthy respect for acute Puritanism, were predictably
surprised, and the captain, no doubt savouring his pay-
off line like all good purveyors of old jokes, duly explained. "You have but eight Commandments," he said,
"for you have nothing to covet, nor nothing to steal."

Defoe had more understanding and more compassion.
"Were any other people," he wrote, "to live under the
same unhappiness, I mean as well of a rocky and moun-
tainous situation, thronged buildings from seven to ten
or twelve storey high, a scarcity of water, and that little
they have difficult to be had, and to the uppermost lodgings far to fetch, we should have a London or Bristol
as dirty as Edinburgh; for though many cities have more
people in them, yet I believe that in no city in the world
so many people live in so little room."

There were, of course, compensations. The crime rate
was extremely low. There were underground clubs
formed to sap the strength of the Kirk. The Tron Kirk
in the High Street was thronged on Sundays by a fashionable crowd, and earned the reputation of being something
of an unofficial marriage market. There was horse-racing
on the sands of Leith, when, that is, no bodies were dang-
ling from the gibbet there. Drinking was allowed until
ten o'clock at night except on Sundays. The so-called
sport of cock-fighting was popular. And there was
always golf. Even so, the lack of theatres, of music, of
anything approaching a readable news-sheet, of the publishing of books other than theological or political
works, indeed of culture as a whole, cannot be ignored.
Religion ruled the roost, and it was a harsh religion,
cruel and unforgiving as the icy gales which assailed the
city walls, which could countenance such iniquities as

the Stool of Repentance, where sinners were forced to stand and receive an interminable diatribe against their wickedness delivered by an elder of the Kirk. It is not difficult to visualise how much English soldiers stationed at the Castle must have longed for a return to comparative civilisation, as they looked down from the battlements at the dingy, black buildings. Edinburgh to them must have seemed as exile in a cold, uncultured provincial town appeared to patrician Romans.

It was against the Castle that the first armed attack of the rising was to be made. Up in the North Mar was displaying to the full his innate lack of decision and general incompetence. True he had issued a number of manifestoes from the house of the unfortunate Farquharson, who had now been induced to return and display modest enthusiasm for the enterprise; and James had been proclaimed at various points throughout the North-East: at Aberdeen by Marischal, at Dunkeld by Tullibardine, at Perth by Colonel Balfour and Colonel Hay, by Huntly at Castle-Gordon and by Panmure at Brechin, at Montrose by Southesk, at Dundee by Graham of Duntroon, and in Inverness by Macintosh of Borlum, who with a force of only 500 men had seized the town before marching to join Mar. On the latter's leisurely march south by the Spittal of Glenshee, he had been joined at Kirkmichael by 300 horse raised by Linlithgow and Drummond, and by 500 foot under Tullibardine, a very welcome reinforcement as the self-appointed leader of the rising had found it unconscionably difficult to fill his own tenants with any sense of urgency. Indeed, he had felt himself obliged to issue a stern rebuke to his baillie at Kildrummy, the redoubtable Black Jock Forbes of Inverernan. Writing during the night of September 9, he took him firmly to task:

"Ye was in the right not to come with the 100 men ye sent up to-night, when I expected four times the number. It is a pretty thing when all the Highlands of Scotland are

now rising upon their King and Country's account, as I
have accounts from them since they were with me, and
the gentlemen of our neighbouring Lowlands expecting
us down to join them, that my men only should be re-
fractory. Is not this the thing we are now about, which
they have been wishing these twenty-six years? And now,
when it is come, and the king and country's cause is at
stake, will they for ever sit still and see all perish? I have
used gentle means too long, and so shall be forced to put
other orders I have in execution. I have sent you enclosed
an order for the lordship of Kildrummy, which you are
immediately to intimate to all my vassals; if they give
ready obedience, it will make some amends, and if not,
ye may tell them from me that it will not be in my power
to save them (though I were willing) from being treated
as enemies by those who are ready soon to join me, and
they may depend on it, that I will be the first to propose
and order their being so. Particularly let my own tenants
in Kildrummy know, that if they come not forth with
their best arms, I will send a party immediately to burn
what they shall miss taking from them. And they may
believe this only a threat but, by all that's sacred, I'll
put it in execution – let my loss be what it will. You
are to tell the gentlemen that I'll expect them in their
best accoutrements, on horseback, and no excuse to
be expected of. Go about this with all diligence, and
come yourself and let me know your having done so. All
this is not only as ye will be answerable to me, but to your
king and country.

Your assured friend and servant,

MAR.

This letter, celebrated though it is, is still worth quoting
in full, as, with its blend of somewhat empty threats and
bland cajolery, it gives an excellent insight into the men-
tality of its writer, a man lacking finesse or incisiveness.
The response from the tenants and vassals was, predict-

ably, only moderate, no more than 400 men eventually appearing. Perhaps, like Farquharson, they knew their chief too well and put less than complete faith in his abilities as a military leader. Perhaps, since he was so often absent in London, they did not know him well enough to give him their firm loyalty.

But while Mar was endeavouring to raise his tenants, indeed only two days after the unfurling of the standard at Braemar, the plot to seize Edinburgh Castle in the name of James had been hatched. The reasoning behind such a plan was excellent. Not only did the Castle contain the great majority of the arms and ammunition available to the English Government in Scotland as well as a sizeable sum of money, but the moral fillip to the Jacobite sympathisers provided by the capture at the very outset of the rising of the main symbol of English interference would have been incalculable. Unfortunately, the execution of the plan did not match its concoction in intelligence.

The chief movers were Lord Drummond, the eldest son of the titular Duke of Perth, still one of James's chief advisers in exile; Charles Forbes of Brux, described by the acerbic Master of Sinclair as "a little broken merchant", and Macgregor of Balhaldy. Three soldiers inside the Castle had been well bribed, Sergeant William Ainsley being promised a lieutenancy, and two sentinels, Thomas and Holland, receiving eight and four guineas respectively on account of future benefits. The attempt was to be made at nine o'clock at night, by scaling the rock-face on the north side near the Sally Port where the incline was less steep; and suitable ladders had been constructed which were to be pulled up by the soldiers on the battlements. As soon as the Castle was in their hands, Drummond was to be appointed governor and three cannon-shots were to be fired. These would be heard over in Fife and a series of beacons ranging northwards would then be lit so that the news of the success could

reach Mar without delay. He would then march rapidly
on Edinburgh and the first phase of the rising would be
triumphantly over.

In principle, it sounds a simple, almost fool-proof
operation, but almost inevitably a series of disasters proceeded to occur. First of all, a certain Lieutenant Arthur,
who had until recently served as an ensign in the Castle
garrison, told his brother, a doctor, of the plan.* The
latter was by no means a confirmed Jacobite and his
wife, realising that something was troubling his peace of
mind, wormed the entire story out of him. She promptly
sent an anonymous letter to the Lord Justice Clerk warning him about the imminent attack. Cockburn communicated at once with the Deputy Governor, Colonel Stuart,
but the latter was inclined to minimise the danger and,
before going to bed, did nothing more than double the
guards. As it transpired, he was right not to have worried, although for his pains he was later relieved of his
post and thrown unceremoniously into the Tolbooth
gaol.

Celebrating their success somewhat prematurely, the
conspirators were drinking happily in a nearby tavern
– Sinclair calls it contemptuously "powdering their
hair" – and did not arrive at the appointed rendezvous
until two hours later. One can imagine the panic of the
two treacherous sentries as the hours went by and there
was still no sign of their presumed friends or benefactors.
At last, however, the conspirators, properly powdered
and no doubt a trifle unsteady, arrived at the foot of the
wall. But just when they were finally hauling up the first
ladder, a party of soldiers under Lieutenant Lindsay
came marching up to the Sally Port. The two sentries let
the ropes and the ladder fall – according to Sinclair, one
of them, understandably rattled, shouted down to the

*There can hardly have been one plot in the history of the
world which failed to come off, when someone did not open his
mouth too wide.

attackers, "God damn you all! you have ruined both yourselves and me! here comes the round I have been telling you of this hour, I can serve you no longer" – but it was too late to escape detection. A few shots were fired and the conspirators fled away ignominiously. Only four men were apprehended, a Captain Maclean who had injured himself falling down the rock-face, a former page of the Duchess of Gordon, and two "writers", Alexander Ramsay and George Boswell. A dozen firelocks and carbines were also picked up and it was discovered, ironically enough, that the ladders had not even been long enough to reach the battlements. One final captive was "a popish priest, with his trinkets", but his connection with the attack seems rather nebulous.

All in all, it had been a fiasco, although with better organisation it could so easily have succeeded. The Lord Justice Clerk, for one, expressed himself as hugely relieved, and even a year later, after the rising had failed, noted that "the remembrance of this day twelve months supports my spirits, we saved the castle".

*

In spite of this severe set-back to the Jacobite hopes, events in the North went on their faltering way. Mar processed on to Dunkeld via Moulin and Logierait, while the other leaders of the rising dispersed to the various regions where they exercised the most influence. And on September 14 the crucial city of Perth fell to a detachment of Mar's forces. For once Mar had acted with despatch. Argyle's army was encamped around Stirling and some 500 men under the command of Lord Rothes were on the way to secure Perth for King George and to supplement the 150 Highlanders provided by the Duke of Atholl as an earnest of his loyalty. In order to prevent Perth from falling irrevocably into Hanoverian hands, Colonel John Hay, Mar's first wife's brother, swept in with a compact body of 200 cavalry and had

little difficulty in taking possession, particularly when
Atholl's men changed sides. Mar now controlled the
whole of the east coast north of the Tay, and he decided
to set up his camp at Perth, such an obvious strategic
position; although he still lingered on until the 28th at
the small village of Moulinearn near the Pass of Killiecrankie, waiting for the clans to join him.

He was disappointed in his most optimistic estimates,
but by October he calculated his forces as consisting of
nearly 1,000 horse, almost half under the command of
Huntly, and just short of 2,700 foot, the lion's share of
which – 1,200 – had again been contributed by the Gordons. In other words, his army already outnumbered that
of Argyle by two to one, and fresh contingents were coming in all the time. Macintosh of Borlum had set out
from Inverness; Tullibardine arrived with 500 men, and
even Breadalbane judged the wind sufficiently favourable
to declare himself at last. Above all, offsetting the news
of Louis XIV's death and the Regency of the more
doubtfully disposed Orléans, there came despatches from
Commercy announcing the imminent departure of twelve
ships loaded with men, provisions, ammunition, and
money, sailing from various French ports.

Argyle himself, who had travelled north very shortly
after Mar's flight, was pessimistic. Government arrangements had not so far been munificent. Three regiments,
commanded by the Earl of Forfar, the Earl of Orrery
and General Hill, had been recalled from Ireland and
had arrived in Edinburgh by August 24. Major-General
Wightman had marched to Stirling, secured the Castle
and the vital bridge over the Forth, and set up his camp
in the Park. Half-pay officers were scraped together and
sent off to organise the local militia. And two Dutch
regiments had left Maastricht, in readiness for transportation to Scotland. But, with only four regiments of foot
and some 500 dragoons, Argyle's total force was quite
inadequate to face the Jacobite army. After the failure of

the attack on Edinburgh Castle, he was reinforced by the Scots Greys, two English regiments of foot and a considerable body of militia, whose efficiency did not match their size; and at least the far North was likely to be secured by the Earl of Sutherland who sailed from Leith on September 25. But, the fact had to be faced, his camp at Stirling still only boasted approximately 1,400 men.

On the 24th, Argyle wrote to Lord Townsend, the Secretary of State for Scotland: "I must end with insisting on considerable reinforcements, for without it, or a miracle, not only this country will be utterly destroyed but the rest of his Majesty's dominions put in the extremest danger." Even the normally phlegmatic Lord Justice Clerk could not forbear noting that Claverhouse's victorious army back in the days of William III had been considerably smaller than Mar's force. The inhabitants of Edinburgh were now filled with gloom, as reports came in of further Jacobite successes. Glasgow and Dumfries were being threatened; Strathmore, Robertson of Struan, Southesk, Panmure, Auchterhouse, Lord Nairn, and General Hamilton had all arrived at Perth with contingents of varying sizes to add to the Jacobite total; the loyal army, under the command of General Whetham now that Argyle had posted off to Edinburgh, lay at Stirling powerless to move; the Earl of Sutherland, now that he was on his way north, could be of no assistance to the frightened Lowlanders; and, perhaps most impertinent of all, an attempt had been made to seize Fort William – it was an attempt doomed to failure, but the fact that it had been made at all was a sign of these nervous times.

There is no doubt at all that if Mar had marched south on Edinburgh at this juncture he could have been in control of the whole of Scotland within a matter of weeks. But, instead, he prevaricated and watched. He had at last arrived at Perth on September 28, and the Master of Sinclair was not over-delighted to see him. "We were

drawn out to the North Inch to receive him, and from that
time did he daily take more and more upon him to act
like our General, and did all of himself, without consulting anybody, as if he had been another Moses, meek
and spotless, and without a blemish, sent from Heaven
with a divine commission to relieve us miserable wret-
ches out of bondage ... He spent a number of weeks in
Perth, issuing edicts which he had not the power fully to
enforce, practising feints against an enemy not equal to
his own army by nine-tenths, in order to cover a petty
village warfare and fortifying a camp which the moment
his antagonist was in sufficient force to attack, he be-
hoved of necessity to abandon." Only one plan emanat-
ing from Perth actually came to fruition, and when it
was first formed it threatened to explode the sole excuse
Mar might have been allowed for failing to take the offensive earlier.

Mar was already so chronically short of money that,
according to the ever-scornful Sinclair, the Highlanders
were mutinying; there was also a desperate lack of arms
and ammunition. "While everyone was building castles
in the air, and making themselves great men, most of our
arms were good for nothing; there was no method fallen
on, nor was the least care taken to repair those old rusty
broken pieces, which, it seems, were to be carried about
more for ornament than use, though gunsmiths were not
wanting; but this was either because he who took upon
him the command expected no powder from the beginning, or because what was everybody's business was nobody's." But a piece of news reported to Sinclair by an
old family friend at six o'clock in the morning of October
2 on the South Inch at Perth seemed to offer the perfect
remedy.

It appeared that a small ship had put in at Burntisland,
across the Forth from the port of Leith, so that the master could go ashore to see his wife and family. This in
itself was hardly of interest, but when Sinclair heard from

his friend that the ship was loaded with arms and ammunition to the number of "at least 3,000" destined for Lord Sutherland, he decided to take immediate action. After a moment's hesitation because of his antagonism towards Mar, he hauled his commander out of bed and duly passed on the information. Mar was as usual averse to making up his mind, but eventually, after two further discussions, he gave Sinclair written orders authorising him to seize the ship and its contents. Too much time had already been wasted, as the ship was due to sail by the midnight tide, and more was squandered while Mar and Sinclair argued over the strength of the foray. Sinclair, mindful that he would have to pass within ten miles of Stirling on the way back and that his speed would be cut by the presence of waggons laden with his spoils, requested an extra hundred men who could be left at Burntisland if necessary to guard any arms which could not be removed at once. Mar refused and finally agreed to dispatch 500 men after Sinclair had actually left.

Sinclair's small troop of eighty horse rode out of Perth at five o'clock in the afternoon and, on arriving at Burntisland, had no difficulty in press-ganging some of the townsmen into helping bring the ship into harbour. But Sinclair was to be disappointed. "I received all the arms from the ship's side, and found, to my great grief, but three hundred, wanting one; we found a bag of flints and two little barrels of ball, and two or three barrels of powder, about a hundred pound each, and some cartridge boxes ... We seized the arms of a big ship which lay in the harbour, which were about twenty-five firelocks, and with them a barrel of powder, and at same time, the arms of the Town Guard, about thirty." He and his men did not need to tarry and they were back in Perth twenty-four hours after their departure, without falling foul of the Stirling garrison. But, although their haul was puny, reports of Sinclair's escapade – no doubt exaggerated – did serve to goad the Jacobites of Fife into definite action. A detachment of the Highland army marched into the shire, and within a few days Kirkcaldy, Dysart, Kinghorn and Wemyss were all in Mar's hands, and Lord Rothes had been forced to withdraw from Leslie.

By the beginning of October, indeed, the Jacobites held virtually the whole of Scotland, with the exception of the country south of Edinburgh and around Glasgow, Argyle's lands in the West and Sutherland's in the far North. The contingents promised by Macintosh of Borlum, Huntly and Marischal had arrived at Perth, and Sinclair estimated the strength of the army at about 7,000.* Again this was a time for Mar to move decisively southwards; again he did nothing.

He would not be offered such an opportunity again. From this moment onwards there would be none but the most transitory triumphs, the occasional bright fanfare sounding briefly out of the fog of indecision and impending disaster, only to be smothered once more. And it was now that Mar's real and manifold deficiencies as a leader of men were most obviously displayed. His failure to inspire his own tenants back at Braemar was no isolated incident, and his much-vaunted silvery tongue, so useful when charming the ladies or delivering emptily grandiose addresses, did not impress those supremely unimpressionable men, the Highland clans. He was, in addition, no expert at staff dispositions. There was no discipline in the camp at Perth and, if Sinclair can be believed, "though orders were given out to form into regiments, everyone did as they pleased. Each commander insisted on having a Regiment under himself, however small, and the same with the troops of horse."

*Rae gives a very different, and improbably large, estimate: "By this Time their Army amounted to 12,600 Men, and being afterwards join'd by General Gordon and the Western Clans, to the Number of 100 Horse and 4,000 Foot, but a short Time before the Battle, made in all 16,700 Men."

James Francis Edward, with Lord Middleton's son, by Trevisani. The background represents the naval action during the 1708 expedition.

Photo: Studio Morgan, Aberdeen

John, Earl of Mar, with his son, by Kneller

Photo: Annan, Glasgow

John, Duke of Argyle, by Kneller

Photo: Scott

The Jacobite Expedition of 1708, by van Salm

A Panorama of the 1715 Rebellion, by Terasson

Photo: Scott

The End of the Rebellion, by Terasson

Photo: Scott

The Execution of the Jacobite Lords

Photo : Scott

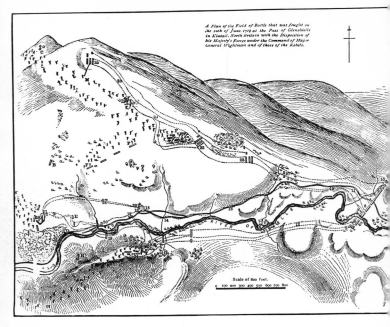

A Plan of the Field of Battle that was fought on the 10th of June, 1719 at the Pass of Glenshiels in Kintail. North Britain with the Disposition of his Majesty's Forces under the Command of Major General Wightman and of those of the Rebels.

Scale of 800 feet.
0 100 200 300 400 500 600 700 800

REFERENCES TO THE PLAN

1. A Sergt. and 12 Grenadiers.
2. An Officer and 24 do.
3. Main Body of Grenadiers, 120 in Num.
4. Col. Montagu's Regmt.
5. Col. Harrison's Detacht Battalion.
6. Huffel's Regmt. and 4 Companies of Amerongen's.
7. Dragoons.
8. Col. Clayton's Regiment.
9. The Monro's Highlanders.
10. The Sutherland's Right.
11. The first march by ye Right.
12. Clayton's march by the Left.
13. The Dragoons march to the Plain.
14. The Dragoons Halt.

15. The Dragoons advance to the middle of the Plain.
16. Clayton's four Plottoons and the Monro's making ye First Attack on ye Rebels' Right.
17. Cohorn Mortars throwing Granades at the Rebels where ye First Attack was Ordered.
18. Cohorn Mortars throwing Granades at ye Spaniards in their Entrenchments.
19. Part of Clayton's attacks the Barricade of the Pass.
20. 35 Dragoons on Foot attack the Spaniards Breast Works.
21. The Dragoons mount the Hill.

22. Our March in line of Battle to the where the Attack began under ye comm of Col. Clayton.
23. Our Right pursue the Rebels.
24. The Plottoons and the Monro's halt upon Hill, having putt the Enemy to the F
25. Our Right halts upon ye Mountain.
26. Part of Clayton's takes possession of y that commanded the Pass.
27. Guard for the Baggage and place fo Hospitall.
28. The Bagage advanced with the wo men for their security.
29. Majr.-Genl. Whightman giving his dire during the Action.

REFERENCES TO THE ENNEMY

A. A Spanish Regiment posted on the Hill that commanded the Plain and the Pass.
B. Spaniards march to ye Mount and Halt.
C. The Spaniards retire to the Top of the mountain.
D. The Barricade that defended the Pass on the River Side.

E. The Breastworks on the Side of the Hill.
F. The Highlanders drawn up before the attack.
G. A straggling number of Highlanders fire upon the Plottoons of Clayton's and the Monro's behind them in the time of the attack.

H. A Body of Highlanders going to sustain Right.
M. The Flight of the Rebels. The Mount Skururan the highest in Scotland Benevis.

A Plan of the Battle of Glenshiel by Lieutenant John Henry Bastide

Commissariat arrangements were equally disorganised. When Huntly marched in with his men, he discovered that no quarters had been prepared and was forced to retrace his steps into Angus. The Highlanders were not being paid, and both Panmure and Southesk preferred to sacrifice £500 apiece in an attempt to ward off possible mutiny; many of the chiefs followed this example, but private fortunes were exceedingly scarce at the time and such hand to mouth operations could not last indefinitely.

Mar finally realised that some sort of finance committee must be set up, not only to elaborate ways and means of raising funds but to evolve a basic system of providing forage and food for the hungry army and its horses. One firm decision was reached, to reintroduce the old cess or land tax which had first been levied in the reign of Alexander III in the thirteenth century. All those who had joined the standard were to pay "twenty shillings on each hundred pounds Scots of valued rent", and those who had not would pay double. But even when money did start to trickle in to Perth, it was not routed towards the most deserving recipients, the ordinary soldiers, but went instead to a number of Mar's more impecunious acquaintances. Sinclair indeed has no hesitation in hinting that an appreciable proportion of these funds vanished straight into Mar's own pockets.

Money was at a premium, but arms, ammunition and above all gunpowder were even scarcer. What there was of this last essential commodity remained almost permanently damp as the Highlanders possessed no powderhorns. Sinclair is scathing about the whole lamentable state of affairs. He points out, for once with perfect justice, that if Mar had had a spark of imagination he could have sent over to Holland for gunpowder, or even have had it manufactured in Aberdeen; the first course was perfectly feasible now that the east-coast ports were in Jacobite hands, and Aberdeen, commercially flourishing, would have welcomed an increase in business. The short-age of powder-horns and flints could have been remedied even more painlessly. As Sinclair says, "ram's horns were there in plenty and gipsies to make them into powder flasks", and there was an abundance of flints lying along the shores ready for the picking. And yet Mar could write on October 10 to the French Regent that he had no pressing need for foreign assistance, though he would of course be happy if it were forthcoming.*

An incident on October 24 did little to raise the morale of his army. A substantial contingent of between two and three hundred foot and some eighty horse had been des-patched to collect the cess tax in the predominantly anti-Jacobite town of Dunfermline; it was presumably considered an important manoeuvre as the two comman-ders were Major Thomas Graham, who had served under Dundee, and Gordon of Glenbucket. They were foolish enough deliberately to pass by the garrison at Dinnen, a mere six miles from Stirling, and consequently gave Argyle ample time to alert Colonel Cathcart's dragoons who were already in the district. On their arrival in Dun-fermline, Graham and his officers behaved even more idiotically, posting no more than two sentries, drinking merrily in the local taverns, and going off to bed as if there were not the remotest chance of counter-measures. Cathcart duly arrived in the early hours of the morning, killed one of the sentries, and totally surprised the sleep-ing officers. His dragoons took seventeen prisoners, of whom eleven were officers, and rode off before the maj-ority of the Highlanders had time to emerge from their beds; they had, in any case, been given no orders and they had no leader. The cess was not levied and the High-landers moved on to Burntisland. It was a trifling affair, certainly, but the Jacobites had hardly distinguished themselves – Sinclair speaks darkly of officers who ran

*Orléans would not have offered any assistance even if Mar had requested it.

away and others who were "hiding under a bed or in a garret" – and Argyle's army was exuberant over this brief but successful passage of arms.

While the duke's forces were beginning to grow, Mar seemed hell-bent on dissipating his own strength. He had already despatched General Alexander Gordon to harry Argyle's Campbells on their own territory, to induce any dissident Campbells to join him and to stir up the Jacobite clans; this particular splinter-movement was less than successful as Islay, Argyle's brother, was in complete control at Inverary, and Colonel Campbell of Finah even managed to persuade the vast majority of his clansmen to remain loyal to the Government and to delay Cameron of Lochiel and Stuart of Appin from joining Mar at Perth. Mar's own approach to this expedition of Gordon's, and to other threatening moves against Argyle by Clanranald and Glengarry and by the Macgregors,* was less than warlike as can be deduced from the contents of a letter he wrote personally to Argyle and in which he promised he would not harm Argyle's gardens at Inverary if the latter refrained from damaging Mar's own fine gardens at Alloa House. This request, although it has its charming aspect, hardly bears the stamp of ruthless determination.

One possibility Mar refused to contemplate was a pitched battle with Argyle, not at least until he was sure of having cut him off at Stirling and entwining him in a "hose-net". He decided therefore that the Lowland Jacobites who were rising under Kenmure, Carnwath and Wintoun should be induced to cooperate with Gordon in the West, and that it would be advisable to send a sizeable force across the Firth of Forth to attack Argyle from the east. With Gordon moving from the west, the

*The activities of the Macgregors, led by the celebrated Rob Roy, are essentially a side-issue to the main narrative, but a full description of the so-called Loch Lomond Expedition can be found in Appendix II.

Lowland lords coming up from the south, this new
splinter-army marching westwards and Mar himself descending from Perth, the net could very easily be joined
and hauled in at Stirling. In the event, Gordon had to be
recalled from Campbell country and Kenmure's army
was destined to veer round with the Northumberland
Jacobites and meet disaster at Preston; but there is no
doubt that Brigadier Macintosh of Borlum's expedition
formed the one great moment of glory in the entire rebellion – it was a choice piece of swashbuckling opportu-
nism which was never emulated.

Old Borlum had been one of the first to come out in
support of James and the Stuart succession, and his capture of Inverness in the opening stages of the rising,
although to be expected, had been none the less crucial.
Macintosh was a hardened soldier and a firm disciplin-
arian, and his control over his clan, which he commanded
since the chief was still a minor, was absolute. Certainly
he lacked finesse and polish – Sinclair referred to him as a
"Highland bull" – and his brief career in the unexpected
and unlooked for rôle of envoy to the exiled Stuart court
in the year before the outbreak of the rising had caused
some raised eye-brows in the less brusque circle of French
diplomacy; Tynemouth, Berwick's son, had dismissed
him as loyal but stupid, but his judgment took no account
of Borlum's real qualities, those of a military commander in the field. Mar, for once, chose the ideal man when
he appointed him to the command of the 2,500 men who
were to cross the Forth.

It was a strong force, consisting as it did of the entire
Macintosh contribution as well as contingents from the
regiments of Mar himself, Strathmore, Nairn, Drummond of Logie-Almond and Lord Charles Murray; and
it set out at the end of the first week in October in the
wake of Sinclair's horse, who were to prepare the way
and to act as protective cover into Fife. Macintosh's
plan was ingenious and simple. 500 men marched quite

openly to Burntisland for all the world as if they intended to cross the Forth at this point. Three English men o' war which had been cruising along the coast immediately changed course and sailed up to Burntisland. The 500 gave every appearance of being about to set out. Boats were being prepared and a battery was established as if to warn off the English ships. The attention of the English was now completely engaged.

While these rather ostentatious manoeuvres were in operation at Burntisland, the remaining 2,000 of Borlum's force had moved with extreme caution and secrecy through the Fife countryside and had arrived at the harbours of Crail, Elie and Pittenweem, twenty miles to the east of Burntisland and out of sight of the marauding men o' war. Macintosh did not delay and the following morning a fleet of small boats could be seen crossing the Forth. The men o' war raised anchor and attempted to give chase, but it was too late. Macintosh had precisely calculated the tide and the wind, and only one boatload fell into English hands. About 300 men under Strathmore were driven on to the Isle of May and prepared to hold out until the last, but fortunately were able to extricate themselves and return to Perth. The great majority of the force, however, made the crossing successfully and landed at Gullan, Aberlady and North Berwick.

Edinburgh, which appeared to be seriously threatened, took leave of its collective sanity, only the Lord Justice Clerk, who had far-sightedly expected just such a development, keeping his head. Barricades were erected, rusty old cannon were brought back into service, and even the ministers were observed to be carrying arms. Urgent requests for help were despatched to Argyle's camp, and the English commander in Edinburgh, General Wightman, set about trying to instil some vestige of military training in the townspeople.

Ironically, Macintosh had previously had no intention

of besieging Edinburgh, indeed such a move would have
been quite contrary to his orders, but the temptation was
too great. He halted at Haddington for one night and the
following morning, Friday, October 14, pressed on towards the capital. He was within a mile of the city walls
when reports reached him of the imminent arrival of
Argyle's relief force, and he decided to make for Leith
and await developments. He took the town with little
difficulty and was even able to release the forty men
who had been captured during the crossing of the Forth
and had been lying in gaol ever since. Then he moved
over to North Leith and set up his headquarters in an
old fort originally built by Cromwell and now partly in
ruins. Argyle was definitely on the way, and Macintosh
was convinced that the fort could withstand any siege.
After erecting make-shift barricades, siting eight cannon
he had taken from some ships in the harbour at the
drawbridge and along the walls, and plundering the well-
stocked custom-house, he waited.

Argyle, when he did arrive, had about a thousand men
under his command, although this number gradually
dwindled as the somewhat cowardly Edinburgh volunteers began to drift away. But he had no artillery and
soon realised that he was in no position to force Macintosh to surrender. Macintosh, for his part, was by now
equally convinced that he had no hope of taking Edinburgh and, soon after Argyle had retired, he decided to
march into East Lothian and continue along his pre-
scribed route. Before leaving the fort, he sent a messenger across the Forth to tell Mar what had occurred, and
as soon as night had fallen made his own stealthy move,
leading his men along the deserted beach and past the
head of the pier. "His march was completely unobserved;
for, in 1715, the people were chiefly retired to rest at nine
o'clock; and no spies had been planted in that unsus-
pected quarter." He reached Musselburgh before midnight and by the Sunday was strongly entrenched in Lord

Wintoun's Seton House, waiting for a further move on the part of Argyle. He did not realise for some time that he had no more to fear in that quarter. Argyle was on his way back to Stirling having received an urgent summons from General Whetham who was convinced, with some reason, that Mar was on the point of attacking from Perth.

Macintosh was now ordered to march into the Border country and join up with the Northumberland volunteers and the Lowland army. He duly crossed Lammermuir and for the first time displayed that pig-headed impulsiveness which Sinclair had remarked upon. Earlier in the month, there had been a curious and tragic incident in Haddington. Lord Tweeddale, the Lord Lieutenant of the shire, had issued injunctions to his deputies to enforce with severity the laws against Catholics and suspected Jacobites. Two of these deputies, Dr. Sinclair of Hermandston and Mr. Hepburn of Humbie, saw it as a perfect opportunity to have their revenge on their Jacobite neighbour, Hepburn of Keith. Sinclair rode up to the latter's house, brandishing Tweeddale's order and confident of Hepburn's immediate submission. Hepburn, however, was made of sterner stuff. He sallied forth, fired his pistol at Sinclair's servant and smote the worthy doctor over the head with his sword. Sinclair's supporters retaliated and in the turmoil Hepburn of Keith's younger son was killed.

Macintosh was incensed when he heard of Sinclair's part in the affair and was all for setting fire to his house at Hermandston, a pointless act of vengeance which could well have started a wave of looting and arson and alienated the country-people still further. Luckily, he was persuaded to hold his hand although he still insisted on allowing Nairn's soldiers to plunder the house; and his army moved on towards Kelso where the joint Northumberland and Lowland forces had already arrived. On the Sunday, everyone dutifully went to church to be edi-

fied by a sermon on the text "The right of the first-born
is his", preached by the Reverend Mr. Patten, at the time
chaplain to Thomas Forster, the self-appointed general
of the Northumberland army, and later to turn his coat
so thoroughly that he was moved to write a history of
the rising with a distinctly Hanoverian flavour to it. And
on the following day, the combined armies were drawn
up at the market cross, "colours flying, drums beating,
and bagpipes playing", while James was solemnly proclaimed and his manifesto read out. The onlookers,
mixing patriotism with self-interest, shouted, "No
Union! No Malt-tax! No Salt-tax!", and everyone dispersed peaceably.

While Macintosh's men were engaged in appropriat-
ing the public revenues, plundering the houses of local
Whigs – Baillie of Jerviswood was one such sufferer –
and burning their corn-fields, the leaders were arguing
furiously over what should be done next. There were
two alternative plans. Either they could march into England and defeat General Carpenter's weak and untrained
army which had recently left Newcastle. Or they could
adhere to Mar's original instructions, and move on Stirling or at the very least circle round westwards, taking
Dumfries and Glasgow en route, and join up with Alexander Gordon in Argyle. But they could not agree, and
the result was one of those ill-begotten compromises
which bedevil mixed forces with no overall commander.
They weakly decided to march along the Border towards
Jedburgh, thus giving the impression that they were in
fact retreating.

The march from Kelso to Jedburgh was not only ill-
conceived but it was carried out with complete incompetence. The horse, instead of protecting the foot from
possible attack by Carpenter's army, trotted gaily on and
arrived at Jedburgh while the infantry were still two miles
off. The latter, mistaking a body of their own troops
which suddenly appeared in the foot-hills to the right of

the road for a detachment sent out by Carpenter, panicked and despatched a messenger who raced into Jedburgh to request immediate assistance from the horse.
When the messenger arrived and began to deliver his
report to Macintosh and Kenmure as they stood in the
High Street, he was so out of breath and incoherent that
they formed the notion that the infantry were being attacked by Lord Lumley's troop of light horse which had
recently been raised in Northumberland. The messenger,
now beside himself with terror and giving his obviously
fertile imagination full scope, then galloped off through
the streets, shouting, "Mount, gentlemen, mount! Mount
for God's sake! Lumley is upon the foot, cutting them
in pieces!" The effect was instantaneous and demoralising. "Some of those who stood beside the general tore
off the white cockades from their hats, to make themselves appear guiltless in the eyes of those by whom they
expected to be immediately taken. Others sought places
of concealment throughout the town. The greater part
eventually mounted their horses and marched out to join
the foot; but yet so strong was the impression that they
were devoted to destruction, that many of even this more
resolute band were observed weeping like children." The
whole affair was most shocking, although these same
men who hid and wept later showed conspicuous gal-
lantry at Preston.

The combined armies rested at Jedburgh for two days,
and the bickering between the leaders continued acrimo-
niously. Forster was in favour of stealing a march on
Carpenter and arriving in England before him, but to
Macintosh this seemed the plan of an arrant coward. He
was determined to fight Carpenter, to fight him north
of the Border, and to defeat him. Matters reached such a
head that on the march to Hawick the Highlanders refused to move another step and the exasperated
Englishmen were reduced to threats and imprecations.
Eventually, it was agreed that they should make for

Dumfries, but the town was so well garrisoned with volunteers that this plan too was abandoned. Finally, Macintosh gave way. Lured on by the prospect of easy pickings in the softer land south of the Border, he declared roundly, "Why the devil not into England, where there is both meat, men and money?" He managed to persuade all but 500 of his men to join him; these 500 marched northwards and were nearly all captured.

The last of the commanders to hold out was Lord Wintoun, but even he at last acceded with the utmost reluctance, announcing that "it shall never be said in history, to after generations, that the Earl of Wintoun deserted King James's interests and his country's good", but adding that he was convinced that they would all rue the day the decision had been made.

On November 1, the Jacobite army crossed the river Esk into England.

Chapter Seven

Preston and Sheriffmuir

His Grace's [Argyle's] army was drawn up upon the heights above Dunblane to the north-east of that place, which lay about a mile and a half from his left, and a wet boggy mire called Sheriff-Moor on his right.

CAMPBELL'S Life of Argyle

TOWARDS the end of September, while Mar was assembling his forces in Scotland, the English Government had issued a number of warrants for the arrest of prominent Jacobite sympathisers in the North Country. Among those listed were Thomas Forster, Member of Parliament for Northumberland, and the Earl of Derwentwater, the son of one of Charles II's many illegitimate daughters and consequently a cousin of James the wrong side of the blanket. Forster was something of a nonentity, lacking any military skill, self-seeking and a coward; but Derwentwater was something different. He was only twenty-five in 1715 and seemed universally popular. Smollett called him "brave, open, generous, hospitable, and human", and Patten went still further in his praise, describing him as "formed by nature to be universally loved for his benevolence was so unbounded that he

seemed only to live for others". What he lacked, however, was political sense, and Kneller's portrait, showing
a somewhat vacuous and fleshy face, not unlike that of
an amiable, not unhandsome pig, bears out this assessment. This was the ill-assorted pair who were to lead the
Jacobite army of the North to destruction.

Trouble had been brewing there for some time. A certain Captain Robert Talbot, "an Irishman and Papist",
had sailed up from London to Newcastle, and began immediately to spread the word that a rising was imminent.
He found a number of eager helpers. "All these rid like
Gentlemen, with Servants and Attendants, and were
armed with Swords and Pistols. They kept always moving, and travelled from Place to Place till things ripen'd
for action." This moment seemed to have come when
the warrant for Derwentwater's arrest was issued, and
messengers were sent from Durham to effect it. Derwentwater escaped in time, and the messenger sent to seize
Forster missed him by a matter of minutes. "Upon this
News they had a full Meeting of the Parties concerned in
Northumberland, where, consulting all the Circumstances of their Friends and of the Interest they were
embark'd in, they boldly resolved, since there was no
Safety any longer in shifting from Place to Place, that
they would immediately appear in arms."

On October 6, they summoned their friends and supporters to gather at a piece of open ground called the
Greenrig near Rothbury, and Forster was nominated as
commander on the slender grounds of his Protestant
faith. The following day they proceeded on to Warkworth where they were joined by Lord Widdrington and
a small troop of horse; and their army began to take
shape as they passed on to Alnwick and Morpeth. The
obvious target was Newcastle which was known to contain a large number of Stuart adherents, but Forster's
lacklustre tactics gave the inhabitants loyal to the Crown
ample time to strengthen the walls and muster volun-

teers; and the arrival of a whole regiment on the 9th removed the town from danger.

Forster approached the situation with total amateurishness. He seemed to have no notion of the absolute necessity of raising at least a small body of infantry, and preferred to concentrate on his fellow-cavaliers whom Sinclair so aptly dubbed "an army of fox-hunters armed with light dress-swords". Finally, after being forced to retreat to Hexham, he came to his senses and sent off a letter to Mar begging for some reinforcements of foot.

It was a dismal beginning and matters were to deteriorate. Only one incident, one example of courage or even enterprise, stands out at this period. This was the capture of Holy Island, on which there was a fort manned by English soldiers who came over and were then relieved every week from the garrison at Berwick. It had always been considered a place of no strategic importance, but a certain Lancelot Errington, a Newcastle skipper, realised its possibilities as a base for receiving supplies from France. Errington was in the habit of sailing close to the island and when his ship hove in sight on October 10, the soldiers in the fort paid no attention. He and his few companions landed and walked coolly into the fort, taking control of it without the least resistance. It was, however, a short-lived triumph. The army at Warkworth failed to send over any form of assistance, and the very next day a contingent from Berwick marched over the sands at low-tide and recaptured the fort. The gallant Errington was shot in the thigh and borne back to Berwick; but he was later able to escape.

Forster now saw that his only hope of success lay in amalgamating his minuscule army with that of the Lowland lords, and he retraced his steps to Rothbury. Here, on October 19, he met Kenmure, and three days later the tripartite force was completed by the arrival at Kelso of Macintosh of Borlum's Highlanders. By November 2, acting on a vague plan of Forster's to make for Liverpool, raise the standard in Lancashire and join up with the Welsh Jacobites, they were encamped at Penrith in Cumberland. The only opposition they had so far encountered was put up by the Westmorland militia and was hardly of a martial nature. "They appeared with their pitchforks on the very ground through which the rebels were to march, and most of their parsons were with them, applauding their zeal and courage. This unanimity and good understanding between priests and people continued till about one o'clock, when no enemy appearing abroad, and great gnawings being felt within, and no opportunity of refreshment in view, the infantry began to drop off, and continued to do so until (about three in the afternoon) we had advice that the rebels were coming towards us. I cannot say that this raised our spirits. They were so much sunk and our enemies knew it. In short they marched on and we marched off." In spite of all the endeavours of Lord Lonsdale and the aggressive Bishop of Carlisle, nothing could be done with these yokels, and Forster's army was able to appropriate a fair quantity of arms, besides the less useful pitch-forks, and on arriving at Penrith to enjoy a supper which had been prepared for the bishop.

The following day, they moved on to Appleby, and by November 9, after passing through Kendal and Lancaster, were at Preston. Peter Clarke had viewed their entry into Kendal with some surprise. "About 12 o'clock of the same day November [5], 6 Quarter Masters came into the Town of Kendal, and about 2 o'clock in the afternoon, Brigadier Mackintosh and his men came both on horseback, having both plaids on, their targets hanging on their backs, either of them a sword by his side, as also either a gun and a case of pistols. The said Brigadier looked with a grim countenance."

Macintosh had little to smile about. It was pouring

with rain, and had been for a number of days past, so that the streets were awash. The rebel army made a poor show of it. "The horse and ye footmen did not draw their swords nor show their colours, neither did any drums beat. Only six Highland bagpipes played." Clarke, who was clerk to the local attorney, went to hear James proclaimed at the Cold Stone and took a professional interest in the proceedings. A nasty incident was only just avoided. "At the end of the proclamation they gave a great shout. A Quaker who stood next to me not pulling off his hat at the end of the said ceremony, a Highlander thrust a halberd at him, but it fortunately went between me and him, so that it did neither of us any damage. So they dispersed."

Forster treated the inhabitants with scant respect. The town crier was despatched to summon the innkeepers and tanners to come and pay the excise due to the Crown, "or else they that denied should be plundered by Jack the Highlander", and the mayor was arrested because he refused to disclose the whereabouts of the local militia's arms. But the Member for Northumberland received short shrift at the hands of his godmother, Mrs. Bellingham, who happened to live in Kendal. She "would not admit her said godson to see her, and he going up stairs for that intent, she met him on the stairs, gave him two or three boxes on the ear, called him a rebel and a Popish tool, which he took patiently". Perhaps he was used to his godmother's outbursts.

The Highlanders did not behave well, breaking into the church on Sunday morning in the hope of discovering a cache of arms; nor did they consider it necessary to pay for their board and lodging, although it is unlikely that they had any money in the first place. At last, Forster's army left, and the citizens of Kendal were highly relieved to see it gone. "The Brigadier looked still with a grim countenance, but the Lords, Forster, and most of the other horsemen were disheartened and full of sorrow. About 9 o'clock the same morning they marched out of the town, but not in ranks. A journeyman weaver," Clarke adds in affronted tones, "joined them here."

Lancaster provided some bottles of claret and a good quantity of brandy, which was unwisely passed out to the Highlanders. Preston was less well-endowed. And they were to go no further. Forster had hoped to seize the bridge at Warrington and so threaten Liverpool, but the countryside was in the hands of General Wills and the Jacobites were forced to remain within the walls of Preston. Wills was on the way from Wigan with six regiments of dragoons and the Cameronians; and Carpenter had left Durham, ill and exhausted but determined to be in at the kill.

Forster appeared overcome with apathy. The local Catholics had joined him, but they and their tenants, in spite of numbering almost 1,200, presented a miserable spectacle. Macintosh exploded with wrath. "Gude faith, man," he shouted at Forster, "an ye had ten thousand of them, I would engage to beat the whole with a squadron of Wills' dragoons." It was a palpable exaggeration, but in the event he was not far from the truth. Forster even failed to put a guard on the bridge over the Ribble, thus presenting Wills with the perfect means of approach. Like a man caught in a nightmare and burying his head beneath the sheets, he withdrew all his men inside the town and proceeded to wait in a spirit of fatalism. An indolent man at the best of times, he was indeed in bed when Kenmure tried to hold a general council of war. It was now that the other leaders realised that Forster was less than useless, and decided to organise the defence of the town without consulting him further. Four barricades were set up at the four points of the compass: the first, in the churchyard, manned by Kenmure and the gentlemen volunteers; the second, in a street leading to the fields, by Lord Charles Murray with his Atholl Highlanders; the third, at a windmill on the road to Lancaster, by the

Macintoshes; and the fourth, on the Liverpool road, by the Northumberland men and Lowland lairds.

On November 12, General Wills arrived in front of the town. Forster had gone out on a reconnaissance beyond the bridge over the Ribble, but had returned hastily when he espied the first dragoons riding up. A small force of a hundred men, commanded by Colonel John Farquharson of Invercauld, was left to guard the bridge. According to Patten, Farquharson "was a good Officer and a very bold Man, and would have defended that important Pass of the Bridge to the last Drop, and till the rest had advanced and drawn themselves out of the Town: but he was order'd to retreat to Preston". It was an insane order. It was imperative that the bridge should be held as long as possible, and as Farquharson had some artillery he could have delayed General Wills for some hours at the least.

Wills proceeded cautiously. He had been informed by his scouts that the enemy had withdrawn, and he suspected a trap. The lane up which he moved was very deep owing to the high hedges growing on both sides, and also extremely narrow. "This is that famous Lane," reports Patten in his guise of schoolmaster, "at the end of which Oliver Cromwell met with a stout Resistance from the King's Forces, who from the Height rolled down upon him and his Men (when they had entered the Lane) huge large Mill-stones; and if Oliver himself had not forced his Horse to jump into a Quick-Sand, he had luckily ended his Days there." But Wills encountered no mill-stones. There was no ambush, the rebels had simply vanished.

Wills immediately put in attacks against two of the barricades. The fighting was predictably fiercest in the vicinity of Borlum's position, but Wills' men could make little headway and were eventually obliged to withdraw, even the Cameronians admitting temporary defeat. The appearance of General Carpenter on the following day

altered the entire picture. Although Carpenter's force
added little to what Wills already had under his command, and regardless of the fact that the defences of
Preston had already proved strong enough to withstand
a lengthy siege, Forster completely lost heart. With the
approval of Lord Widdrington, but unknown to the
other leaders, Colonel Oxburgh was sent out to parley
with the enemy. He met with a frosty welcome. Wills
was not well disposed towards treating with rebels, particularly with one who still held His Majesty's commission. But Oxburgh persevered and at last obtained a
promise that if all the soldiers in Preston laid down their
arms he would guarantee to hold his own men in check.
It was little enough, but Oxburgh returned to Forster
reasonably satisfied; they had one hour in which to make
up their minds.

A further appeal was made by Carnwath's brother,
Captain James Dalzell, on behalf of the Scottish contingent, but Wills was not prepared to wait any longer.
"About Three in the Afternoon, Colonel Cotton, with a
Dragoon and a Drum beating a Chamade before them,
came up the street from the King's General; The Colonel
alighted at the Sign of the Mitre, where the Chief of the
Rebel-Officers were got together, and told them he came
to receive their positive Answer." There were more arguments and a request for a cessation of hostilities until
seven o'clock the following morning; this was granted
by Cotton, provided a number of hostages returned with
him to Wills' camp. Macintosh and Derwentwater were
among those selected for this doubtful honour. Forster
became the target for violent abuse and even one attempt
at assassination, and prudently remained indoors.

The following morning, at the agreed hour, he sent a
message to Wills accepting the terms of surrender. Macintosh, who happened to be in the tent at the time, refused
to believe that his Highlanders would give themselves up
with so little guarantee for their lives; but, after Wills

had sent him back into the town to verify the facts for
himself, he returned with the assurance that Kenmure
and the other Scots would indeed surrender on the same
terms with the English. Wills' army then marched in
"with Sound of Trumpets and Beat of Drums", in two
detachments, and the prisoners were marshalled in the
market square. "Here the Highlanders stood drawn up
with their Arms; the Lords, Gentlemen, and Officers were
first secured and placed under a Guard in several Rooms
in the Inns, where they remained for some time. The
Highlanders laid down their Arms in the Place where they
stood drawn up, and then were put into the Church under
a sufficient Guard." All in all, seventy-five English and
143 Scottish noblemen and gentlemen surrendered, together with some 1,400 ordinary soldiers of whom a
thousand were Scottish. Only seventeen men had been
killed in the defence of Preston, as opposed to 200 on
the Government side. The rising in the North of England
was over. In the words of Robert Campbell, Argyle's
official biographer, "none but fools would have stayed to
be attacked in that position, and none but the knaves
would have acted when there as they did".

*

The battle of Sheriffmuir, or Dunblane as it was often
referred to by contemporary historians, was fought on
the very same day as the surrender of Preston. Although
neither side could reasonably have claimed total victory, its after-effects were to seal the fate of the whole
rising.

Since the departure of Macintosh's men over the
Forth and on into England, Mar had remained virtually
immovable, as if transfixed by the thought that sooner or
later he must come to some, to any, decision. His feint
in the direction of Stirling in order to draw off Argyle
from Edinburgh had been his sole contribution to the
campaign. But with news coming in of Ormonde's failure to land in the West of England, he reluctantly con-

cluded that he must take action. And now that he had
been joined by over 3,000 men under Lord Seaforth and
that General Gordon had reappeared from the West,
his army numbered some 12,000, more than four times
larger than Argyle's force.

The camp at Perth gave a very motley appearance.
"There were country gentlemen from Angus and Aberdeenshire, riding on stout horses, with sword and pistol,
each dressed in his best laced attire, and each attended
by serving-men, also armed, and also on horseback. Then
there were Highland gentlemen in the more picturesque
garb of their country, with obeisant retinues of clansmen
on foot. The mass of the army was composed of Lowland
peasants, with arms slung over their plain gray clothes,
and of mountaineers, nearly naked, or at least wearing
little more than one shirt-like garment. Two squadrons
of cavalry, which Huntly had brought with him, excited,
under the name of light-horse, the derision of friends and
foes; being composed of stout bulky Highlandmen,
mounted on little horses, each with his petit blue bonnet
on his head, a long rusty musket slung athwart his back,
and not one possessed of boots or pistols, those articles
so requisite to the idea of a trooper. On arriving at Dunblane, this puissant body of cavalry took two hours to
dismount; and it is the opinion of one who observed
them, that, if attacked by an enemy, they would have
been as long before they were in readiness to receive
him."

A council of war was held on November 9, and a plan
evolved: three battalions would be left to hold Perth
and the remainder of the army would march to Dunblane, as the first point on a route which was intended
to lead them over the Forth, into Edinburgh and on to
England. At Dunblane, a further 3,000 men would be
detached to hold Argyle's force of approximately the
same numerical strength. The Dunblane contingent
would make a three-pronged attack aimed at certain

strategic positions and, while Argyle's attention was entirely taken up, the main part of Mar's army would cross the Forth higher up and march on unmolested; the fact that no investigation of the chances of fording the river had been undertaken, and that Mar was apparently in ignorance of the necessity of crossing the river Teith first, underlines the complete absence of even the most rudimentary intelligence system. Argyle's agents were more effective and he heard about the plan the day after it had been concocted. Leaving Lord Buchan, the Lord Lieutenant of Stirlingshire, in command of the local militia which had been strengthened by a volunteer regiment raised by the Provost of Glasgow, and summoning General Wightman to join him from Edinburgh, Argyle went to meet the danger. His small but compact army now totalled some 3,000 and was made up of eight battalions of foot and five regiments of dragoons. They marched out of Stirling on the 12th and bivouacked two miles to the north-east of Dunblane on rising ground above Kippendavie.

The weather was bitingly cold and there was such a heavy frost that night that the river nearby showed signs of freezing over. Argyle, though, was not one to pamper his men, and they were ordered to lie down in the open in their exact order of battle. The general himself set up his headquarters in a sheep-cote and slept on a pile of straw. Before the morning, rounds of ammunition were distributed.

Mar's army had quitted Perth on the 10th with sufficient provisions for twelve days, and that night they encamped at Auchterarder where they were met by General Gordon and the western clans. Morale was low. The Frasers deserted during the night and, says Sinclair, "two hundred of my Lord Huntly's best men who were under the command of Glenbucket deserted us, as his Lordship said, because they had been designedly more oppressed with duty than any other". Sinclair continued to

bicker with Mar and to comment scathingly on an army
which was "never so constant in any thing as our being
disorderly".

Early in the morning of the 12th, they marched as far
as the old Roman camp at Ardoch, about five miles from
Dunblane. There the main body halted while a detachment was sent off to seize Dunblane, and Mar himself
departed to confer with Breadalbane at Drummond
Castle; the first operation was abortive, as Argyle had
been there first, and there is no record of Mar's conversation with the old grey fox. The Jacobite army finally
took up its quarters for the night at Kinbuck, some three
miles away from Argyle's position.

Between the two armies lay the bleak and desolate
Sheriffmuir, so-called from once having been used as a
training ground for the Menteith militia. The moor is far
from flat, taking rather the form of a series of low hills.
Towards the east rise the Ochills, with Beneleuch their
highest point at over 2,300 feet. Towards the west, the
ground slopes down to the river Allan and in the direction of the Perth–Stirling road. Away to the north are
Braco and the Roman camp, and, over the Muir of
Orchill, Crieff and Auchterarder. To the south lie Dunblane, Bridge of Allan and Stirling. The siting was far
from ideal for a battle because of the short hills, but
Argyle at least was satisfied. Arriving first, he had been
able to draw up his cavalry at the most favourable vantage point. Mar's army, on the other hand, was clustered
together entirely haphazard and presented an ideal target
for attack if Argyle had shown more enterprise. Sinclair
doubted whether "since the invention of powder were so
many troops packed in one small place. It cannot properly be said we had a front or rear any more than has a
barrel of herrings." However, they managed to survive
the night.

On the Sunday morning, the two armies were under
arms soon after daybreak, Mar forming his troops up to

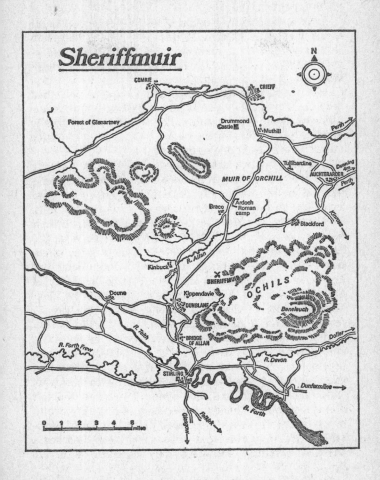

Sheriffmuir

N

COMRIE
CRIEFF
Forest of Glenartney
Drummond Castle
Muthill
Perth
Tullibardine
AUCHTERARDER
Dunning 4m.
MUIR OF ORCHILL
Perth
Braco
Ardoch Roman camp
Blackford
Kinross
R. Allan
Kinbuck
X SHERIFFMUIR
OCHILS
Kippendavie
DUNBLANE
Beneleuch
Doune
R. Teith
BRIDGE OF ALLAN
Dollar
R. Forth Frew
R. Devon
STIRLING
Dunfermline
Glasgow
Falkirk
R. Forth

0 1 2 3 4 5 6 miles

the east of the Dunblane road with the sweep of the moor
in front. His first line of battle consisted of ten battalions
of foot, mainly Highlanders, under the overall command
of General Gordon; among the more important leaders
in this front line were Glengarry, Clanranald, Ogilvy of
Boyne, Gordon of Glenbucket, Sir John Maclean, and
two brothers of Macdonald of Sleat. Mar himself was in
the right centre. The second line, from right to left, contained three battalions of Seaforth's foot, two battalions
under Huntly, Panmure's men, Tullibardine's Atholl
Highlanders, and detachments under Strathallan, Drummond of Logie-Almond and Robertson of Struan. At
either flank there were troops of horse, the Perthshire and
Angus squadrons to the left; and Huntly's two squadrons, the Stirling squadron with the royal standard, and
two squadrons under Marischal to the right. A further
800 men were held in reserve.

Argyle's army was also drawn up in two lines, although the front had only six battalions and the second
a mere couple to strengthen the centre. His only advantage – and it was a vital one – lay in the dragoons at either
flank, although many of the front-line men, under the
command of General Wightman, were at least seasoned
soldiers. Argyle himself commanded three squadrons of
dragoons, including the Scots Greys, on the right wing.

The first move was made by Argyle. Being unable to
view the whole battlefield because of the hilly ground, he
decided to reconnoitre personally and rode with his staff
to the top of a hill above Dunblane where his advance
guard had already been positioned. "From that point he
could easily perceive the dark cloud-like masses of the
clans, as they wheeled into order at the distance of about
two miles. At first, their advanced guards were pointed
in the direction of the highway to Dunblane, as if they
designed to march thither; but by and by he observed a
large body move up the face of the moor towards his
right, as if to take his army in flank. Judging this troop

to be the principal body of the clans – for their right wing
was entirely concealed from his view by a rising ground
– he at once came to the conclusion that they wished to
gain the ascent of the hill, in order to descend in their
usual impetuous manner upon the right wing of his
army." He realised that he was in some danger. Marshy
ground to his right, which might have acted as a barrier,
had frozen over during the night and was now quite pas-
sable. His plans must clearly be altered. He decided to
advance his troops to meet the Jacobite army, and to
trust that they could be re-formed in time.

Mar had sighted this reconnoitring party and was
greatly alarmed by its implications. He still appeared to
be in doubt as to whether he should fight Argyle at all,
but compromised by calling another council of war to
decide the issue for him. Sinclair was scathing about
his continued prevarication, describing him as "stunned,
finding there was something more requisite than lies, for
it was not with us he was to have to do, but with the
enemy and blows must decide it"; but he had to admit
grudgingly that Mar made a fine speech on this occasion, "the only good action of his life". He asked whether
they should fight or not. Huntly, who was becoming increasingly disenchanted at the progress of the campaign,
voiced some doubts, pointing out that if they crossed the
Forth they would be cut off from James when he eventually landed in Scotland. A few less influential members
of the council were in favour of marching back to Perth,
but the vote was finally given unanimously for battle.
The news was greeted with great enthusiasm. "We were
no sooner got to our posts when a huzza begun, with tossing up of hats and bonnets, and run through our whole
army on the hearing we had resolved to fight; and no
man, who had a drop of Scots blood in him, but must
have been elevated to see the cheerfulness of his countrymen on that occasion; and for my own part, in spite of
my reason, I made no manner of doubt of gaining the

victory, and by that unaffected liveliness that appear'd in every man's looks, I begin to think that Highlandmen were Highlandmen." Marischal was sent forward to reconnoitre the ground, Mar made yet another speech to his men, and the left wing was abruptly launched into the attack.

It was too abrupt. General Hamilton, who commanded, had not been given sufficient time to make proper dispositions, indeed Mar's overall orders were far from precise. Even so the accurate musket-fire of the Highlanders was highly effective. Sinclair describes the charge: "The order to attack being given, the two thousand Highlandmen ... run towards the enemy in a disorderly manner, always firing some dropping shots, which drew upon them a general salvo from the enemy, which begun at their left, opposite to us, and run to their right. No sooner that begun, the Highlandmen threw themselves flat on their bellies; and when it slackened, they started to their feet. Most throw away their fuzils, and drawing their swords, pierced them every where with an incredible vigour and rapidity, in four minutes' time from their receiving the order to attack."

It was not until a troop of Argyle's cavalry under Colonel Cathcart rode across the marshy ground which had been frosted over and took them in the flank that the Highlanders gave way. For three hours the struggle on Mar's left flank continued, every inch disputed and the Highlanders facing about no less than six times. Finally, though, they could hold on no longer and were forced into the river Allan where a number of them were drowned. It was noticeable, however, that Argyle's men were not pressing their advantage as ruthlessly as might have been expected. In this battle, cousin often found himself opposed to cousin, and friend charging friend, and quarter was given lavishly. Argyle himself – and by so doing he later laid himself open to vicious political attack – did his utmost to control his dragoons when they threatened to cut down the Highlanders indiscriminately, and on one occasion was heard to cry, "Oh, spare the poor Bluebonnets!" In the heat of battle, emotion and recognition of his Scottish blood were stronger than the killer instinct.

But while Argyle's right wing was winning the day, his left was in a state of total disarray. Because of the lie of the ground, it was impossible for one wing to see what was happening to the other, and when the two armies had first marched against each other Mar's right wing, by accident, heavily outflanked Argyle's left wing. As a consequence, when Mar put in his assault at this point he carried all before him. His men suffered one tragic casualty when the Captain of Clanranald, a chief possessed of "an almost Ossianic degree of heroism" according to a nineteenth-century commentator, was killed by the first volley. But Glengarry rallied Clanranald's Highlanders with the promise of revenge, and within seven minutes Whetham's cavalry were fleeing away towards Dunblane, closely followed by the terrified infantry and hotly pursued by the triumphant Jacobite cavalry. It was a total rout and Mar was convinced that his was the victory. Not until he reached the village of Corntown near Stirling, after pursuing the panic-stricken infantry for half an hour and cutting swathes through their disorganised ranks, did the realisation dawn on him that his left wing had not emulated his own success. The field of battle had, in fact, been almost completely vacated, only part of Argyle's right wing and the infantry on Mar's right remaining more or less intact.

Mar re-formed his men as rapidly as possible and marched them back to Sheriffmuir. But at this crucial stage he again seemed overcome with lethargy. If he had moved immediately, he might well have been able to attack what remained of Argyle's army and drive it from the field. Instead, he spent the whole afternoon quite inactive and watched the return of Argyle's exhausted right wing and the arrival of three fresh regiments. Sinclair describes the rather ridiculous stalemate: "The enemy made the first halt, and we, in complaisance to them, did as much, and stood looking at one another about four hundred yards distance, for half an hour." From his vantage point on top of a hill, Mar could have swept down to deliver the coup de grâce at any moment of his choosing. Instead, he had the doubtful satisfaction of having an excellent view of Argyle's army re-forming and marching safely away to Dunblane. It is hardly surprising that Gordon of Glenbucket was heard to groan, "Oh, for an hour of Dundee!" The great Claverhouse would not have hesitated – and lost.

There is no doubt that Mar should have won the battle of Sheriffmuir. He had overwhelming superiority of numbers and he had the moral advantage of his Highlanders who, charging half-naked and shouting blood-chilling war-cries, could have put terror into hearts much stouter than those of Argyle's regiments. Argyle, too, had not shown the intelligence to be expected of a general trained under Marlborough. Perhaps he had no desire to cut down his fellow-countrymen, certainly it was later said of him that he was a better Christian than a general, as he did not let his left hand know what his right was doing. Both generals displayed indecision, but Mar committed other faults. His orders to his cavalry were open to misunderstanding and his control over his subordinates was often non-existent. Sinclair's squadron of cavalry was never engaged, although its assistance was urgently called for on three occasions; the Macphersons never came under fire, and Rob Roy Macgregor, waiting to see the probable winner before committing himself, marched his clan away for the simple reason that he could perceive no winner; the majority of Seaforth's men ran away and so did the Camerons, the Stuarts of Appin and the Gordons; Marischal's horse were later criticised for their lack of vigour in dealing with Whetham's dragoons. It is a sorry catalogue of inefficiency and downright cowardice.

When Argyle marched his men away to Dunblane as night was falling, Mar turned in the direction of Ardoch. Sheriffmuir was left abandoned. The following morning, however, Argyle returned to the field of battle to collect the spoils, the standards and broadswords, the muskets and the plaids, the few pieces of artillery which had never been used. Thus, technically, he remained in control of the fighting area. Then he too departed, for Stirling.

Accounts of the casualties at Sheriffmuir differ. Mar himself says that he only lost sixty men, but a Government report of approximately 600 deaths on either side has the stamp of truth. Clanranald was dead, and so were Auchterhouse and Strathmore, while Lord Forfar, one of Argyle's commanders, subsequently died of his wounds. Nearly 200 Jacobites, including Lord Strathallan and Drummond of Logie-Almond, were taken prisoner and sent off to Stirling. At one time both Panmure and Robertson of Struan were in enemy hands but they managed to escape. Sinclair's report that Huntly too was at one time captive is unlikely to be very strongly based as the leader of the Gordons took remarkably good care of himself during the battle.

As Rae puts it succinctly, "by this battle the heart of the Rebellion was broke". But perhaps the final comment can be left to one of the many Jacobite songs which contain a peculiar brand of sharp truth:

> There's some say that we wan,
> Some say that they wan,
> And some say that nane wan ava, man;
> There's but ae thing, I'm sure,
> That, at Shirramuir,
> A battle there was, that I saw, man.
> And we ran, and they ran,
> And they ran, and we ran,
> And we ran, and they ran awa, man.

Chapter Eight

The Coming of the Pretender

> At the first news [of James's Landing] it is impossible
> to express the joy and vigour of our men. Now we
> hoped the day was come when we should live more
> like soldiers, and should be led on to face our enemies.

> *The Proceedings at Perth*

By the evening of November 13 the rising lay in ruins.
Preston had capitulated; Sheriffmuir, although strictly
speaking a drawn contest, was as good as lost; and three
days earlier, an improbable alliance of Lord Sutherland,
Duncan Forbes of Culloden and the egregious Simon
Fraser, turning his coat at the right moment for the first
and last time in his disgraceful career, had effected the
recapture of Inverness for King George (it was not entirely by the way that Mackenzie of Fraserdale, who had
married the famous Lovat heiress, had also brought out
the Frasers on the Jacobite side; the fall of Inverness
demonstrated to the clan where their loyalties lay and,
indeed, two days before Sheriffmuir they had all gone
home).

Mar's army now seemed to vanish before his eyes. He
wrote later that "amongst many good qualities the
Highlanders have one unlucky custom not easy to be

reformed, which is, that generally after an action they return home". Auchterarder's and Strathmore's men departed after their leaders had been killed. The Camerons had slunk home, fearful of the reaction of the chief, old Lochiel. And soon both Seaforth and Huntly were gone, ostensibly to counter any hostile attacks on their property by the victorious Sutherland but in effect because they were heartily sick of the whole affair. It is doubtful indeed whether Huntly had ever had the faintest wish to declare himself for James, and he certainly never forgave Mar for being appointed commander-in-chief in the heart of Gordon country.

A final problem was set by the attitude of the majority of the clans. Mar should have realised that they would always return home in three eventualities. If they were defeated, they would take refuge in the hills; if they were victorious, they would make off to squander any booty as rapidly as possible; and on no account would they have patience with a protracted and indeterminate campaign. The long wait at Perth and the indecisive battle at Sheriffmuir fulfilled all three conditionals admirably, and there was no personal loyalty to Mar himself to detain them.

Even so, Mar, if he had possessed more energy or more imagination, could have withdrawn the forces he still commanded gradually northwards, forcing Argyle to lengthen his lines of supply and communication and to leave a series of garrisons at strategic points until his army was vulnerable once more to attack. But it is clear that shortly after the news of Preston* and of the fall of Inverness Mar gave up all hope of continuing the rebellion. He had received no help from France, nor from

*Predictably, Sinclair was not surprised. "I never expected better; it was not to be imagin'd that a handful of raw, undisciplined men, without arms, care, or thought, could march so far into a country, without any man of authority or knowledge at their head, without falling into a snare."

England. A general election in England was imminent and its result might offer a better chance of negotiation. Finally, Argyle had been reinforced, by two regiments which had marched from Preston to Glasgow, by the promised 6,000 Dutch troops, and by the far more ruthless General Cadogan, sent to ensure that there was no leniency shown towards the rebels. It is possible to sympathise with Mar's situation, and the last iota of optimism must have been driven from him when he discovered that the Macdonalds of Keppoch who had mysteriously arrived at Perth, presumably as reinforcements, had in fact merely come in hopes of plunder after the battle. Mar put out blandishments and Keppoch himself stayed on; but his clansmen, finding no booty, proceeded to depart in high dudgeon, seizing anything they could lay their hands on along the road.

And yet, amazingly, Argyle too seems to have been filled with gloom as November passed into December, writing pathetic letters to Townshend and wildly overestimating Mar's strength. With Cadogan at his elbow, spying on him and despatching confidential reports to London, something akin to melancholia took hold of the King's General, and one finds him writing on November 27, "if the Pretender lands, a very few days will put him at the head of 20,000 men." He did not even have the powers necessary to open negotiations with Mar's representatives. It was perhaps a relief when in February 1716 his commission in Scotland was not renewed and he was forced to hand over to the watchful Cadogan.

It was now that James Francis Edward, the old Pretender, the unlucky chief guest at a banquet which would never take place, chose to land in Scotland. A small boat put ashore on December 22 from an eight-gun ship lying at anchor off Peterhead on the north Aberdeenshire coast. Signals had been made,* and soon the son of

*Mar had issued, on October 7, a complicated set of signals and passwords, expecting James to land on the west coast: "A

James II was being carried on to dry land on the shoulders of Captain Park. It was hardly a dramatic or romantic landing. The coast was bleak and unwelcoming, and there was no unfurling of standards or waving of bonnets in the air. James had only five or six companions who had sailed with him from Dunkirk. He had set out from Bar-le-Duc as long ago as October 28, but he was no doubt lucky to arrive at all in his "own ancient kingdom".

His experiences during these two months had been hair-raising. Since the death of Louis XIV, his position vis-à-vis Torcy and the French Government had deteriorated rapidly. Orléans, the Regent during the minority of Louis XV, was strongly in favour of a rapprochement with England (malicious observers noted that his own position was not unlike that of George I's – they were both in a sense usurpers) and extremely unwilling to assist James even as far as the French coast. In addition, the British ambassador in Paris, Lord Stair, had his spies well-paid to watch the roads to the ports.

James had been staying with the Prince de Vaudémont at the Château de Commercy. One evening a fête was being given and it was suddenly announced that King James was ill and unable to attend. There was a flutter of interest but none of the guests thought anything more of it. The following morning, Vaudémont remarked that James had not been ill at all but had left forty-eight hours previously for the coast. On October 30, James, disguised as a priest, was in Paris, having so far eluded

---

White Flag on any of the Topmast-heads, pulled up and down for several times; and the Answer from the Shore, a white Cloath shown on the nearest Eminence. Upon the Signal, a Boat to be sent off, and the Word from the Boat, *Lochaber*. The Answer from the Ship, *Lochyeal*. The People who make the Signal, to know of Horses and Carriages. If any Ship be seen chas'd, Boats to be immediately sent off." It is not known whether all this was put into practice at Peterhead.

Stair's agents. The next day, he visited his mother at the convent of Chaillot and, after spending the night at the Duc de Lauzun's, pressed on towards Nantes. But Stair's men were too close on his heels and he decided to return to Paris before making a further attempt to reach the coast at Saint-Malo.

In the meanwhile, Stair had been endeavouring to persuade Orléans to have James arrested as he passed through Château-Thierry. The Regent, as usual ready to promise anything provided he was not implicated, duly gave orders to a major in his Guards, Contades, and two sergeants to appear to intercept James, although in fact deliberately to miss him. It was a piece of double-dealing which Stair, himself a pastmaster in such matters, immediately saw through; and he decided to take the law into his own hands and arrange James's assassination.

For this unsavoury task he employed a renegade Irish officer down on his luck called Douglas and two other men of an equally dubious nature. The murderers waited for James at Nonancourt, a small village near Evreux, but made such strenuous enquiries for a fair, thin young man with the scars of small-pox on his face that the local postmistress, a certain Madame l'Hôpital, grew suspicious. First of all she lavished so much wine on Douglas's two accomplices that they went fast asleep, then she capped this feat by arranging for them to be arrested. Douglas she misdirected along the wrong road, so that when James arrived in his chaise there was time to conceal him in the house of one of the postmistress's friends. Douglas gave up the unequal struggle and returned to Paris, while James, after waiting for three days, obtained another chaise and travelled safely on to Saint-Malo, where he arrived on November 8. There he found the hapless Duke of Ormonde waiting to launch yet another expedition to the English West Country, and a storm raging off the Normandy coast.

As usual, atrocious ill-luck seemed to surround James.

The weather was always bad at the crucial moments of his life, the winds always veered too soon. As he lingered on in Saint-Malo, waiting for a change in the weather, he became more and more depressed. The presence of Ormonde, whom he liked personally, was a living reminder of the futility of the Jacobites. James had not patched up his bitter quarrel with Berwick, after the latter had refused to resign his commission in the French army and lead the expedition to Scotland; and he could only pour out his unhappiness in a stream of pathetic letters to Bolingbroke, who had prudent and pressing reasons, among whom could be listed the delectable Mme de Tencin, for remaining safely in France. On November 15, James wrote: "I never wanted you so much in my life, for we have been in a strange, confused chaos here these eight days ... I have been harass'd to death since I am here, and have been a little sick to boot, but I hope 'twill be nothing, for I am well today, but if I have life in me, shall not let slip the first fair wind."

But the fair wind did not materialise and, after one attempt to set sail, he decided to leave Saint-Malo and make for Dunkirk. Accompanied by Berwick's son Tynemouth, he rode through the wintry countryside of Normandy and Picardy, along the muddy, pot-holed tracks which served as roads. One of his grooms described his bravery in the face of so many dispirited setbacks: "I never knew any have better temper, be more familiar and good, always pleased and in good humour, notwithstanding all the crosses and accidents that happened during his journey; never the least disquieted, but with the greatest courage and firmness resolved to go through with what he had designed on; ... in fine possessing eminently all the qualities of a great Prince with those of a most honest private gentleman." No better tribute could have been paid him.

At last they reached Dunkirk. The news here was little better. Ormonde had failed again, and Byng's Channel fleet was still hovering in the area. But at least the weather had slightly improved and, on December 16, the small ship sailed. Five days later, Peterhead was sighted.

On his first night ashore, James stayed at a house in Peterhead, but by Christmas Eve he was ensconced at Fetteresso, Marischal's principal seat. The minute he had landed, Lieutenant Cameron, one of the officers accompanying him from France, had ridden off to Perth to spread the news, and Mar, Marischal, General Hamilton and a score of "Persons of Quality on Horseback" had immediately set out to greet him. At Fetteresso, he could at last discard his naval officer's disguise and receive the Scottish leaders with some dignity. Every attempt was made to convert a sad occasion into a royal progress. James was proclaimed at the castle gate and received addresses from the Episcopal clergy and the Aberdeen magistrates and university. Peers were created and Bannerman, the Provost of Aberdeen, was knighted. But James failed to inspire his followers with confidence. It was remarked that he rarely smiled – he perhaps had little to excite his mirth – and he had arrived without men, money or arms. He wrote to Huntly on three occasions requesting him to bestir himself and march on Inverness, but his letters made no impression on this reluctant nobleman.

Having recovered from a feverish cold which kept him at Fetteresso for nine days, James eventually moved on to Brechin. He formally entered Dundee on January 6 and Perth on the 9th, and then took up his residence in the old palace at Scone. His coronation was fixed for the 23rd, and offers came in from the wives of the Scottish lords of diamonds and other jewels to be made into a crown. But there was not enough time and the crown was not to be needed in any case. There was no coronation.

James's spirits had not been raised by what he saw of the army at Perth, and the army returned the insult. The anonymous author of *A True Account of the Proceedings at Perth*,* in a long, often unfair, always vivid description, gives his own reaction. "His person was tall and thin, seeming to incline to be lean rather than to fill as he grows in years. His countenance was pale, but perhaps looked more so than usual, by reason he had three fits of an ague, which took him two days after his coming on shore. Yet he seems to be sanguine in his constitution; and there is something of a vivacity in his eye, that perhaps would have been more visible, if he had not been under dejected circumstances, and surrounded with discouragement; which, it must be acknowledged, were sufficient to alter the complexion even of his soul, as well as of his body. His speech was grave, and not very clearly expressive of his thoughts, nor overmuch to the purpose; but his words were few, and his behaviour and temper seemed always composed. What he was in his diversions, we know not; here was no room for such things." The writer then becomes more critical: "When we saw the man whom they called our king, we found ourselves not at all animated by his presence; if he was disappointed in us, we were tenfold more so in him. We saw nothing in him that looked like spirit. He never appeared with cheerfulness and vigour to animate us. Our men began to despise him; some asked if he could speak. His countenance looked extremely heavy. He cared not to come abroad amongst us soldiers, or to see us handle our arms or do our exercise. Some said the circumstances he found us in dejected him; I am sure the figure he made dejected us; and, had he sent us but five thousand men of good troops, and never himself come among us, we had done other things than we have now done." This evaluation set beside that of James's Irish groom at Dunkirk would

*The author of this tract never revealed his real name, but preferred to masquerade under the hardly debatable nom de plume or de guerre of "A Rebel". Some authorities have credited the writing to the Master of Sinclair, others to Daniel Defoe.

seem to be of a completely different person. It is, as must be emphasised, an unfair assessment – for instance, James was particularly fond of reviewing his troops, even if they hardly reached the standards of a French military display – but something of this cold attitude must have been shared by many at Perth.

Mar himself saw the wisdom of improving James's image and composed a rather curious letter which was circulated from Glamis. Unfortunately, even he was unable to dwell on James's warrior qualities, contenting himself instead with remarks about his sweet temper, his fine writing and the fact that he closely resembled Charles II (perhaps Mar was still trying to scotch the warming-pan rumours of illegitimacy). James's fine writing, although not his sweet temper, was exercised when he signed the notorious Auchterarder Burning Order "at our court at Scoon the 17th day of January in the fifteenth year of our reign 1715–16". This was a directive to James Graham of Braco, one of Mar's principal agents, to ensure the destruction of a number of Perthshire towns and villages, Auchterarder, Muthill, Crieff, Blackford and Dunning. It was thought necessary to carry out this scorched earth policy, common enough in modern warfare but rarer then, so as to remove from Argyle and Cadogan both shelter and provisions in the event of their marching northwards.

The leader of the party which carried out the order was Ranald Macdonald, brother of the dead Clanranald; it is possible that he was chosen for the very reason that he was mourning his brother and might be glad of an opportunity to avenge his death. With a detachment of between five and six hundred men, he arrived at Auchterarder at four o'clock in the morning of January 25 and immediately sent a party off to Blackford, ordering his men to "go and burn all the houses in the town, spare none except the church and Mrs. Paterson's"; "this Mrs. Paterson's was the house where the Jacobites kept their

Conventicles during the time of the late Ministry and before the Rebellion."

The houses were fired within a few moments and Ranald Macdonald marched his men away. As he went, "he prayed the people whom he saw weeping to forgive him, but was answered with silence, and so departed to do the like in other places. His men, before they went, seized all the horses they could find to carry off their plunder." Being January, the weather was freezing cold and the villagers were left standing in the thick snow.

Similar attacks were carried out on the other villages during the next few days, and in none was there the least resistance. One eye-witness, no lover of the Jacobites, describes the scene after the flames had ceased to rage luridly against the pure-white background of the snow-drifts.

"Sir, from these few instances of the many severities we met with, it's easier for you to conjecture what must have been the sad and fatal consequences of such inhumane, barbarous, popishlike, and hellish cruelty ... The poor women (*horresco referens*) exposed to the open fields with their sucking infants, and scarce a rag left to cover them from any extremity of cold; likeways several vigorous men and women were struck with such terror that they survived the burning but a very few days ... Many have died since, and no doubt their deaths occasioned by cold contracted in barns, stables, and old huts where they were obliged to lodge, and that in a very rigorous season as has been of many years, having no clothes save what honest, charitable neighbours were pleased of their goodness to bestow ... Were there a particular account given of the bad usage the people met with from the Rebels, it could not miss to produce an utter abhorrence of a popish Pretender in the heart of any thinking man, who countenanced, yea even ordered the execution of such cruelties."

This account is no doubt highly-coloured and partial, making the incident take on the horror of a Glencoe in miniature, but the burning of the villages did the reputation of James little good. Cadogan made as much capital out of it as he could, and Argyle magnified its effects as evidence of the impracticality of marching on Perth. But it is known that James bitterly regretted signing the order and one of his final acts before abandoning Scotland was to request the payment of funds to compensate the destitute villagers.

The time for this abandonment was now very close. On the 29th, Argyle at last left Stirling with a much reinforced army, and two days later James gave the order to strike camp. According to Tynemouth, it was a command he gave reluctantly. "I am in despair," he said, "at finding myself compelled to withdraw from Perth without a fight; but to offer battle would be to expose brave men for no reason, since the enemy is twice as strong as we are, and I wish to preserve them for a more fitting occasion. I hope that when we have joined our friends in the north all will go well, and as you are waiting for the French I will use a proverb in that language which says *Nous ne reculons que mieux sauter.*" James still seemed to expect help from France, and he wrote letters to Orléans and even to Berwick asking for assistance; but it was at last borne in upon him that the rising had failed, totally and irrevocably, and that he owed it to the future of the Stuart dynasty to leave Scotland and return to France.

On February 4, at Montrose, he penned his long "letter of adieu to the Scotch" and also wrote to Argyle, justifying his own behaviour and reproaching the King's General for fighting against him. Then, empowering General Gordon to make use of any money left for paying the troops, and to treat with Argyle for the best terms he could obtain, he went on board the small Dieppe ship, the *Marie-Thérèse,* accompanied by Mar, Melfort,

Drummond and a few others it was considered inadvisable to leave in Scotland. They sailed by the evening tide, eluded the two English men o' war lying in wait, and reached Waldam, between Gravelines and Calais, six days later. James had been on Scottish soil a mere forty-five days. He left his supporters with these words: "Convinced as I am that you would never abandon me, and that therefore my stay could only involve you in greater difficulties, I took the party to repass the seas that by that I might leave such as cannot make their mistake (towards which nothing on my side have been neglected) in full liberty to take the properest measures for avoiding at least utter ruin." It was cold comfort indeed.

The remnants of the Jacobite army, now under General Gordon, did not realise that James had left Scotland until they were on the road to Aberdeen, and the news was not greeted with marked rapture; the general consensus seemed to be that he had come too late and gone too early. Up to Aberdeen the Highlanders retained their discipline but after Gordon had opened James's letter and communicated its contents, a sense of *sauve qui peut* took hold of them. Argyle was close behind – he entered Aberdeen the day after Gordon left it – and the clansmen simply melted away, a few escaping by sea from Peterhead and Fraserburgh and others vanishing up Strathspey. According to Robert Campbell, "they dispersed so effectually that, though his Grace the Duke of Argyle used all the diligence in his power to come up with them and gave himself or his army no rest; yet he never could overtake one party of them, and did not in all the pursuit from Perth to the Highlands make a hundred prisoners".

From Ruthven a letter, with ten signatures including those of Gordon, Southesk, Linlithgow and Ogilvy of Boyne, was sent to Argyle, requesting favourable surrender terms. Argyle did not answer and the last of the Jacobites dispersed, making their escape as best they could. And on February 16 Adam Cockburn noted, doubtless with a degree of complacency: "Here is this formidable rebellion evanish like Smoak." Now, inescapably, it was the time for revenge. And Cadogan was the man to carry it out.

John, second Duke of Argyle, Earl of Greenwich, Knight of the Garter, Knight of the Thistle, Chief of the Clan Campbell, the King's General in North Britain, returned to Edinburgh on February 27 and left for London a few days later. He was an unhappy and disillusioned man. His position had always been difficult. At Ramillies and Oudenarde and Malplaquet he had known who his enemies were. In Scotland he had never been certain. Mar and James Stuart were his ostensible quarry, but in the later stages of the campaign Cadogan seemed a more ruthless adversary. Argyle suspected that his colleague was by no means a true friend, but he cannot have been aware that Cadogan was continually writing to the Government and to his mentor the Duke of Marlborough, accusing him of leniency and deliberate delaying tactics. Cadogan did not scruple to suggest that the wrong man was in command when he complained about Argyle's treatment of the rebels; and he gave it as his firm opinion that "any Acts of Grace and mercy should pass through other hands than those of Argyle". It is true that Argyle had always let pessimism – or realism, depending on one's attitude – dominate any sense of urgency, but he did have a number of reasons for his doubts. His own troops were raw and few, whereas Mar seemed to command a Scottish horde. To all outward appearances, the Jacobite cause had triumphed in three-quarters of the country and was maintaining its popularity to the extent that even the Campbells were a divided clan: Breadalbane, Glendaruel, Glenlyon and others had all declared for the Stuarts. The support from Edinburgh and London was negligible. And finally, sensibly refusing to under-estimate his opponent, he cannot have believed that Mar was as inept and manifestly ill-suited for high command as he later showed himself beyond all shadow of doubt. It is no compliment to Argyle that the campaign was lost by Mar rather than won by himself, but civil war, which the rising essentially was, is notoriously the most complex and demoralising of all types of warfare.

As Argyle was posting south towards London, he encountered the funeral procession of the recently executed Derwentwater, and he was seen to be deeply moved; his reaction summed up pathetically all that he must have been feeling. When he arrived in the capital he soon realised that Cadogan had done his job well. Argyle was removed from all his high offices of state in July, losing even his pension, and he was to languish in disfavour for a number of years. Eventually, though, the pendulum swung back and he ended his life in 1743, at the age of sixty-three, with the rank of Field Marshal and a monument in Poets' Corner in Westminster Abbey. In retrospect, it is intriguing to conjecture on his possible standpoint had he lived two more years and seen the Jacobite pattern repeat itself.

With Argyle safely out of the way in London and in disgrace, Cadogan set about pacifying Scotland. The anti-Jacobite lords and chiefs, who had previously hesitated to make their positions crystal-clear for fear of their neighbours' disapproval, now appeared in their true colours, and the Grants, the Forbeses, the Mackays and the Brodies were fierce and diligent in the execution of the new Government measures, convening courts to inquire into the behaviour of men who had been out and had now returned home, and calling in a vast and motley collection of offensive weapons by the terms of the Disarming Act. Cadogan's Dutch troops, with no social niceties to observe and no irritating patriotic feelings to restrain them, were still more vigorous in their efforts to stamp out any last flicker of rebellion. According to one eye-witness, they did not leave "a chair or a stool, nor a barrel or a bottle, *enfin* nothing earthly undestroyed, and the English troops very little more merciful".

But, although harsh, Cadogan's measures were directed more against property than against life, and he set no precedent for the brutalities perpetrated by Cumberland's officers thirty years later. A number of the leaders of the rising, including General Gordon, Seaforth and the dead Clanranald's brother, eventually made their way to the Western Isles and from there to safety in France. Marischal and his brother James Keith were two more who used this route. The Master of Sinclair and Colonel Hay, the officer who had taken Perth, escaped to Orkney before joining the other refugees in France. But the great majority of the Jacobites vanished into the hills, some like Rob Roy Macgregor to carry on a form of guerrilla warfare long into the future, others to sit and wait for the hue and cry to die down.

A few prominent Jacobites simply gave themselves up and threw their lives on the mercy of the Government. One of these was Huntly, who because his title was only a courtesy one, his father the Duke of Gordon still being alive, was ordered to join the prisoners who were on their way to stand trial at Carlisle. He actually set out with the third contingent, which included Gordon of Glenbucket and John Gordon of Aboyne, but the order was rescinded and he was brought back to Edinburgh Castle. There he had a number of conversations with General Carpenter who was convinced that he would cause no more trouble and would indeed be very helpful in promoting the Government's case. Carpenter had no illusions on the score of why Huntly would be prepared to cooperate. "One reason I have to think this is that the Pretender's friends hate him morally and would be glad he were put to death, but the continuance of his great interest in the north is by the vast number of tenants he has in those parts." Sure enough, Huntly's remission ar-

rived at the beginning of November and he was promptly
set at liberty.

It is difficult to valuate fairly Huntly's contribution
to the rising. Without doubt, no other man involved
earned for himself so much opprobrium, even loathing.
The ballad-mongers sharpened their tongues and their
quills, and there were few defenders of his conduct at
and after Sheriffmuir. His detractors thought back to
more glorious examples of the house of Huntly, particularly perhaps to the days of Mary when the Gordons
had wielded great power and had been prepared to lead
a rebellion rather than avoid one; but the sixteenth century had been an age of fierce beliefs fiercely held, now a
century had passed and dissimulation was the popular
political manner. Men, indeed, were more careful of their
heads, and equivocation had replaced Celtic devil-may-
care bravado. Alexander, Marquess of Huntly was a man
of this new era, a palimpsest from which too much of
the old had been erased. His father George, first Duke of
Gordon, had once held Edinburgh Castle for James II
before the latter's cause was seen to be hopeless, but it
was the single action in his life governed by emotion,
and his son strove to emulate this example.

At the time of the 1715 rising Huntly was about thirty-
seven and he had been back in Scotland some ten years
after an extensive Grand Tour during the course of
which he had struck up a firm but improbable friendship
with the Duke of Tuscany, Cosimo de' Medici. He was
a handsome man, tall, thin and elegant in his dress. The
veneer of the Continent had rubbed away the starker
manners of a Scottish boy and, according to Macky, he
was "certainly a very fine gentleman, and understands
conversation, and the Belles Lettres; is well bred; made
for the company of ladies". He was accused of cynicism
and covetousness, acquired no doubt from the French,
but his chief sin seemed to be his Catholic faith, although
he was certainly not a religious man. His mother, a force-

ful and dynamic *grande dame* and a committed Jacobite, had been before her marriage to Gordon Lady Elizabeth Howard, daughter of the Duke of Norfolk, and had imported to Scotland all the assurance of the greatest English Catholic dynasty. Indeed, many observers attributed Huntly's involvement in the rising to his mother's prompting, and Sir Hew Dalrymple echoed this feeling when he wrote to Stair in February 1716 that "the Marquess owes his misfortune in a great measure to the Duchess, who both drew him into the snare and discouraged all means of bringing him out of it". But there was a second, conflicting influence in Huntly's life – his wife, Henrietta Mordaunt, the Whiggish daughter of Lord Peterborough – and from the moment of their marriage any Jacobite leanings he might formerly have possessed began to dwindle rapidly. Caught between these two female persuaders and annoyed that the leadership of the rising had not been entrusted to him, it is scarcely surprising that Huntly should have appeared lukewarm to his more aggressive and less polished companions in arms. Although he made reasonable efforts to bring out his men, he was no military leader and Gordon of Glenbucket noted that the Huntly contingent was little better than a rabble, "not a third of them being armed". Certainly Sheriffmuir was not to his liking, and the Countess of Seaforth accused him of palpable cowardice – "he did not go near the line of battle, but went off as soon as he heard the first fire". But the Master of Sinclair, another member of what Mar termed the "Grumblers' Club", disagreed and put a more charitable and persuasive gloss on his defection. Huntly, for all his uncertainty, was perfectly well aware of Mar's crass stupidity and was merely facing inevitable reality when he abandoned the Jacobite army and rode north into Aberdeenshire.

But though Sinclair might say that Huntly was "shamefully traduced over Sheriffmuir fight", and though the Seaforth evidence is at the least highly dubious owing to the fact that the noble earl himself was not seen in the thick of the fighting, it does seem that he was only too glad to witness the collapse of the rising and the speedy departure of the Stuart claimant. The ballads have caught him like a fly in amber, unable to stir himself from the miasma of suspicion; and the barbed sarcasm shown in the following example is mild compared with countless other vituperative verses:

> Near to him [Atholl] let His Grace of Gordon stand
> For these two Dukes may well go hand in hand.
> And if you mount him on his Tuscan steed,
> Pray leave him room to gallop off with speed.

But perhaps Macky's astute appraisal is nearer the mark: "He hath a great many good links in him, but they do not all make a complete chain."

Before his release from Edinburgh Castle, Huntly no doubt spent much of his time assuring General Carpenter of his good intentions towards the Hanoverian dynasty and reminding him of the fact that he had been one of the first to open secret negotiations with Argyle, and that he had kept his word and not attempted to escape into the Highlands or overseas. But he also managed to help those of his clan who had been taken at Preston, sending them money and pressing for their release. And he continued to keep his word. A month later his father died and he succeeded to the dukedom. He ignored Ormonde's blandishments to support the 1719 rebellion and did not even flirt with the Jacobites as he had done so disastrously during the '15. Alexander, second Duke of Gordon, died on November 22, 1728. Cosmo, so-called out of respect for the Duke of Tuscany, followed his father's advice and refused to dabble in politics, and two of his brothers whole-heartedly supported the Government; only Lord Lewis Gordon broke out of the pattern of judiciousness and joined the Stuart army in the '45. Patten, the historian of the '15, had called Huntly "one

of the most inconsistent men of his Age, having in this
very Rebellion acted so much the Trimmer, that whenever opportunity served, he sided with the rising party".
His obituary notice referred to "consummate Honour
and integrity, an extensive Charity, innate love of virtue
and a scrupulous aversion to whatever was vicious or
irregular, all sweetened with a blest natural temper".
Both writers erred in different directions. The enigmatic
Huntly could not so easily be classified.

*

The absence of outright vengeance on the part of Government supporters in Scotland after the final scattering
of the Jacobite army is remarkable. The motions were
gone through, courts were set up, evidence was heard,
but the lairds and chieftains had friends in high places.
The estates of such prominent leaders as Mar, Marischal
and Southesk were declared forfeit and sold off and the
Act of Attainder indicated to certain Jacobites the wisdom of remaining outside the country. But even the prisoners who were marched from Stirling and Edinburgh
to stand trial at Carlisle eluded hanging juries and judges. The conditions in which they found themselves in
the overcrowded prisons excited the compassion of men
like Duncan Forbes of Culloden, certainly one of the
greatest humanitarians of his age who had been appalled
by the judicial murder of Captain Green and was to earn
the contempt of Cumberland for his decent treatment of
the wretched prisoners in the aftermath of the '45; and
dreadful these conditions undoubtedly were. But not one
Scot who was tried at Carlisle felt the hangman's noose.
And during the succeeding months the gaols and Tol-
booths began to render up their bedraggled inmates.
Starving, destitute, diseased they very often were, but at
least they were alive. Cadogan's unimaginative Dutch
troops continued to burn and lay waste, but they did not
kill. Curiously, the Government did not feel any passion-

ate anger towards the Scottish rebels. They considered that the country was already pacified and the inhabitants sufficiently cowed. And when the Act of Pardon was passed less than a year and a half later, the only prominent Highlander to be exempted from the general amnesty was Rob Roy Macgregor, and his clan had been outlawed for a century. It is true that four of the captured Scottish lords were arraigned for high treason, but only one was executed.

The full rigour of English law was directed against the English rebels – and here there was no compassion.

Chapter Nine

The Prisoners

> Albeit that here in London town
>   It is my fate to die;
> Oh, carry me to Northumberland,
>   In my father's grave to lie!
> Then chant my solemn requiem
>   In Hexham's holy towers;
> And let six maids of fair Tynedale
>   Scatter my grave with flowers.
>
> Jacobite ballad

AT the end of the first week of December 1715, two events attracted the attention of inquisitive Londoners: three Jacobites, who had failed in their attempt to secure Oxford for the Stuarts, were drawn up Holborn Hill in carts towards Tyburn and execution; and a detachment of Guards marched up Gray's Inn Lane to Highgate and took up their posts in readiness for the imminent arrival of the prisoners taken at Preston who had been gradually approaching the capital after the long trail from the North. The weather was cold and wintry, but crowds began to gather, eager to inspect the bizarre Highlanders and to hurl abuse at the English rebels.

The treatment of the prisoners at Preston had veered

towards the barbarous. No provision for even bread and
water had been made, and some of the men, incarcerated
in the church, had been forced to rip out the linings of
the pews to give themselves slight protection from the
cold. A few officers were shot out of hand for desertion,
and one eye-witness, probably exaggerating, speaks of
seventy being tortured to death and great numbers being
shipped off as slaves for the plantations in America. Certainly, however, the victorious General Wills was dis-
inclined to show any leniency or even common humanity.
And when the melancholy procession at last set out for
London, even the officers were often fettered, an egali-
tarian but unusual condition. There were about 300
prisoners, headed by the officers, followed by the
gentlemen-volunteers, with the Highlanders bringing up
the rear. A few tried to escape, but almost none succeeded.

As they reached Highgate, precautions became more
strict. "Every one of them had his arms tied with a cord
coming across his back, and being thus pinioned they
were not allowed to hold the reins of the bridle but each
of them had a foot soldier leading his horse." According
to Lady Cowper, whose husband was shortly to be appointed Lord High Steward and to sit in trial over the
Jacobite peers, the spectators enjoyed themselves hugely.
"The mob insulted them terribly, carrying a warming-pan
before them, and saying a thousand barbarous things
which some of the prisoners returned with spirit." She
forbade her children to watch the proceedings, nor did
she go herself, not only from nervousness that the crowd
might run amok, but also out of respect for a number of
her relations who were among the prisoners. There were
many others, equally highly placed, who viewed the collapse of the rising in the North of England with mixed
feelings.

The two leaders of the rising, Forster and Derwentwater, behaved very differently. The renegade Member
of Parliament, idiotic even within sight of the hangman's

noose, appeared certain that they would all be rescued
by a Tory mob, and when this happy event failed to
materialise contented himself with grumbling because he
was being taken to Newgate instead of to the Tower. But
his optimism was hardly boosted when he saw the remains of the three Jacobites who had been hanged, drawn
and quartered the previous day waiting to be placed on
the gates as a warning to all traitors. Derwentwater, on
the other hand, had no illusions and displayed much of
the coolness inherited from his grandfather Charles II.
As he rode through Barnet he asked an officer in Lord
Lumley's regiment of horse where the prisoners would be
lodged once they reached London. The officer said that
he believed they would be divided between the Tower,
Newgate, the Fleet prison, and the Marshalsea, according to their rank and importance. Derwentwater then
remarked cryptically that "there's one house would hold
us all, and we have a better title to it than any other
people in Great Britain". The officer asked for clarifica-
tion. "It is Bedlam," answered Derwentwater. It was not
the first time that the lunacy inherent in the northern
rising had struck home to him, indeed it is doubtful
whether he would have joined the insurgents in the first
place if the order for his arrest had not been issued.

As the prisoners passed on to their various prisons,
the crowd was able to catch a glimpse of men of the
highest quality who had chosen the wrong moment to
prove their loyalty to the wrong claimant to the throne
of England and Scotland. Derwentwater rode with his
brother Charles Radcliffe; Lord Widdrington was accompanied by his two brothers; Lord Carnwath was with
his uncle James Dalzell; the most powerful Northumberland families were well represented; Nithsdale and
Kenmure, Nairn and Wintoun, even old Lord Edward
Howard, Norfolk's brother. Particular interest was
shown in Forster and his chaplain, Mr. Patten, as they
rode past together, and this less than worthy clergyman

later testified to the vastness of the mob and the shouts of
"Long live King George and down with the Pretender".*
As the *Flying-Post* aptly put it, the cavalcade "gave a
very lively idea of the triumphs of the ancient Romans
when they led their captives to Rome". The right-wing
Tories, reluctant at this stage to allow Whig certainty
of victory over the Jacobites, pricked this particular
bubble of conceit as they proceeded to spread a rumour
to the effect that a high proportion of the so-called
prisoners had been in reality out-of-work actors hired
for the occasion who had slipped away home after the
procession had vanished. The crowd merely enjoyed itself in an uncritical way and prepared for the hangings
and executions.

But before the final retribution there were the laborious
investigations in the Secretary of State's room at the
Cockpit in Whitehall, the continuing arrests of suspect
persons and the preparations for the state trials with all
their empty ritual and panoply.† The Jacobite lords were
lodged in the Tower and treated with considerable courtesy by the Lieutenant-Governor. But the unlucky common soldiers who were walled up in Newgate and the
other prisons knew hard times. Newgate itself was run
on highly commercial lines by the drunken Governor Pitt
and his band of gaolers. The act of Parliament which laid
it down that a rent of half a crown a week could be
levied was ignored, and guineas were the negotiable cur-

---

*The Reverend Mr. Patten's ears were both selective and ad-
aptable. The book he wrote was primarily self-justification, but
he seized any opportunity to overlay his own innocence and
readiness to atone with a general atmosphere of Hanoverian
popularity and magnanimity.

†The state trials of the early eighteenth century bear a strong
resemblance to the great public trials organised periodically in
Communist countries. In both there is a sensation of theatri-
cality – much is made of the honest legal processes and the
accused's ability to rely on them, but the dénouement is certain
before the judge even takes his seat.

rency. Twenty guineas could buy the privileges of residence in the Governor's own house, but even this
arrangement was a hollow mockery bringing with it
merely the right to take exercise in the foul press yard
and to eat in the squalid pothouse adjoining it. The fee
payable for the removal of a prisoner's fetters rose as
high as twenty-five guineas, and the amused news-sheets
reported that the wretched officers were forced to advance
more money to the turnkeys "that would almost have
paid the rent of the best house in St. James's Square, or
Piccadilly, for several years".

Even after some faint privacy had been dearly bought,
there was little enough to occupy the minds of the prisoners as they waited for death or transportation. Forster
and Macintosh of Borlum quarrelled more fiercely than
ever and fought every incident in the battle at Preston
over and over again. Some took to writing poetry,
others to treachery. Mr. Patten decided rapidly that val-
our was no part of the make-up of a man of God, and
opted for a complete confession of his manifold sins
and wickedness in return for an unstretched neck. Lord
Townshend, eager for some reliable witnesses, dispatched
a certain Reverend Doctor Cannon to converse with the
wavering Patten in Newgate. Cannon, it appears, was a
man "of singular good temper and literature, who applied
his best endeavours to satisfy me [Patten] in every point
and query I proposed. In which, his learning and solid
reasoning prevailed upon me." Patten did not need
strenuous persuading and he promptly became "an Evidence for the King; which I am far from being ashamed
of, let what calumnies will follow". His experience in the
pulpit stood him in good stead and the commissioners
hearing his evidence had some difficulty in halting the
flow of testimony and self-accusation. Mr. Patten,
though, "was used in the most gentleman-like manner".

But while the officers and clergy languished in comparative comfort, those foolish enough not to have pro-

vided themselves with the requisite horde of guineas received short shrift at the hands of their gaolers. "The Lions' Den", "the Middle Dark", and "the Common Side" have an ominous ring to them, and these were the appalling holes where the destitute were left regardless of old age or illness. And if any man dared object to his treatment, there was always the "Condemned Hold", a dungeon beneath the arches of Newgate, where the offender could spend the night in total darkness; once this was experienced, few complained a second time.

It is difficult to equate the treatment of prisoners at the beginning of the eighteenth century with modern attitudes and conditions. Certainly there was no psychological approach – how could there have been? – and the legal system was hardly equipped to interfere. The Fleet, Newgate and the Marshalsea were merely half-way houses to the gallows, to transportation for life or, possibly the most terrible punishment of all, permanent imprisonment, not necessarily because a life sentence had been passed but very often simply because forgetfulness superseded justice. It would have needed a combination of Hieronymus Bosch and Hogarth to paint the scene. Gin was cheap and so were the sluts prepared, even eager, to sell their favours. But these were Dead Sea fruit, aids to oblivion, a more than transitory pleasure in an atmosphere of filth and crudeness.

The rebel lords in the Tower knew nothing of these horrors. In that icy winter their apartments may have been depressingly bleak, but they met with politeness and even a reluctant admiration. Humanity respects a doomed man so long as he possesses a title, and the spurious glamour of a lost cause clung to these noble peers like a counterfeit aureole. Their estates were up for sale and, after the first days, they were refused visitors; but they had many influential sympathisers who were pressing for their release.

On January 9, 1716, Mr. Lechmere rose in the House

of Commons to deliver himself of a lengthy speech, much
of which was concerned with George I's virtues and good
qualities but during whose course he stressed the absolute necessity to "put an end to this rebellion, not only
to quiet the present commotions, but to extinguish the
very possibility of their being renewed". His peroration
duly reached its expected climax: "And therefore I now
impeach James, Earl of Derwentwater of high treason;
which Impeachment I undertake to make good." Similar
motions dealt with Widdrington, Nithsdale, Wintoun,
Carnwath, Kenmure and Nairn, and the same evening
the Articles of Impeachment were carried up to the
Lords. The following day the seven peers were brought
to the Bar of the House, charged and allowed until the
16th to submit their answers with the full help of counsel
(this date was extended to the 19th).

During this intervening period the Privy Council
undertook the preliminary examinations, and there was
much excitement as the great coach bore the accused
from the Tower to Westminster. Sometimes they went by
water but only after the Thames had thawed out. A few
weeks earlier it had frozen over and a fair had been set
up. Oxen were roasted, and one day even the Prince of
Wales and the Duke of Marlborough were adventurous
enough to emerge from their sedan chairs and cross the
ice to Lambeth. Finally, on the 19th, the rebel lords
entered Westminster Hall to plead and make their
answers. Only Wintoun made any attempt at delaying
tactics, and his trial was postponed. The other six all
pleaded guilty.

The proceedings were organised with elaborate ceremony. Lord Cowper had been nominated Lord High
Steward and was to be referred to as Your Grace for the
duration of the trial. His servants were provided with
new liveries, although Lady Cowper insisted on their
plainness. "I think it very wrong," she noted, "to make
a parade upon so dismal an occasion as that of putting

to death one's fellow creatures." A parade, however, was obligatory, and its form was strictly governed. "On the morning of the Trial, at the hour appointed by the Lord High Steward, the judges in their scarlet robes, together with Garter, and the Black Rod, and the serjeant at arms, who is to make the proclamations, are to assemble at the Lord High Steward's house, and are to wait on him above stairs, or where he pleases to receive them, Garter being in his coat of arms, the Black Rod having the white staff [it was eight to nine feet in length], and the serjeant at arms bearing his mace, where they all have a collation."

The collation successfully terminated, the procession formed up. Cowper entered his coach, followed by Garter and the seal bearer; Black Rod and the serjeant at arms disposed themselves less regally in the boots. The Lord High Steward's coach was drawn by six horses, while the carriages containing the judges and the Lord High Steward's retainers were provided with a mere couple. The cavalcade then set out for Westminster and eventually drew up in Old Palace Yard. Cowper descended, passed through the Painted Chamber and on into the Lord Chancellor's room, donned his parliamentary robes and entered the House. Prayers were said, the peers present were called over, and yet another procession gathered before moving on to Westminster Hall. The line of dignitaries, walking solemnly out of the House, seemed interminable. First went Cowper's gentlemen attendants, followed by the clerks assistant to the House of Lords, the clerk of the Parliament and the clerk of the crown in the Court of Chancery. They were followed by the masters in Chancery, the judges and chief justices, the peers' eldest sons and peers minor, four serjeants at arms bearing maces, and the yeomen ushers of the House of Lords. Then came the peers, "the Lords spiritual and temporal, according to their degrees and precedencies, two and two. The youngest barons first, all covered." Four more

serjeants at arms, the Lord High Steward's serjeant at
arms and seal bearer, Black Rod and Garter King of
Arms, and finally, clothed in the panoply of his awe-
inspiring office, stepped Lord Cowper himself.

Through the Painted Chamber they marched, on into
the Court of Requests and part of the Court of Wards,
under a doorway between the Court of Chancery and
King's Bench, and at last into the great space of Westminster Hall with its superb timbered roof. Lord Cowper
took his place on the woolsack. The clerk of the crown
in the Court of Chancery directed the Lord High Steward's serjeant at arms to make proclamation of silence,
bowed three times to Cowper, and presented the King's
commission, which was then read in its full Latin text.
The Lord High Steward left the woolsack and, now bearing the white staff of his office, seated himself in a large
and impressive chair; the serjeant at arms called once
more for silence and then uttered the long awaited
words: "O Yes, O Yes, O Yes! Lieutenant of the Tower
of London, bring forth your prisoners to the bar,
according to the order of the House of Lords to you
directed." But besides the six peers and the Lieutenant
Governor of the Tower, there was an additional member
of this far more exiguous procession. This was the Gentleman Jailer and he carried the ceremonial axe with the
blade turned away from him.

Even at this point the courtesies were maintained. The
prisoners knelt and then bowed to the Lord High Steward, and to their fellow peers. The compliment was returned, and finally more serious matters were reached.
The Articles of Impeachment were read and, one by one,
the arraigned peers made their answers. Derwentwater,
Widdrington, Nithsdale read their prepared answers,
pleading for mercy and expressing deep sorrow at their
past actions; Carnwath and Kenmure had no statements
but again threw themselves on the king's mercy; Nairn
presented a petition in which he stressed his adherence

to the Protestant faith and minimised his own participation in the rising. They were so many words falling in a vacuum of antagonism. Not one peer would, not one peer could, vote for their acquittal. And there were yet more words to be wasted on the hostile air. Cowper enquired why judgment should not be passed upon them according to the law, and once again the six peers fumbled out their excuses and pleas for mercy. Widdrington had complained of gout, Nairn said that his family would starve without him, Derwentwater and Nithsdale, according to their testimony, had barely been connected with the rebellion. Only Carnwath and Kenmure retained some dignity, by the simple expedient of saying little.

It was Derwentwater, cool no longer, who perhaps best exemplified the tenor of the speeches: "The terrors of your lordships' just sentence, which at once deprives me of my life and innocent children, are so heavy upon my mind that I am scarcely able to allege what may extenuate my offence, if anything can do it. I have confessed myself guilty; but, my lords, that guilt was rashly incurred, without any premeditation." This was certainly no fighting address, and it wrung no tears from his audience.

Cowper, in his closing speech, rapidly demolished the accused peers' pleas of mitigation and, after referring to George I as "the best of kings" and becoming positively carried away by his eloquence, arrived at the inevitable sentence: "And now, my lords, nothing remains, but that I pronounce upon you (and sorry I am that it falls to my lot to do it) that terrible sentence of the law, which must be the same that is usually given against the meanest offender in the like kind. The most ignominious and painful parts of it are usually remitted by the grace of the crown to persons of your quality; but the law in this case being deaf to all distinctions of persons, requires I should pronounce, and accordingly it is adjudged by this Court, that you, James, Earl of Derwentwater, William, Lord

Widdrington, William, Earl of Nithsdale, Robert, Earl
of Carnwath, William, Viscount Kenmure, and William
Lord Nairn, and every of you, return to the prison of the
Tower from whence you came; from thence you must be
drawn to the place of execution; when you come there,
you must be hanged by the neck, but not till you be dead;
for you must be cut down alive, then your bowels must
be taken out, and burnt before your faces; then your
heads must be severed from your bodies, and your bodies
divided each into four quarters; and these must be at
the king's disposal. And God Almighty be merciful to
your souls."*

The prisoners were removed, the white staff was cere-
monially broken, and the assembled peers adjourned to
the House of Lords. The great trial was at an end. Less
than a month later, on March 15, the whole empty show
would be revived for the trial of George, Earl of Wintoun, on an impeachment for high treason; by that date
two noble heads had parted from their bodies on Tower
Green.

*

Among those who listened to the sentences being passed
was the Prince of Wales and, according to Lady Cowper,
who was greatly elated at the praise for her husband's
oratory, "he came home much touched with compassion
for them". But although the prince did not involve himself in the campaign to save the lives of the condemned
men, his wife determined to help Lord Carnwath, perhaps because of his youth. She used Sir David Hamilton
as a go-between to persuade Carnwath to make a full
confession. Carnwath did indeed write a letter along such
lines, but the Princess of Wales was not satisfied. "He
must say more to save himself," she exclaimed. "Bid Sir
David Hamilton go to him again, and beg of him, for

*This barbarous sentence was almost invariably commuted to
simple beheading in the case of a peer of the realm.

God's sake, to save himself by confessing. There is no other way, and I will give him my honour to save him, if he will confess; but," she added tartly, "he must not think to impose on people by professing to know nothing, when his mother goes about talking as violently for Jacobitism as ever, and says that her son falls in a glorious cause." Carnwath did his utmost to comply and his life was indeed spared; the date of his execution was postponed a number of times and he was eventually released under the terms of the Act of Grace in the following year. When he emerged from the Tower he found himself without money or property, and even deserted by his friends who considered his confession far from admirable. He lived on only a further nine years.

Lady Nithsdale made a gallant attempt to plead her husband's case with the king, but it was quite unsuccessful, George showing himself at his most boorish. The unfortunate woman later described the whole embarrassing scene in a letter to her sister. "The first day, I heard that the King was to go to the Drawing Room. I dressed myself in black, as if I had been in mourning, and sent for Mrs. Morgan, because, as I did not know his Majesty personally, I might have mistaken some other person for him. She stayed by me and told me when he was coming. I had also another lady with me, and we three remained in a room between the King's apartments and the Drawing Room, so that he was obliged to go through it; and, as there were three windows in it, we sat in the middle one, that I might have time enough to meet him before he could pass. I threw myself at his feet, and told him in French that I was the unfortunate Countess of Nithsdale, that he might not pretend to be ignorant of my person. But, perceiving that he wanted to go off without receiving my petition, I caught hold of the skirt of his coat, that he might stop and hear me. He endeavoured to escape out of my hands; but I kept such strong hold that he dragged me upon my knees from the middle of

the room to the very door of the Drawing Room. At last
one of the blue-ribands, who attended his Majesty, took
me around the waist, while another wrested the coat out
of my hands. The petition, which I had endeavoured to
thrust into his pocket, fell down in the scuffle and I
almost fainted away through grief and disappointment."[5]

It was a disgraceful scene but the intrepid Lady Nithsdale was not daunted. The evening before her husband's
execution a coach with three ladies inside, Mrs. Morgan,
a Mrs. Mills, who gave every appearance of pregnancy,
and Lady Nithsdale herself approached the Tower. Her
plan was simple and foolhardy. The last hope of a legal
reprieve had vanished when the petition which Lady
Derwentwater had prepared for the House of Lords
failed in its objective. A number of influential peers had
spoken in favour of hearing the petition read and even
of recommending clemency – the Dukes of Bolton,
Montrose, Richmond and St. Albans, besides Lords
Nottingham and Pembroke, were all well disposed – but
the king was annoyed at the suggestion that he should
pardon the rebel lords whether or not they made a full
confession, and he gave as his answer that "on this and
all other occasions he would do what he thought most
consistent with the dignity of his crown, and the safety
of his people". Lady Nithsdale realised that she must act
immediately.

She had already taken the wise precaution of ingratiat-
ing herself with the guards at the Tower and of giving
them occasional bribes, and she later confessed to more
than a pang of conscience at deliberately cheating them.
It was also convenient that Mrs. Mills' delicate condition
made her "not only of the same height, but nearly of the
same size as my lord". Mrs. Morgan, on the other hand,
was very tall and slender, so that she was able to wear a
second riding-hood under her own cloak without appearing abnormally fat. Lady Nithsdale chattered away at
such a rate in the coach that her two accomplices had no

time in which to reflect upon their own participation in
the affair.

Once inside the Tower her plan went without a hitch.
The women went into Nithsdale's room one by one, various items of clothing were removed and re-allotted, and
the redoubtable Lady Nithsdale proceeded to make up
her husband's face. Mrs. Mills' eyebrows "were rather
inclined to be sandy, and my lord's were dark and very
thick; however, I had prepared some paint of the colour
of hers, to disguise his hair as hers; and I painted his face
with white, and his cheeks with rouge, to hide his long
beard, which he had not had time to shave". The guards
who fondly imagined that they were eavesdropping on
three distraught women taking leave for the last time of a
man on the point of execution were embarrassed and
sympathetic. The first to leave was Mrs. Morgan, whose
part in the masquerade was brief if vital, and Mrs. Mills
soon followed her. Finally, Lady Nithsdale shooed her
transvestite husband out of the door and down the stairs,
calling him "my dear Mrs. Betty" for the sake of the
guards' ears and urging him or her to run to her lodgings
as quickly as possible as if on an errand. Then, her husband clear away, she returned to the room and pretended
to be talking to her husband, bidding him farewell and
promising to return later in the evening, if the gate to the
Tower were still open, but failing that early the following morning. She arranged the latch so that the door could
only be opened from the inside, told the servant not to
disturb Lord Nithsdale as he wished to finish saying his
prayers, and calmly took the first available coach back
to her lodgings.

The news of Nithsdale's escape was received with consternation and delight, depending on the loyalties and
politics of the recipient. According to the Duchess of
Montrose, the king "flew into an excess of passion, and
said he was betrayed; for it could not have been done
without some confederacy. He instantly despatched two

persons to the Tower to see that the other prisoners were well secured." But there is another story which credits him with more grace: he is said to have remarked drily, "it is the best thing that a man in his situation could have done".

The Nithsdales lay low for a few days and he was then smuggled into the Venetian ambassador's house by one of the latter's servants, a certain Mitchell. Conveniently, the ambassador was due to meet his brother at Dover, and it was an easy matter for Nithsdale to don livery and travel down with the coach and six. The ingenious servant hired a small boat and they set sail for Calais. "The passage was so remarkably short that the captain threw out a reflection that the wind could not have served better if his passengers had been flying for their lives, little thinking it to be really the case." It is not known how the Venetian ambassador received the information of his unwitting assistance or of the loss of such a resourceful servant.

It is pleasant to record that Lady Nithsdale joined her husband shortly afterwards and that they lived on in Rome until his death in 1744; she survived him by five years. And, although his life-rent from his estate had been forfeited, it was decided in 1723 after interminable legal wrangling that the estates themselves could pass intact to his son, Lord Maxwell. The Nithsdales, if one can forget their actual support of the Jacobite rising, were evidently not lacking in foresight or intelligence.

Widdrington and Nairn, like Carnwath, had no need of such desperate measures, although Lady Nairn received the same rough treatment at the king's hands as had been meted out to Lady Nithsdale. Both men were eventually released, Widdrington to live in poverty and obscurity until his death in Bath in 1743, and Nairn never ceasing to reproach himself for his behaviour at his trial and for pleading for mercy from a king who, in his eyes, was so clearly a usurper. But Derwentwater and Kenmure

could not escape the executioner's axe however strenuous the efforts on their behalf. The day set for their
deaths was February 24.

Both men met their ends with consummate dignity.
Derwentwater, on the afternoon of the 23rd, summoned
an undertaker and gave him very precise instructions for
his burial. He asked that the coffin-plate should be in-
scribed with a brief statement that he died for his lawful
and legitimate sovereign, but the undertaker was understandably appalled by the notion. Derwentwater also
prepared his speech on the scaffold. At ten o'clock on
the following morning he drove in a coach to Tower Hill
and then walked through the ranks of soldiers to the
scaffold draped in black. His face was ashen as he mounted the steps to the block, but he retained his calm com-
posure. A few prayers were followed by his speech. It
was an extraordinarily moving address in which he retraced his plea of guilty made at his trial, spoke with
great warmth and feeling of James III, and assured his
audience that the country could have no lasting peace or
happiness until the restoration of the Stuarts. His last
words were devoid of bitterness: "I die a Roman Catholic; I am in perfect charity with all the world, I thank God
for it, even with those of the present Government, who
are most instrumental in my death. I freely forgive such
as ungenerously reported false things of me; and I hope
to be forgiven the trespass of my youth, by the Father of
infinite mercy, into whose hand I commend my soul."
And then, curiously, he added these words: "If that
prince who now governs, had given me my life, I should
have thought myself obliged never more to have taken
up arms against him."

Derwentwater handed the paper to the sheriff and
turned towards the block. He espied a rough bit and
asked the executioner to chip it off in case he hurt his
neck on it. He took off his coat and waistcoat, and laid
his head on the block. Three times he said "Lord Jesu

receive my soul" and the axe fell. The executioner needed only one stroke. Holding up the head, he proclaimed the ritual epitaph: "Behold the head of a traitor! God save King George!" The head was then wrapped in a handkerchief and the body in a black cloth, and both were removed back into the Tower.

Minutes later, Lord Kenmure took Derwentwater's place. The previous night he had compiled a letter to a friend, also regretting his behaviour in Westminster Hall, and he made no speech on the scaffold; earlier he had remarked that "I had so little thoughts of suffering so soon, that I did not provide myself with a suit of black, that I might have died with more decency; for which I am very sorry". A moment praying, a word or two with the executioner, his head on the block, it was all over mercifully quickly. Two strokes of the axe and a second Jacobite epitaph.

Both men died bravely, even gallantly. Their bodies received decent burials, Derwentwater's probably at St. Giles's in the Fields. From there it was removed by his family to the ancestral vault at Dilston, the funeral procession moving only at night. But his passing did not eradicate his name. A few days later strange flashes of light were seen away to the north-west. The scientists explained them scientifically, but the ordinary superstitious citizens spoke of giants flying through the air with flaming swords and dragons breathing fire. Lady Cowper described "a black cloud, from whence smoke and light issued forth at once, on every side, and then the cloud opened and there was a great body of pale fire, that rolled up and down and sent forth all sorts of colours – like the rainbow on every side; but this did not last above two or three minutes". At one o'clock in the morning the light was so intense that she could see people crossing Lincoln's Inn Fields although there was no moon. The streets were packed with terrified crowds expecting the end of the world. And this heavenly phenomenon was duly christened "The Earl of Derwentwater's Lights". Not everyone, however, appeared to care about the executions and their strange aftermath. The Duke of Montagu was host at a ball and masquerade to which the king and his court were invited. Also remarkable for his presence was d'Herville, the French envoy sent over specially to announce the death of Louis XIV, and he did not scruple to remind any who cared to listen that the rebellion in Scotland was by no means at an end and that help from the French Regent was probably even now on its way. This groundless gossip spread widely but the Whig peers continued to make merry. Lord Lumley, who had helped to destroy the rising in the North of England, erected a vast bonfire outside his house in Gerrard Street and ordered three barrels of ale to be broached so that passers-by could drink to the health of the Prince of Wales whose birthday it was.

The legal proceedings, though, were not at an end. On March 15, the state trial of George Seton, Earl of Wintoun finally commenced. Many people hinted at the time that he was insane, certainly he was an eccentric, having worked once as a bellows-blower and blacksmith's assistant. But his ingenious delaying tactics to effect a postponement of his trial, his behaviour and conduct of his case when the patience of his fellow-peers was exhausted, and his audacious escape from the Tower, all bear witness to a remarkable shrewdness and native wit in such a young man. He was only twenty-six.

Again the ceremonial mummery was lavished on the interested spectators. Processions, obeisances, uncovering of heads, impressive proclamations in Latin and in English, this ballet of etiquette seemed never-ending. At last, however, Wintoun, the Lieutenant-Governor of the Tower and the Gentleman Jailer with his axe made their appearance, and the charges were read; they referred to rebellion, regicide, murder and robbery. The verdict, of course, was a foregone conclusion, but Wintoun had no

intention of merely pleading guilty like the other six lords
and of receiving his sentence without a fight.

Arrayed against him were the best, or most devious,
legal brains which the House of Commons could put up.
Wintoun, for his part, was allowed counsel, although
this was an empty farce as this gentleman, in such an
unenviable position, was not permitted to cross-examine
witnesses, a task exclusively granted to Wintoun himself; more important, and something of a legal novelty,
Wintoun's witnesses were to give their testimony under
oath, so that their word could be on an equal with that
of the prosecution witnesses. Unfortunately, or perhaps
deliberately, Wintoun's witnesses were generally conspicuous by their absence, and the noble lord made great
play throughout the trial with the fact that they had not
been given sufficient time in which to travel southwards
to London.

In turn, Mr. Hampden, Sir Joseph Jekyll, and the Attorney General Sir Edward Northey made their speeches
for the Crown, the first two aiming to ridicule Wintoun's
plea of comparative innocence, and Sir Edward concen-
trating on a purely factual account of the rising and
Wintoun's part in it. Witnesses of the calibre of Patten
and Calderwood, an ex-quartermaster, were called,
treated with marked politeness and cascaded with ques-
tions. Cowper, retaining his commission as Lord High
Steward, asked Wintoun at various stages whether he
wished to interrogate the witnesses, but the accused man
insisted that he knew nothing of the law and that his
counsel should be the one to undertake the cross-
examination. At one point he interjected with some
vehemence: "My Lords, I am not prepared, so I hope
your Lordships will do me justice. I was not prepared
for my trial. I did not think it would come up so soon;
my material witnesses not being come up; and therefore
I hope you will do me justice, and not make use of Cowper Law, as we used to say in our country, 'Hang a man

first, and then judge him!' " He was referring to the town of Cupar in Fife, but the play on words was not lost on the Lord High Steward who was unable to believe his ears.

Lord Forrester, who had commanded a regiment at Preston, General Carpenter, summoned by Wintoun, and General Wills then gave their evidence. They, and the other senior officers who followed them, hardly contributed to any important development, and Lord Cowper then called on Wintoun for his defence. The earl promptly asked for a further month in which to prepare it, a request which was almost equally promptly refused after learned exclamations by the Attorney General. Wintoun's valid point that his witnesses would be no use to him if they arrived after he was dead failed to influence the assembled peers. The proceedings of the first day were over.

The second day of the trial opened with a prolonged and monotonous battle between Wintoun and Cowper over the vexed question of when counsel was and was not allowed to speak. Cowper persisted that counsel could only do so on a point of law and that Wintoun must first state what this mythical point of law was. The earl in exasperation remarked that he could not do a thing which he could not understand. "I don't know what the point of law is no more than a man that knows nothing about it!" This sally was greeted with a certain amount of audible amusement, and Wintoun had no hesitation in reminding his mockers of the gravity of the situation: "I am only speaking in my own defence. I do not expect to be laughed at!" The Lord High Steward agreed: "I think his Lordship does observe well. I hope everyone will forbear that!" But the sniping continued. Wintoun pleaded the absolute necessity of waiting for his witnesses from the North and stated blandly that his counsel would be able to demonstrate that he, Wintoun, was incapable of committing treason against the monarch and the constitution. His tongue was in his cheek, as he was no doubt referring to James III and the Stuart constitution.

Final speeches were contributed by counsel for the Commons, and, without more ado, the verdict of the peers was requested. One by one, from Thomas, Lord Parker, whose coronet was less than a week old and who one day would be the Earl of Macclesfield and Lord Chancellor, through the barons, viscounts, earls, the single marquess present and the dukes, until the Duke of Devonshire, the Lord Steward, and the Earl of Sunderland, the Lord Privy Seal, were reached, the ninety peers assembled gave their verdict. Placing their right hands over their hearts, they uttered the inevitable words, "Guilty, upon my honour!" Wintoun listened calmly but, as he left Westminster Hall on that Friday evening and drove away to the Tower, he must have inwardly shivered as he saw that the edge of the ceremonial axe carried by the Gentleman Jailer was now turned towards him.

Monday the 19th was set aside for Wintoun's application and for sentence. Sir Constantine Phipps, the great Jacobite lawyer, rose to his feet and attempted to speak. He was instantly cut off by the Attorney General but, after receiving a sharp rebuke from Cowper for not first having asked the permission of the House to make his address (which is precisely what he was trying to do when he was interrupted), was eventually permitted to put his point. It was a good speech, reinforced by the eloquent Mr. Williams, who was also representing Lord Wintoun, but the legal points were exploded by the vociferousness of the Attorney General, Robert Walpole and others. Wintoun, on being asked whether he had anything to say why the sentence of the law should not be carried out against him, resumed his fencing with Cowper to no avail. His last words were "since your Lordships will not allow my counsel to speak, I don't know nothing".

The Lord High Steward then rose, spoke a number of platitudes about the heinous crime of rebellion and the duty of punishing rebels, and proceeded to the identical sentence as had been passed on the other lords. Repetition, however, did not minimise the brutality of its references to disembowelling and quartering. Lady Cowper was not impressed by Wintoun's demeanour while sentence was being passed. "He behaved himself in a manner to persuade a world of people that he was a natural fool, or mad, though his natural character is that of a stubborn, illiterate, ill-bred brute. He has eight wives. I can't but be peevish at all this fuss to go Fool-hunting. Sure, if it is as people say, he might have been declared incapable of committing Treason." It was waspish, Whiggish opinion, and one not shared by many of the onlookers who were greatly struck by Wintoun's dignity and sang-froid. Without an iota of legal knowledge he had delayed some of the best juridical brains in the country for three days. It was, of course, an empty success, but the struggle had been excellent value for even the most sensation-saturated. With his trial the impeachments of the seven rebel lords were terminated and, as Wintoun was preparing to leave the Tower somewhat precipitately, the Government turned its attention to those lesser mortals in the Fleet, the Marshalsea and Newgate. Wintoun never appealed for mercy to the king nor did he sanction any plea on his behalf. Instead, he set about persuading his servants to help him and sawing through his prison bars. He reached the Continent safely and, like so many of his fellow-Jacobites, made for Rome to join James Francis Edward. He died, aged fifty-nine, in 1749.

*

The prisoners up at Carlisle, Liverpool and in Chester Castle had been dealt with long ago. About twenty-two had been hanged in Lancashire, and approximately a thousand had been transported to the plantations. They were probably only too glad to exchange the ghastly conditions of their gaols for America; indeed a certain Wrigglesden, who had already removed His Majesty's plate from the Chapel Royal in Whitehall, did very well for himself in Maryland. One Whig news-sheet showed considerable disapproval: "He had got a cargo of cutlery ware, and a Mistress like a Woman of Fashion, in rich clothes and a gold striking watch, with other proper equipage, at Annapolis, where they live with great show of affluence." It all seemed shockingly unfair, and even the Jacobite prisoners still in the London gaols had begun to enjoy life once more. Rich sympathisers poured money into the hands of the turnkeys, and the lucky ones ate and drank to their hearts' content. Indeed an apparently bottomless cellar greatly assisted that cardboard cavalier, Thomas Forster, once Member of Parliament and commander at Preston, to make his escape. By getting Governor Pitt drunk and incapable, bribing the turnkeys and obtaining a duplicate master-key, he walked coolly out into the street. The alarm was given by Pitt, who was shortly afterwards confined to his own dungeons, a reward of a thousand pounds was offered, and the ports were watched. But Forster and his companions rode with such express that they were on the Essex coast by four in the morning, and soon the ship which had been alerted was sailing for France. Forster had saved his neck but there was no future for him as an influence in Jacobite circles. He died in Paris eighteen years later, unmourned and forgotten.

On the evening of May 4, a further outrage occurred at Newgate. A lavish dinner with attendant wines and punch had been under way for some considerable time when about sixty prisoners gathered in the press-yard, ostensibly for a breath of highly tainted air. Suddenly they rushed at the turnkey guarding the gate, knocked him down and charged through towards liberty. A great many were recaptured, simply because they had no idea where they were and blundered about rather aimlessly, but about a dozen got clean away; among them were Macintosh of Borlum, his son and his brother. A meagre reward of two hundred pounds was offered for the brigadier's apprehension, and a highly unflattering description circulated: "A tall, raw-boned man, about 60 years, speaks broad Scotch." The king was so enraged that he personally raised the reward to a thousand pounds, but Macintosh and his son safely reached the Thames, took ship and sailed off over the Channel; his brother, however, was re-taken at Rochester.

One last prisoner of importance, Robert Hepburn of Keith, took advantage of the confusion and made off. Sir Walter Scott describes the scene with a wealth of circumstantial colour: "He had pinioned the arms of the turnkey by an effort of strength, and effected his escape into the open street without pursuit. But he was at a loss whither to fly, or where to find a friendly place of refuge. His wife and family were, he knew, in London; but how, in that great city, was he to discover them, especially as they most probably were residing there under feigned names? While he was agitated by this uncertainty, and fearful of making the least enquiry, even had he known in what words to express it [he too spoke "broad Scotch"], he saw at a window in the street an ancient piece of plate, called the Keith Tankard, which had belonged to his family." Needless to say, his family were inside the house, having deliberately taken lodgings near Newgate. Needless to say, they all escaped to France. Such was the stuff of Jacobite legend.

Three days later, however, the remaining prisoners of apparent importance, including Derwentwater's brother Charles Radcliffe, Widdrington's two brothers, Richard Gascogne and Colonel Oxburgh, were arraigned at the Exchequer Bar in Westminster. The sentences were again predictable; all were condemned to death, and there were no thoughts of dignified and comparatively humane executions by the axe. Oxburgh was hanged at Tyburn on the 14th, and even anti-Jacobite eye-witnesses were forced to admit that he behaved like a prototype officer and gentleman. The Whig "Mercurius Politicus" reported the event: "He was drawn in a sledge, with a book in his hand, on which he fixed his eyes, without once looking up till he came to the place of execution." Oxburgh died without a word of regret for having supported the Stuart cause; Gascogne, too, died at Tyburn. The two Widdrington brothers, however, like the head of their family, survived. And so too did Charles Radcliffe, if only temporarily. One evening, he simply strolled out of Newgate, wearing a mourning suit and a brown tie-wig. If he had waited a little longer, he would have been pardoned under the Act of Grace and might not have lost his head after the collapse of the '45.

The trials went on, but seemingly without purpose. The obviously guilty were often acquitted whereas men who had merely uttered faintly seditious sentiments while in their cups were sentenced to savage floggings. There were rumours that one in twenty prisoners was selected for transportation while the other nineteen were set free. Non-juring clergymen were hanged, and foolish young soldiers were shot. Sir William Wyndham, as guilty as any, was acquitted. Justice had no rules and set no precedents. The prisoners in Newgate simply hoped to last it out until the Whig thirst for vengeance had been assuaged. The lords in the Tower, until they were released in 1717, paid out and continued to pay out. Nairn, for instance, estimated that his incarceration had cost him some four thousand pounds, mainly to legal advisers and supposedly influential and sympathetic ladies at court. His account book bears the following blunt entry, a sign of the times if ever there was one: "Gave to Lawyers and Bitches, during that time, £1,500."

But for all the apparent brutality and judicial backsliding, for all the beheadings at the Tower, the hangings at Tyburn and the transportations to the American colonies, it is surprising how many people escaped, particularly in Scotland but also even in England where the authorities were far more eager to make an example of the rebels. Lord John Russell, writing long after the bitterness and the hard memories had died and when the romanticism of the Stuarts was being vigorously fostered, summed up very reasonably: "If we consider the object of the rebels, the blood which they spilt in their enterprise, and the necessity of securing the kingdom by some examples of severity from further disturbance, we shall probably be of the opinion that as much mercy was shown as was consistent with the safety of the established government and the vindication of the rights of the people." This was not the whole story, but it was an understandable verdict.

Part Four

Rebellion 1719

Chapter Ten

Sweden and Spain

During the first period of these ticklish times, the Scots Tories were obliged to keep themselves very quiet and live in the most retired way.

Lockhart Papers

THE great enterprise had come to nothing. In 1715, the supporters of James could produce convincing reasons, for public consumption as well as their own consciences, why a Stuart should sit once again on the throne of England and Scotland. The interval of twenty-seven years between the Glorious Revolution and the raising of the standard of rebellion at Braemar was not long enough to impose a patina of age and rust on the precept of Stuart legitimacy. The Hanoverians were unpopular and barely established; the Whig Government vacillated; high Toryism was vociferous; the British army was unreliable when faced with civil war. Even James's advisers were, with obvious and crucial exceptions, shrewd and intelligent; and in Bolingbroke he possessed the most brilliant statesman of the age as his confidential secretary. The rebellion in England was a clear and immediate failure, and it might be wondered whether even the rising in the North and in Scotland could have had the faintest hope of success entrusted as it was to commanders of the imagination and energy so rarely displayed by Mar and Forster. But there is no gainsaying that with a modicum of luck allied to a heavier measure of courage and insight the Hanoverian dynasty might have been cut off in its infancy.

Thackeray, adding the reminder that he did not aspire to be an expounder of history, was one to play the conditional game which always leads to entertaining, if pointless, results. Suppose, he says, that the attackers of Edinburgh Castle had not stopped to "powder their hair" and so missed the hour of rendezvous? "Edinburgh Castle, and town, and all Scotland were King James's. The north of England rises, and marches over Barnet Heath upon London. Wyndham is up in Somersetshire; Packington in Worcestershire; and Vivian in Cornwall. The Elector of Hanover, and his hideous mistresses, pack up the plate, and perhaps the crown jewels in London, and are off *via* Harwich and Helvoetsluys, for dear old Deutschland. The king – God save him! – lands at Dover, with tumultuous applause; shouting multitudes, roaring cannon, the Duke of Marlborough weeping tears of joy, and all the bishops kneeling in the mud. In a few years, mass is said in St. Paul's; matins and vespers are sung in York Minster; and Dr. Swift is turned out of his stall and deanery house at St. Patrick's, to give place to Father Dominic, from Salamanca." All very cynical and overstated, but there is a kernel of possibility. Certainly, never again would the Jacobites be closer to ultimate triumph, not even before that extraordinary day at Derby, December 5, 1745, when Charles Edward's advisers dissuaded him from marching on to London.

In the early months of 1716, however, the air of deep despondency in Jacobite circles did not go entirely untempered by optimism. Things could have been worse. James was alive, and only a handful of his more prominent supporters lay in the Tower. Government reprisals had avoided wholesale savagery. The spark of Jacobitism still smouldered in the Highlands and the West Country. Admittedly, James had quarrelled violently and disastrously with Bolingbroke, and the latter had departed in a magisterial rage with the uncompromising oath: "May my arm rot off if I ever use my sword or my pen in their service again!" But Ormonde and Mar were still available, and James was either too blind or too generous to see their faults. James's chief worry, indeed, concerned a permanent place of residence. The Duc d'Orléans, still acting as regent for the infant Louis XV, was more than reluctant to see an enclave of Stuart conspiracy established permanently in his country. Orléans was determined to reverse the old king's policy and to foster closer relations with England. He and his chief minister Dubois would have maintained that this was for the general good of France, but there was also a more personal consideration: Orléans was heir to the throne.

When the Duc d'Anjou, the Grand Dauphin's second son and Louis XIV's grandson, had assumed the crown of Spain in 1700 as Philip V, he had surrendered all rights of inheritance to the French throne. If, therefore, the young Louis XV were to die – and this was a distinct possibility, remembering the high mortality rate among his relations and the fact that he had already nearly succumbed to the dubious attentions of the royal physicians – then Orléans, Louis XIV's nephew and his closest surviving relation, would succeed. But only if Philip of Spain kept faithfully to his act of renunciation, an eventuality in which the French Regent put little trust. Inevitably, Orléans turned to George of England as a potential ally. And inevitably James must leave French soil.

Ever since the Utrecht peace treaty he had had asylum at Bar-le-Duc in the lands of the sympathetic Duc de Lorraine, but now even this was prohibited. Like a rather pathetic travelling circus which has known better days, his court took to the road and travelled at the end of March to Avignon, which lay in Papal territory. James was allowed to remain there only ten and a half months before he was forced on over the Alps. The British Government considered Avignon too close for comfort and looked askance at the growing numbers of Jacobite sympathisers who flocked there. An ultimatum alluding to the possible bombardment of Civitavecchia was sent to the Pope, and in February 1717 James travelled over the Mont Cenis pass to Turin. After a short stay in his mother's home of Modena, he stopped briefly in Rome and then finally arrived in Urbino. Clement IX received him and presented him with the old palace. And with the discontinuance of his French pension James's final link with France was gone. Italy would be his home for the rest of his life.

Urbino was as remote a centre for Jacobite intrigue as the English Government could have desired, and the rustic tedium of the court was only rarely broken. There were walks on the hills and a little music-making and the nine-day wonder of the Earl of Peterborough's arrest by order of the Pope on suspicion of planning the assassination of James, an affair which terminated in thunderous protests from London, the release of the unfortunate and quite innocent peer, and Papal apologies. But the peaceful tenor of life gave no indication of the concealed plotting and diplomatic negotiations. These were directed towards an unexpected source of possible assistance.

Charles XII of Sweden, considered by some a great warrior-king, by others a foolhardy eccentric whose personal habits and peculiar ideas of statecraft bordered on the lunatic, had been in close contact with the Jacobite court on a previous occasion. Back in 1712, James had suggested his sister Princess Louise as a suitable match for the Swedish king, but the plan had foundered on her sudden death. Now, the time seemed to be ripe for forging a definite alliance. Charles, always a prey to strong reactions and a full-blooded patriot if nothing else, was consumed with a passionate desire for revenge against George I. The reasons were territorial. The bishoprics of Bremen and Verden, secularised and ceded to Sweden by the Peace of Westphalia at the end of the Thirty Years War, had been seized, together with Schleswig and Holstein, by Frederick IV of Denmark in 1712. This was a sharp enough goad to Charles's fiery temper, but his rage became manic when he heard in July 1715 that Frederick had sold the two ex-bishopics to George for £150,000 and the support of an English fleet against Sweden. Only the fact that he was besieged in Stralsund at the time of the 1715 rising prevented him from sending Swedish troops over to Scotland, and now he encouraged an immediate expedition aimed at dethroning his Hanoverian *bête noire* in London.

The main instigator of the conspiracy was Baron Gortz, Charles's chief minister, who during the winter of 1716–17 was at the Hague as Swedish envoy. From there a stream of letters went out, to Count Gyllenborg in London, Baron Spaar in Paris, to Ormonde and to James himself. At the end of September 1716 Gyllenborg had written to Gortz: "People go so far here as to lay wagers that the young King of France will be dispatched before a certain time to make way for his uncle." And after giving it as his opinion that Scotland was once more ready to rise, he ended uncompromisingly: "The intimations which have been made me terminate in bringing in the Pretender . . . Ten thousand men transported hither from Sweden would do the business, and I believe we shall not be at a loss for money."

A month later, he mentions the sum of £60,000 which could be raised as soon as Charles XII gave a written assurance of help, and finally Charles agreed to lead personally an army of 12,000. With the promise of a heavy subsidy from Cardinal Alberoni, Philip of Spain's chief minister, the Swedish plot seemed to go from strength to strength, only to vanish overnight. Some of Gyllenborg's letters fell into Government hands and were deciphered. And on January 29, 1717 Stanhope proposed to the Council that the Swedish minister and his papers should be seized on the grounds that he had violated the law of nations, as well as the rules of hospitality, by plotting against the king to whom he was accredited. The Council approved this almost unprecedented step and that same night Gyllenborg's house was surrounded by a detachment of foot guards under General Wade. A cabinet, which Gyllenborg's wife claimed contained only plate and linen, was broken open and enough documentary evidence to satisfy any critics in Parliament was discovered.

Gortz, too, fell into the net. He was at Calais, about to cross to England, when he heard the news of Gyllenborg's arrest, and immediately returned to Holland. But even his status as envoy at the Hague could not give him immunity, and he was also arrested, at Arnhem. Charles remained silent, neither approving nor disowning his two ministers' undiplomatic conduct, and after protracted negotiations Gortz and Gyllenborg were finally released. The Swedish plot, over-optimistic and reckless (Gortz had once written blandly that the only material they lacked was men o' war and transport ships, without which no expedition could have progressed very far), had been blown, and the sphere of influence moved from the Baltic to Madrid.

Cardinal Alberoni, who now became the master-mind of the Jacobite cause, was the most powerful man in Spain – indeed, many said he was the only powerful man in Spain. Born in 1664, the son of a gardener, he had risen to a degree of influence as secretary to one of Louis XIV's least attractive bastards, the syphilitic Duc de Vendôme, by a mixture of flattery and native wit. He is, perhaps unfairly, remembered for his amazing remark on seeing Vendôme rise from his *chaise-percée* – "Oh! Cul d'ange" – but this does less than credit to his astounding career. After the death of Vendôme, which some people attributed to Alberoni's expertise with poisons, the redoubtable abbé moved on to the court of the Duke of Parma and was intimately involved in the negotiations for the marriage between Philip of Spain and Elizabeth Farnese, daughter of the Duke. From that moment his rise was meteoric and by 1717 he was a cardinal and Philip's chief minister. Intent on placing his master on the French throne, he was ready to seize upon the happy chance of Jacobite dissidence and set about devising a grandiose plan of operations, designed at one breathtaking stage to involve those arch-enemies Charles XII of Sweden and Peter the Great of Russia in an alliance against England.

War had broken out between the Emperor Charles VI and Spain, and Spanish soldiers occupied Sardinia. Early in 1718, a great fleet was fitted out in the port of Barcelona; its destination was Sicily. England, bound by treaty to guarantee Imperial territory in Italy, dispatched a fleet of twenty ships under the ubiquitous Sir George Byng, with the prime object of restoring peace in the Mediterranean but, failing that, to obstruct Spanish aggression. Byng's efforts to convince Alberoni by diplomatic means failed, and his hand was forced when news filtered in that the Barcelona fleet had arrived off Sicily on July 2; that Palermo and Messina had already fallen, and that a large part of the island was under Spanish control. Byng, his fleet by now anchored in the Bay of Naples, made a last attempt to end the conflict, but the Spanish admiral did not agree to an armistice, and on August 11 his ships were decisively beaten by Byng off Cape Passaro.

The results were predictable. The Spanish ambassador in London was recalled, English ships lying in Spanish ports were seized, and English consuls were ordered out of the country. Alberoni determined to cripple England, or at the very least to prevent her from interfering further in the Mediterranean. An expedition in support of the Jacobites was the obvious answer.

Spanish help came just in time for James's adherents. They were rapidly running out of money, and one of their last firm sources of revenue had recently been removed by the death of the saintly Mary of Modena, James's mother. They could expect sanctuary from the Pope, but positive assistance, pecuniary or military, from no one. Lord Stair, still English ambassador in Paris, was bringing strong pressure to bear on the Regent to expel the last remaining Jacobites at Saint-Germain, and elsewhere in France; and even the Duke of Ormonde was threatened with arrest and only managed to remain by pretending to be seriously ill. It was he who was chosen by Alberoni to lead the projected expedition and he duly left Paris for Spain at the beginning of November, after receiving Alberoni's invitation by the hand of Cellamare, Spanish ambassador in Paris.

Ormonde set out on November 5, 1718 and succeeded in avoiding arrest by disguising himself as a valet during the crossing of the Pyrenees. Alberoni, eager to conceal the real reason behind Ormonde's precipitate journey, put it about that he was simply seeking the asylum which the inhuman Orléans refused to grant him. Ormonde arrived in Madrid in the first week of December, and he and Alberoni immediately began a series of discussions, the gist of which Ormonde forwarded to James in Rome in a long letter dated December 17. Its contents were sufficiently encouraging to compensate for the death of Charles of Sweden and the consequent removal from the European scene of one of the Jacobites' most fervent and reliable supporters. After touching briefly on negotiations with Sweden, Ormonde pressed on to give definite figures: "The next time I saw Alberoni, he asked me what I demanded as necessary to make an attempt to restore 289 [the cipher for James]. I told him seven or eight thousand men, with 15,000 arms and ammunition proportionable.''

At first Alberoni refused to contribute an army, merely arms, ammunition and money, but when he realised that Charles XII's death removed the likelihood of Swedish intervention, he compromised with the offer of "five thousand men, of which four thousand are to be foot, a thousand troopers, of which three hundred with their horses, the rest with their arms and accoutrements, and two months pay for them, ten field pieces, and a thousand barrels of powder and fifteen thousand arms for foot, with everything necessary to convoy them". Ormonde pointed out the need to create a diversion in Scotland while the main force was directed against England, and named the Earl Marischal, who was then in Paris, as a possible commander. Finally, it was decided that James should come to Spain. There were considerable fears for his safety, as his wife-to-be, Princess Clementina Sobieski, had been arrested by the Emperor at Innsbruck as she travelled from Poland to Rome and had only been rescued after much cloak and dagger adventure; and in addition it was thought that he should be prepared either to accompany the expedition or to follow it later.

James did not leave Rome until February 1719, and by then France had dramatically declared war on Spain, following the discovery of a plot to seize the Regent and to replace him by the King of Spain. Although the prime mover in this conspiracy was the Duchesse du Maine, granddaughter of the great Condé and married to another of Louis XIV's bastards, Cellamare was seriously implicated and ordered to leave the country. This declaration of hostilities coming on top of the news of Charles XII's death in Norway gave the Jacobite expedition a sense of even greater urgency.

The departure of James was clothed in secrecy. On February 8, he apparently set out for the north of Italy, accompanied by Mar and the Duke of Perth. A number of extravagant rumours were circulated, ranging from his election as Regent of Sweden to his return to England at the eager behest of the Government following George's death. It was all wildly improbable, but the truth was successfully masked. The supposed royal party pressed on into Imperial territory and were promptly arrested at Voghera and locked up in Milan Castle. The English resident at Genoa was beside himself with joy and wrote to Stair in Paris to report that the Pretender had been taken. Much to his chagrin the Pretender was precisely that, a member of the royal household called Paterson, and during all the uproar the quarry had slipped away quietly to Nettuno, a small fishing village about thirty miles south of Rome.

James boarded a small ship flying Genoese colours and under the command of Admiral Cammock, an Englishman serving Spain, and after the invariable rough voyage which he appears to have experienced whenever putting to sea, landed at Las Rosas on March 8. From there he travelled to Gerona, where he saw Berwick's son Tynemouth, now Duke of Liria, and eventually arrived at Madrid where he was given a royal welcome and housed in the palace of Buen Retiro.

The day after James landed on Spanish soil after his harrowing journey, the Spanish expeditionary force, which had been assembling at Cadiz, sailed for Corunna. Ormonde had been kicking his heels at Valladolid, writing letters to prominent Jacobites in England to warn them of the rising, and giving the general impression of doing nothing in the least suspicious. It was arranged that he should join the fleet at Corunna.

But while these preparations were in hand, another force was gathering at San Sebastian. This was the part of the expedition to be commanded by Marischal, who had posted down from Paris with his brother James Keith. Marischal conferred with Ormonde at Astorga, and then returned to Madrid in order to see Alberoni and to wheedle some concrete help out of him. He was duly promised two frigates, some 2,000 muskets, money and ammunition, and a small complement of regular Spanish troops. James Keith returned to Paris to stir the remaining Jacobites resident in France.

Marischal's small force sailed out of Passage, the port of San Sebastian, on March 8. The previous day, the main part of the expedition had left Cadiz. On March 16, Ormonde had confirmation of this. And on March 29 the entire fleet was scattered by a storm. The expedition was officially cancelled. Marischal, with his 307 Spanish soldiers, had sailed too early by weeks for this shattering news. The success or failure of the 1719 enterprise, on which so much care and optimism had been lavished, rested on Marischal's shoulders alone.

Chapter Eleven

The Pass of Glenshiel

I am not worried about these few rebels who have
landed in Scotland, they will soon die of hunger in
the mountains, and if some of the Spaniards manage to
escape, that will discourage others from going again
to Scotland.

Stair in a letter to Robethon

ALBERONI'S plans had been known in France and England for some considerable time. As early as January 16
Dubois had written to Secretary Craggs in Whitehall that
something was in the wind, and any information filtering
through to the French Government was instantly passed
on to Stair. The precise destination of the Cadiz fleet was
at first thought to be Ireland but Stair, writing to Craggs
on March 12, suggested that Ormonde's plan was to sail
to Liverpool, seize Chester, march down the Severn and
consolidate in the West Country before striking east-
wards.

There were few signs of panic in England. The Commons agreed to underwrite any expenses which might be
incurred in the defence of the country, and a commissioner was sent down to the West to report on possible
signs of unrest or preparation; he found nothing of inter-

est. Inevitably, a price of £5,000 was placed on Ormonde's head, as a matter of form rather than with the hope of persuading anyone to betray him. Four battalions were brought back from Ireland to stiffen the defences in the West, and by mid-April three Dutch battalions had landed in the North and a further two battalions of Swiss mercenaries in the pay of the States-General sailed up the Thames. The French regent's offer of troops was not accepted.

Naval preparations were also put into effect without delay. Sir John Norris sailed from Spithead to patrol the Lizard, and by March 24 he had sixteen ships under his command. Three frigates waited for the appearance of the Spanish fleet in the Bay of Biscay, but the terrible storm of the 29th ensured that it would never double Cape Finisterre, and only ten ships limped into Corunna, their masts gone and their sails in shreds. The only threat now was from Scotland.

While Marischal's ships were sailing in the direction of Stornoway, his brother James Keith had been active in France. He had set out with 18,000 crowns and a letter of authority from Ormonde, and after a brief stay at San Sebastian in order to pay over the sum of 12,000 crowns to the Prince of Campo Florido for the equipping of the frigates destined for Scotland, was in Bordeaux by the end of February. There he met General Gordon and also Brigadier Campbell of Ormidale; Gordon took no part in the expedition because of illness, and Campbell went south to join Ormonde at Corunna. On March 3, Keith arrived in Orléans to find Tullibardine, the outlawed son of the Duke of Atholl. Together they posted on to Paris. And it was perhaps now that any hope for the expedition vanished in a haze of jealousy. After a talk with Seaforth and Campbell of Glendaruel it became obvious to Keith that the Jacobites were split into two factions, and that Mar and his supporters favoured Tullibardine as commander-in-chief of the whole Scottish expedition.

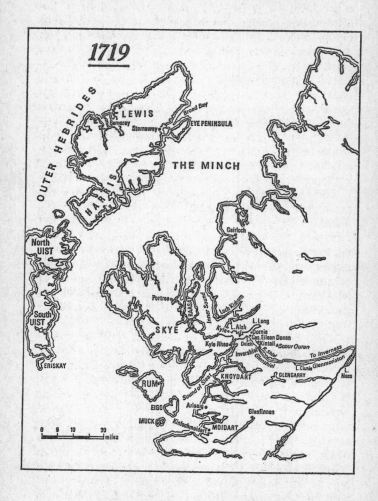

Keith set about preparing a boat to take him and the other Jacobites from Havre de Grâce to Scotland, but Glendaruel insisted that he should also go to Saint-Germain to see General Dillon and to recover from him the commission which had been drawn up in 1717 when plans for the Swedish enterprise were afoot. "This Glendaruel thought absolutely necessary for his own private ends, being surer to govern the easy temper of the Marquess [of Tullibardine] than of those who otherwise would naturally have the command of the army, and particularly falling into the hands of General Gordon, with whom he was not in very good intelligence." In the event, all that Dillon sent was a letter containing "common place advices". There was no word about commissions.

The small party – Clanranald and Lochiel were two prominent members – sailed from the mouth of the Seine on March 19 in a small ship of about twenty-five tons, and a course was set between Dover and Calais, up round the Orkneys to the Isle of Lewis where the rendezvous with Marischal had been set. However, the continuing easterly wind forced them to alter course for St. George's Channel, where they narrowly escaped detection and capture by a squadron of English men o' war transporting troops from Ireland.

Keith, whose memoirs give the most vivid account of the expedition, takes up the story. "From thence we stood for Cape Clear and the west coast of Ireland, and after favourable but blowing weather, arrived the 4 of April, N.S., in the isle of Lewis." There was no sign of his brother, and they waited for a few days in a state of some nervousness. At last, they were told that two frigates had dropped anchor on the other side of the island. Keith, eager to reach his brother first and to warn him about the ominous developments in Paris, rushed off only to find that they had already sailed, luckily no further than Stornoway, the only other village on the island. Keith was there the same evening, before the men had

even landed, pouring out his fears and suspicions about
Mar, Dillon, Glendaruel and Tullibardine. But Marischal declared himself quite ready to serve under anyone
with a superior commission to his own.

The following day, Seaforth and Tullibardine came
over to Stornoway, and in the evening a council of war
was held. Tullibardine did not mention any commission
he had received at Dillon's hands, so the overall command remained for the time being with Marischal. They
then moved on to more important matters. Should they
land at once on the mainland, or should they remain on
Lewis until they had news of Ormonde's fleet? Tullibardine and Glendaruel were in favour of caution, but Marischal was eager to land as quickly as possible, to march
straight on Inverness, which was garrisoned by a mere
300 soldiers, and to wait in the security of the castle for
reinforcements. This plan was agreed on, the Spanish
troops were told to disembark, and the expedition
would cross to the mainland in three days' time.

The acceptance of Marischal's proposal was illusory.
The very next day, Tullibardine revealed his hand. Insisting on a second council of war, he made "a sort of
speech, which no body understood but himself", and presented his commission as Lieutenant-General. Marischal, true to his word and apparently not wanting to
discover the reason for Tullibardine's strange and devious behaviour, resigned his command of the troops
but refused to relinquish control over the ships which had
been specifically entrusted to him by Alberoni. But, in
spite of a fresh attempt on the part of Tullibardine and
Glendaruel to remain inactive on Lewis, the decision to
cross to the mainland was upheld. And on April 4 (O.S.),
the small ships sailed out of Broad Bay and past Eye
Peninsula. The intention was to cross the Minch, pass
down the Inner Sound, leaving Skye and Raasay on the
starboard side, and sail up Loch Alsh and Loch Duich
as far as Kintail, which lay in Seaforth country and

from where they might hope to raise as many as 500 Highlanders.

Unfortunately, the winds were contrary and they only managed to reach Gairloch, across from the northern tip of Skye. Glendaruel landed and set out with letters for a number of Highland chiefs. The ships left again on the 6th but were driven back by a storm as far as Lewis. Finally, much battered and in no fit state for serious fighting, the miniature fleet made the comparative safety of Loch Alsh, and on the following day, the 14th, Glendaruel returned with various promises of help as soon as news of Ormonde's successful landing was forthcoming. That determined Jacobite Lockhart of Carnwath had already dispatched some kind of *aide-mémoire* to Marischal, advising him on what to do next; but even he refused to come out with such slender prospects. And he was also instrumental in dissuading Nairn and Dalhousie from joining the rising, after false information announcing Ormonde's landing had caused some premature excitement. As it transpired, the only two sources for this news were distinctly unreliable, one being probably a Government *agent provocateur*, and the other Lord Stormont. Lockhart commented acidly on the latter: "As for my Lord Stormont's information, I gave it the less credit when I perceived his lordship's letter was dated at one in the morning, about which time I knew he was apt to credit any news that pleased him."

In the meanwhile, the expeditionary force set up its headquarters at Castle Eilean Donan, a stronghold of the Clan Mackenzie, on an islet opposite the village of Dornie, at the point where Loch Alsh branches into Loch Long and Loch Duich. The time which might have been spent in organising the projected attack on Inverness was instead frittered away in a series of pointless and often acrimonious councils. Keith was scathing about these fatal delaying tactics which were still being promoted by Glendaruel and Tullibardine: "The same demon who had inspired them with the design of staying in Lewis, hindered them from accepting this proposition. We were all in the dark what could be the meaning of these dilatory proceedings." Lochiel and Clanranald had returned, the latter also counselling delay, and finally the news of Ormonde came in. It was a cruel blow, and the depressing effect on men who were already markedly lacking fire in their bellies is easily imagined.

Tullibardine wanted to sail back to Spain and this move was only baulked by dramatic action on the part of Marischal, who ordered the two frigates to put to sea. They were just in time. One week later, an English squadron of five ships lay off the coast. The Spanish frigates would have been blown out of the water.*

The small expeditionary force was now virtually surrounded. The Inverness garrison had been substantially reinforced, and any escape by sea was utterly out of the question. Two of the English ships, the *Assistance* and the *Dartmouth*, sailed round the north of Skye and anchored in Loch Kishorn; while the remaining three, the *Worcester*,† the *Enterprise* and the *Flamborough*, under the command of Captain Boyle, passed through Kyle Rhea and anchored at the mouth of Loch Alsh.

Boyle's first objective was the old stone keep where most of the ammunition and provisions were kept, guarded only by forty-five Spaniards. It was no match for artillery fire. After a request for the castle's surrender had been rejected, Boyle's guns opened up on the evening of May 10. There was little resistance and the Spanish garrison was captured, to be sent eventually round to Leith in the *Flamborough*. Also seized were 343 barrels of powder and fifty-two barrels of musket bullets. The

*It could also be argued, in fairness to Tullibardine, that if his suggestion had been accepted the whole expeditionary force would very likely have reached the safety of Spain unscathed. On the other hand, such an obvious piece of cowardice would not have been good propaganda for the Stuart cause.

†Not to be confused with Captain Green's *Worcester*.

castle was blown up, the buildings were destroyed, and a second magazine near the head of the loch was eliminated.

Tullibardine at last decided that action must be taken, and made a half-hearted attempt to raise the Clans. It was far too late. The Dutch regiments had landed and the news of the dispersal of Ormonde's armada had percolated into the hills and glens. Furthermore, as Keith noted, Tullibardine's "circular letters had given those who were not very willing an excellent excuse, he himself having already wrote to them that they should not take arms". Lord George Murray, Tullibardine's younger brother, had come in from Perthshire with a small contingent, and Rob Roy Macgregor, who had little to lose since he and his clan had been specifically excluded from the general pardon under the terms of the 1717 Act of Grace, arrived with some Stirlingshire men and a few from the northern part of Argyll. On June 5, Lochiel's return added a further 150, and two days later Seaforth came in with his promised 500. Finally, on the 8th, one of Rob Roy Macgregor's sons led in eighty recruits to the forlorn cause. As Keith noted, even the men who agreed to fight "seemed not very fond of the enterprise".

General Wightman, the veteran of Sheriffmuir, marched out of Inverness on June 5 with an army consisting of about 850 infantry, 130 Highlanders raised from the loyal Whig clans, and 120 dragoons. He also carried with him four light bronze mortars. His route took him to the head of Loch Ness, where the army rested for a day, and then over Glenmoriston to Kintail. Tullibardine's council of war, with the full realisation that their only chance lay in fighting and forcing their way out of the encircling cordon, decided to take up position in Glenshiel, a desolate glen running inland from the head of Loch Duich. Wightman, in his despatch after the battle, called the site the Pass of Strachell, whereas Tullibardine referred to it as Glenshielbeg. To add to the confusion, the local Gaelic name for the spot is Lub-innis-na-seangan, translated curiously as "the bend of the river at the island of ants".

The editor of Ormonde's letters referring to the 1719 rebellion, writing in 1895, describes the ground: "The position selected for defence was at the place where the present road crosses the river Shiel by a stone bridge, some five miles above Invershiel. Here a shoulder of the mountain juts into the glen on its northern side, and the glen contracts into a narrow gorge, down which the Shiel, at this point a roaring torrent, runs in a deep rocky channel, between steep declivities covered with heather, bracken, and scattered birches. Above the pass the glen opens out into a little strath. Then, as now, the road ran through the strath on the north side of the river and entered the pass along a narrow shelf between the river and the hill, from which it was entirely commanded." The setting was undeniably impressive, a sombre, melancholy spot ideally suited to the death pangs of the Jacobite endeavour. The Highlanders began to take up their positions on June 9, and that same evening Lord George Murray, in command of the outposts, reported that Wightman's army was a mere four or five miles away, having camped for the night at Strathloan at the head of Loch Clunie.

A few more recruits had come in, probably at the instigation of Glengarry, and no doubt to his surprise Tullibardine now found himself in command of a sizeable force. In addition he had the great benefit of a strong position. The contours of nature were helped by a series of entrenchments thrown up on the hill to the north of the river, and by a barricade across the road. Keith drew attention to the defences, impregnable provided they were directed with any tactical intelligence and flexibility: "Our right was covered by a rivulet which was difficult to pass, and our left by a ravine, and in the front the ground was so rugged and steep that it was almost impossible to come at us." And so it should have been, as General Wightman later agreed. "Their dispositions for defence," he noted in his despatch, "were extraordinary, with the advantages of rocks, mountains, and intrenchments." It was precisely the terrain best suited to the Highlanders' method of fighting, and Wightman's English regiments, as Sheriffmuir depressingly revealed, were at the best variable in quality and courage. Tullibardine possessed the element of surprise, the advantage of position, and superiority in numbers. Wightman's force consisted of 1,100 men, and even Tullibardine's calculations estimated his own army at fractionally above this figure, while Wightman himself, although possibly exaggerating in order to underline the spectacular nature of his success, put it at "1,640 Highlanders, besides 300 Spaniards, and a Corps apart of 500 Highlanders who were posted on a hill in order to make themselves masters of our baggage". All these advantages were cast away in the most prodigal manner.

On the morning of the 10th, James Stuart's birthday, Lord George Murray reported that Wightman had struck his camp by Loch Clunie and was marching towards Glenshiel. Murray's outposts began to retire, keeping a half-mile gap between them and the enemy, and the two armies finally came within sight of each other at about two o'clock in the afternoon. Wightman halted his men and gave his dispositions. His right wing, under the command of Colonel Clayton, was the stronger of the two, made up as it was of Montagu's Regiment, Ruffel's Dutch regiment supplemented by four companies from Amerongen's, an additional detachment of fifty men under Colonel Harrison, and 150 dragoons; on the flank, Ensign Mackay had fifty-six of Lord Strathnaver's men. The weaker left wing, on the south side of the river, consisted only of Clayton's Regiment, with Munro of Culcairn and about eighty of his clansmen on the flank. The dragoons and the mortars were deployed on the road.

The Jacobites, with their natural advantages, had rather more scope for their dispositions. The Spanish regulars under Don Nicolas Bolano, Lochiel's and Glengarry's contingents, some Macgregors and M'Kinnons, and 200 of Seaforth's men under the command of Sir John Mackenzie of Coul were all placed along the entrenchments on the north side of the river, with Seaforth himself and the pick of his men on the extreme left. Lord George Murray with 150 men was given the hill on the south side of the river. Tullibardine and Glendaruel commanded in the centre, while Marischal was with Seaforth.

The fighting began between five and six o'clock, and the first position to come under fire was Lord George Murray's. The mortars opened up from the road, and then four platoons of Clayton's Regiment with some of the Munroes advanced up the hill. Murray beat off this attack, but reinforcements came up and he was forced to retire beyond the burn, where he was safe from a further assault because of the high banks. If Murray had received any support, he might well have swept down on the English left wing and altered the whole course of the conflict; but Tullibardine continued to show a pronounced reluctance to seize any opportunity.

Wightman now turned his attention to Seaforth's position on the Jacobite far left, and sent Montagu's and Harrison's men to attack this crucial defensive post. Seaforth, shaken by such a vigorous assault, asked for reinforcements, and Rob Roy Macgregor hurried up. But it was too late. Mar, no doubt relying on subsequent information from Tullibardine, describes the scene: "However, before they could get up so as to be fairly in hands with the enemy, the most of all Lord Seaforth's people were gone off, and himself left wounded in the arm, so that with difficulty he got out of the place." The Macgregors also retreated, and they were soon followed by Glengarry's men. The Jacobite left was in tatters, and Wightman could now concentrate on the Spanish troops in the centre. The mortars were trained on them, but they stood up to the fire very creditably. Isolated in a strange country among wild-looking men speaking a strange language, with scant prospect of ever seeing Spain again, and accurate mortar fire raining down on them, it is surprising that they did not throw down their arms and surrender on the spot. Bolano, however, even offered to attack the enemy once more, a gallant suggestion which was hardly practicable.

Tullibardine's letter to Mar puts a suspiciously self-absolving gloss on the final minutes of the skirmish: "I proposed to my Lord Marischal, Lochiel, Brigadier Campbell, and all present, that we should keep in a body with the Spaniards and march through the Highlands for some time till we could gather again in case of a landing, or else should the King send instructions, the Highlanders would then rise and soon make up all that was past. But everybody declared against doing anything further, for as things stood they thought it impracticable, and my Lord Marischal with Brigadier Campbell of Ormidale went off without any more ado or so much as taking leave. The Spaniards themselves declared they could neither live without bread nor make any hard marches through the country, therefore I was obliged to give them leave to capitulate the best way they could." It is doubtful whether there was time for so much discussion, or whether Tullibardine would have shown sufficient coolness while his men were already in headlong flight over Scour Ouran and up towards the top of the mountain. But, whatever Tullibardine's final words of counsel or command might have been, it was quite obvious that the day was irretrievably lost.

The losses on the English side were negligible, twenty-one men killed and 121 wounded, the highest number of casualties being recorded in Montagu's Regiment which had endured the fiercest fighting. The Jacobite losses are impossible to calculate, but it seems likely that more Highlanders ran than stayed to be bayoneted by their pursuers. Certainly Keith fixes the total number of killed and wounded on both sides together at not much above a hundred.

On the following day, the Spaniards surrendered to Wightman, and as Keith drily puts it, "everybody else took the road he liked best". Keith himself was sick of a fever. He was "forced to lurk some months in the mountains, and in the beginning of September having got a ship, I embarked at Peterhead, and four days after landed in Holland at the Texel, and from thence, with the Earl Marischal, went to the Hague". The other main participants, some with prices on their heads, waited for the right moment in the wilds of Glengarry and Knoydart and then slipped away to the Continent. Only Lord George Murray and Seaforth had been wounded and no one fell into Wightman's hands. The victorious general himself began a march through Seaforth's country to demonstrate the inadvisability of supporting the Jacobite cause, "burning the houses of the Guilty and preserving those of the Honest".

The unhappy Spaniards, 274 of them, were moved to Inverness and then to Edinburgh, where their condition aroused much sympathy. Lockhart describes their misfortune: "The Government for a long time refused to advance subsistence money to them, by which in a little time they were reduced to great straits, which appeared even in their looks though their Spanish pride would not allow them to complain. As I was well acquainted with Don Nicolas who commanded them, I took the liberty to ask him if he wanted money; and finding it was so, I told him it was unkind in him to be thus straitened, when he knew our King [James] for whose cause he suffered had so many friends in town that would cheerfully assist him; so I immediately got him credit for as much money as was necessary for himself and his men." At last, in

October, the Spaniards were sent home. Their only memorial is a corrie far up the hill overlooking the fight at Glenshiel which is called Bealach-na-Spainnteach, the Spaniards' Pass.

*

Back in Spain, Cardinal Alberoni still hoped to relaunch the expedition. Stair wrote scornfully to Craggs: "He has given orders for victualling the ships anew, and for reassembling the troops, but everybody in Spain laughs at that project, and indeed they do pretty much in France, excepting our Jacobites, who have faith enough to believe everything that makes for them, let it be ever so impossible." But Alberoni was only putting on a show. He realised that the fleet would take months to refit, that he had more pressing internal matters to concern him, above all that the weak Jacobite sun had once more set. What was left of the Cadiz fleet attempted to create a diversion in Britanny which might topple the French Regent, but the enterprise was idiotic to an extreme and failed utterly. The French were in any case winning the war and, after the fall of San Sebastian, Alberoni knew that terms would be dictated before long. One of the clauses in any peace treaty would inevitably insist on James's departure from Spanish soil, and it was now imperative for him to leave for Italy while he could still do so with some vestige of dignity. He sailed in August, landed at Leghorn, and at last met his bride Clementina Sobieski at the beginning of September. It was the final occasion that James would take an active part in the attempts to recover the British crown for the Stuart dynasty. A quarter of a century later, a younger and more romantic representative of the court in exile would watch as the Jacobite standard was unfurled by no less a person than the Marquess of Tullibardine at Glenfinnan.

Tullibardine was to die in the Tower after the collapse

of the '45. The other main instigators of the 1719 attempt
had very different careers. Alberoni fell from power, his
policies discredited, in December 1719, and retired to
Italy where he remained until his death in 1752. The Duke
of Ormonde stayed in Spain, living on a pension offered
to him by King Philip and occasionally dabbling in in-
effectual Jacobite plots. The last few years of his life
were spent at Avignon where he died in 1745. Seaforth
was pardoned in 1726 and never troubled the Hanoverians again.

For the Earl Marischal and his brother James Keith,
however, the '19 was only a prelude to outstanding military and diplomatic careers. Both men entered the service
of Frederick the Great of Prussia and contributed to the
meteoric rise in European importance of that country.
The elder brother was Prussian ambassador to France
and to Spain, and was appointed Governor of Neuf-
châtel. He lived on till 1778, dying in Potsdam on May
25. Two days before his death, he asked to see the British
minister at the Court of Berlin. "I have asked for you to
be sent for," he explained, "because it amuses me that a
minister of King George should hear the last sighs of an
old Jacobite. Besides, you will perhaps have some mes-
sages for me to pass on to my Lord Chatham [the elder
Pitt had died a fortnight earlier]. As I expect to be seeing
him tomorrow or the day after, I will be delighted to
undertake them." His brother became one of Frederick's
greatest marshals and was killed at the battle of Hoch-
kirch in 1758.

*

The 1719 rebellion was little more than a chimera, blasted
away by mortar and musket-fire in the Pass of Glenshiel.
In London, reactions to the news of the landing on
Lewis were in general indifferent. The Government acted
swiftly and there were few cases of unrest. A number of
dragoons mutinied, and a certain Captain Lennard, who

had tried to enlist men for the Jacobite cause, was allowed to leave the country. The sale of Ormonde's house in
St. James's Square to an Irish gentleman for the sum of
£7,500 greatly annoyed the High Tories, and when the
Prince of Wales occupied Ormonde's superb White
House at Richmond, which had also been forfeited, they
could not contain their indignation. But the Government
continued to behave almost benevolently towards the
occasional agitator or pro-Stuart printer. Only now and
then were their powers revealed, to encourage the others.
A soldier called Devenish was tied to a tree in Hyde Park
and flogged by fourteen companies of his regiment, a
peculiarly savage torture which, not surprisingly, he
failed to survive. And a chairman, who had spat three
times in the face of the Princess of Wales as she was being
carried in her sedan-chair from Leicester Fields to St.
James's, was whipped at the cart's tail from Somerset
House to the Haymarket.

But these were isolated incidents, and King George felt
so secure that he had no compunction in leaving for
Holland with his hideous mistresses.

In Scotland, Wightman continued his pilgrimage of
grace, and there were no further disturbances. It was left
to General Wade to compile his reports on the Highlands and to advise on security measures. Roads and
bridges were constructed, so that garrison forces could
manoeuvre more easily; two strong forts were built at
Inverness and Fort Augustus; square look-out towers
were dotted about in the glens; and an armed galley was
floated on Loch Ness. It was a remarkable feat of en-
gineering, and Wade's improvements have stood the test
of time. Where before there had been nothing but rough
mountain tracks and flimsy, makeshift bridges over
streams which could easily become foaming torrents,
now there were miles of solid road and quantities of
firm stone bridges. Wade's chief engineer, Burt, testified
to the change: "The roads on these moors are now as

smooth as Constitution Hill; and I have galloped on
some of them for miles together in great tranquillity,
which was heightened by reflection on my former
fatigue." The ordinary Highlander was inclined to ig-
nore these newfangled amenities, but the chiefs knew
that this was basically a military operation designed
more for soldiers than for the comfort of the Scots. And,
in the twenty-six years before the last and most famous
manifestation of Jacobite upsurge, little or nothing was
done to improve the common lot of the crofters and
clansmen. They continued to live near the starvation
level, and even the lairds and once powerful noblemen
suffered from forfeiture of estates and creeping poverty.
The notorious Highland Clearances were far in the
future, but the English never ceased to look with suspicion bordering on disbelief and even disgust on their
enforced countrymen north of the border.

Where nothing altered in Scotland, except superfici-
ally, a profound change was gradually seen in the Jacobite hierarchy on the Continent. Bolingbroke had fallen
from favour before the 1719 expedition had even started.
Courageous men like Marischal and Keith went off to
serve less shadowy and more reliable masters. Middleton and Caryll were dead or retired. Only Mar still held
sway, as always a disastrous influence. He had destroyed
the excellent chances of the '15, and he had intrigued at
the time of the '19. Now a Duke, a Knight of the Garter,
and a Knight of the Thistle, he remained as James's Secretary of State until 1724. During his term of office,
Jacobite hopes, and Jacobite credibility, reached a nadir.
The truth was that supporters of the Jacobite cause were
less and less motivated by loyalty and disinterest, and
increasingly by a simple hope for preferment. Rome,
and James's court there, became a mecca for adventurers
and renegades. Anyone who nursed a grievance against
authority, whether real or imagined, felt that the Jacobites offered a chance of reversal. Memories, too, are

short. The departure of James II seemed a long time
ago, the Hanoverian dynasty, though hardly popular,
was tolerated, there was a general reaction against civil
war, against interference, whether from Spain, France
or the Pope, against disorder. And in Robert Walpole
England had the ideal chief minister for the times. A
policy of *laissez faire*, of letting sleeping dogs lie, of a
rising economy at home allied to non-intervention
abroad, suited the merchants of the City and the spreading middle classes in the towns and more prosperous
rural areas. Even the bugbear of religion seemed to have
lost some of its inflammatory element. The Roman Catholics and the Non-Jurors naturally continued to complain, with ample reason, but these were a small minority.
The threat of the scarlet woman of Rome still wove its
mesmeric spell, but that was only to the discredit of the
Jacobites, for after all did not James reside at the very
heart of Catholicism?

Occasionally, the peace of London was rent by a
Jacobite scare. In the spring of 1722 a Non-Juring Irish
clergyman, George Kelly, was arrested in his lodgings,
and only just had time to burn some highly incriminat-
ing papers. Kelly himself was imprisoned in the Tower,
from where he escaped fourteen years later in ample time
to join Charles Edward on his way to Scotland, but a
number of more distinguished names were cast up on
the dead waters of treachery. The Duke of Norfolk,
Lord North and Lord Orrery all found themselves abruptly incarcerated, but the biggest and most slippery
fish to be landed was Francis Atterbury, Bishop of
Rochester, who had never resigned himself to George I's
accession. Walpole preferred not to exile Atterbury and
thus present James with such an astute counsellor, and
attempted bribery instead. Atterbury refused the offer
of the see of Winchester, and, after a Bill of Pains and
Penalties had passed through the House of Lords, left
the country. Ironically, just as he set foot in Calais, Bol-

ingbroke was preparing to return to England, having patched up his differences with the king and the Government. Atterbury continued on to Rome. It is not known whether he ever suspected that the man who had laid evidence against him was none other than the Duke of Mar, who had also decided that the time was ripe to turn his coat.

Atterbury was a distinct asset to the Jacobite court in Rome, but he was a rare exception in the dreary procession of disappointed and bankrupt men who appeared from time to time. Whether it was the Duke of Wharton, heavily in debt, or some Irish nonentity, they added little lustre to the already tarnished image of Jacobitism.

And so, with James ageing prematurely, one of his sons, the Cardinal of York, lost to the Church, and the other, Charles Edward, displaying the first signs of selfishness and petulance which were to lead to the tragic sense of failure and drunkenness of his last years, the life of the exiles went on its weary way through the 1720's and 1730's. Then, like a brief, illusory rainbow of hope outlined against the thunderclouds, came the '45, and the creation of a legend.

Epilogue

Rebellion 1745

Chapter Twelve

The Eight Men of Moidart

The eldest son of the Chevalier de St George is tall, above the common stature, his limbs cast in the most exact mould, his complexion has in it somewhat of an uncommon delicacy; all his features are perfectly regular and well turned, and his eyes the finest I ever saw.

John Murray of Broughton

ON July 22, 1745, a small vessel, the *Du Teillay*, could be seen off Barra Head in Berneray, a small island off South Uist at the southern end of the Outer Hebrides. It seemed an insignificant arrival, except for the fact that at night the ship had been shrouded in darkness, as if to escape detection by any other vessels that might be keeping watch for possible smuggling activities. Besides the captain and the crew, there were eleven somewhat ill-assorted passengers on board. Aeneas Macdonald was a banker who years later would perish during the French Revolution. Sir Thomas Sheridan was an old man of seventy and seemed too frail for such a voyage. The three other Irishmen comprised Sir John Macdonald, John William O'Sullivan, and the Reverend Mr. Kelly. There was one Englishman on board, Francis Strickland. The seventh member of the party was William Murray,

Marquess of Tullibardine, recognised by some as the rightful Duke of Atholl. With them were three attendants, an Italian valet, Macdonald the banker's clerk, was a certain Duncan Cameron. The last of the eleven was a handsome young man of twenty-five. A few hours before the *Du Teillay* dropped anchor, Tullibardine had noticed an eagle hovering above the ship. "Sir," he said to the handsome young man, "I hope this is an excellent omen, and promises good things to us. The King of birds is come to welcome. Your Royal Highness upon your arrival in Scotland."

Charles Edward Stuart landed on the west coast of the island of Eriskay in drenching rain. It was a depressing first glimpse of Scotland. All there was to eat was a dish of flounders, and the tacksman's cottage where the prince, disguised as a student from the Scotch College in Rome, and his companions – the Seven Men of Moidart, as they came to be called – spent the night, was full of smoke from the open peat fire. No encouragement was forthcoming on the next day. Alexander Macdonald of Boisdale, Clanranald's younger brother, came across from South Uist, and was the first man to whom Charles revealed his identity. Macdonald was aghast at the dangers and bluntly advised the whole party to return to France. He knew perfectly well that his brother would not raise the clan, and that Macdonald of Sleat and Macleod of Macleod, two of the chiefs on whose support Charles relied, would be at the very best neutral. Charles swept his cautious advice aside. "I am come home, sir," he declared, "and I will entertain no notion at all of returning to that place whence I came, for I am persuaded my faithful Highlanders will stand by me."

Macdonald of Boisdale continued to pour the cold water of reason on the whole ill-planned enterprise, but Charles sailed on to Loch na-Nuagh, between Moidart and Arisaig. There, his redoubtable charm and youthful enthusiasm reaped their first adherent in the person of

Kinlochmoidart, Aeneas Macdonald's brother; and soon other chiefs, Glenaladale and Young Clanranald in particular, began to arrive. The effect which Charles had on the men gathering on the deck of the *Du Teillay* was extraordinary. One of the Macdonalds describes the scene: "About half an hour after there entered the tent [a kind of pavilion had been erected on deck] a tall youth of a most agreeable aspect, in a plain black coat, with a plain shirt, not very clean, and a cambric stock fixed with a plain silver buckle, a fair round wig out of the buckle, a plain hat with a canvas string having one end fixed to one of his coat buttons; he had black stockings and brass buckles in his shoes; at his first appearance I found my heart swell to my very throat." Perhaps the black and white clothes were a *coup de théâtre*, perhaps the sheer youth of Charles was the deciding factor, but few people seemed able or willing to resist his charm and eloquence. Even Cameron of Lochiel, old and reluctant to commit himself, fell a prey to this charismatic mixture when, during an interview on the *Du Teillay*, he was converted from opposition through doubt to ultimate enthusiasm.

With Lochiel's declaration, the tide turned. Keppoch and Glencoe began to raise their men, and an increasing number of waverers decided to descend into the arena. On August 6, Charles left the *Du Teillay* and moved into the farm-house at Borodale. And on the 9th the *Du Teillay* sailed for France. Any retreat was now cut; the rebellion had begun in earnest. On the 18th, John Murray of Broughton joined Charles at Kinlochmoidart and was appointed Secretary of State. The following day was set for the important ritual which surrounded the gathering of the clans.

Early in the morning, three boats proceeded along Loch Shiel in the direction of the selected spot. Charles was greeted on landing by the Laird of Morar, and the whole party moved up to Glenfinnan, a narrow valley overlooked by craggy mountains. The glen itself was empty. Charles waited with increasing anxiety for several hours. Then, heralded by the music of the pipes, the Camerons began to arrive. They marched in two long lines and before long all 700 of them were crowded into the glen.

Charles, always ready to improve on an already dramatic moment, decided to raise his standard. There is some doubt as to whether it was made of red, white or blue silk, or of red silk with a white space in the middle; but as it was unfurled by Tullibardine a wave of romantic fervour ran through the onlookers. James VIII was proclaimed, a commission appointing Charles as Regent was read, and a manifesto of intent communicated to the listeners.

Finally, Charles himself stepped forward to speak. He had not yet donned the Highland costume which he was to wear later, and he stood there, dressed simply in a fawn coat, knee-breeches, a scarlet-laced waistcoat and a yellow-bobbed hat. He spoke shortly but with obvious effect. The standard of rebellion floated above him.

The glamour of the ball at Holyroodhouse; the trouncing of Cope's army at Prestonpans; the march southwards and the internecine bickering among his advisers; the fateful decision at Derby; the holding operation of Falkirk; the horrors of Culloden and the long, nerve-racked wanderings; the escape to France; the weary years of exile, the drunkenness and the scandals; the attempts to beget an heir; and the death from apoplexy in Rome on January 31, 1788, at the age of sixty-seven: all this lay ahead. But for one brief hour the excitement, the unanimity, the optimism and the panache of the prelude to the death of an already dying cause held sway on a rocky glen looking out towards the loch, the sea and the Western Isles.

Appendix One

A List of the most considerable Chiefs in Scotland, and the Number of Men they can raise, with an Account of their Disposition for or against the Government [in 1715–16].*

The Duke of *Hamilton* can raise 1,000 Men, all, with their Chief, dispos'd well for the Government.

The Dutchess of *Buccleugh* 1000 Men, all, with their Chief, for the Government.

The Duke of *Gordon* 3000 Men, with their Chief, who is Neutral; but most of them with his Son the Marquis of *Huntley*, who is against the Government, and in the Rebellion.

The Duke of *Argyle* 4000 Men, most of them with their Chief, for the Government. . . .

The Duke of *Douglass* 500 Men, all, with their Chief, for the Government.

The Duke of *Athol* 6000 Men, few with their Chief, who is for the Government; and most of them with his Son the Marquis of *Tullibardine*, who is against it, and in the Rebellion.

The Duke of *Montrose* 2000 Men, few with their Chief, who is for the Government, but most against it.

The Duke of *Roxburgh* 500 Men, all, with their Chief, for the Government. . . .

The Marquis of *Annandale* 500 Men, all, with their Chief, for the Government.

The Earl of *Errol* 500 Men, few with their Chief, who is Neutral; but most of them against the Government.

*From Patten's *History of the Rebellion*.

The Earl *Marischall* 500 Men, most, with their Chief, against the Government, and in the Rebellion.

The Earl of *Sutherland* 1000 Men, most, with their Chief, for the Government. . . .

The Earl of *Mar* 1000 Men, most, with their Chief, against the Government, and in the Rebellion.

The Earl of *Rothes* 500 Men, all, with their Chief, for the Government.

The Earl of *Mortoun* 300 Men, all, with their Chief, for the Government.

The Earl of *Glencairn* 300 Men, most, with their Chief, for the Government.

The Earl of *Eglingtoun* 300 Men, most, with [their] Chief, for the Government.

The Earl of *Cassils* 500 Men, all, with their Chief, for the Government.

The Earl of *Cathness* 300 Men, few with their Chief, who is Neutral; but most of them against the Government.

The Earl of *Murray* 500 Men, few with their Chief, who was lately against the Government, and is now for it; but most against it.

The Earl of *Nithsdale* 300 Men, with their Chief, against the Gouernment, and in the Rebellion.

The Earl of *Wintoun* 300 Men, most, with their Chief, against the Government, and in the Rebellion.

The Earl of *Linlithglow* 300 Men, most, with their Chief, against the Government, and in the Rebellion.

The Earl of *Hume* 500 Men. He was confin'd in the Castle of *Edinburgh*; but most of his Men, with his Brother, against the Government, and in the Rebellion.

The Earl of *Perth* 1500 Men, most with their Chief, who lives Abroad, with his Son the Lord *Drummond*, against the Government, and in the Rebellion.

The Earl of *Wigtoun* 300 Men, most, with their Chief, against the Government.

The Earl of *Strathmore* 300 Men, in the Rebellion.

The Earl of *Lauderdale* 300 Men, all, with their Chief, for the Government.

The Earl of *Seaforth* 3000 Men, most, with their Chief, against the Government, and in the Rebellion.

The Countess of *Dumfries* 200 Men, for the Government.

The Earl of *Southesk* 300 Men, most, with their Chief, against the Government, and in the Rebellion.

The Earl of *Weems* 300 Men, all, with their Chief, for the Government.

The Earl of *Airly* 500 Men, few with their Chief, who is Neutral; but most with his Son the Lord *Ogilvie*, against the Government, and in the Rebellion.

The Earl of *Carnwath* 300 Men, most, with their Chief, against the Government, and in the Rebellion.

The Earl of *Penmure* 500 Men, most, with their Chief, against the Government, and in the Rebellion.

The Earl of *Kilmarnock* 300 Men, all, with their Chief, for the Government.

The Earl of *Dondonald* 300 Men, all, with their Chief, for the Government.

The Earl of *Broadalbine* 2000 Men, most, with their Chief, against the Government, and in the Rebellion.

The Viscount of *Stormount* 300 Men, all, with their Chief, against the Government.

The Viscount *Kenmure* 300 Men, most, with their Chief, against the Government, and in the Rebellion.

The Lord *Forbes* 500 Men, most, with their Chief, for the Government.

The Lady *Lovat* 800 Men, most, with their Chief, against the Government, and in the Rebellion.

The Lord *Ross* 500 Men, all, with their Chief, for the Government.

The Lord *Rae* 500 Men, all, with their Chief, for the Government.

The Lord *Nairn* 1000 Men, most, with their Chief, against the Government, and in the Rebellion.

Here follow the CLANS.

Sir *Donald Mac-Donald* 1000 Men, all, with their Chief, against the Government, and in the Rebellion.

The Laird of *Glengary* 500 Men, all, with their Chief, against the Government, and in the Rebellion. This Gentleman was inferior to none for Bravery.

The Captain of *Clanranald* 1000 Men, all, with their Chief, against the Government, and in the Rebellion. . . .

The Laird of *Keppoch* 300 Men, all, with their Chief, against the Government, and in the Rebellion. . . .

The Laird of *Mackintosh* 1000 Men, all, with their Chief, against the Government, and in the Rebellion. Most of this Clan were in *England*, and others were posted off *Inverness*.

The Laird of *MacGregor* 500 Men, most, with their Chief, against the Government, and in the Rebellion. This Clan did nothing worth mentioning at *Sheriff-Moor*.

The Laird of *Strowen Robertson* 500 Men, all, with their Chief, against the Government, and in the Rebellion.

The Laird of *Mac-Pherson* 500 Men, all, with their Chief, against the Government, and in the Rebellion. This Clan is Part of the *Mackintosh*'s Family.

Sir *Evan Cameron* [of Lochiel] 1000 Men, most, with their Chief, against the Government, and in the Rebellion. This Knight is so old and infirm that he could not lead his Vassals to the Field, but were commanded by his Son. . . .

Sir *John Mac-Lean* 1000 Men, most, with their Chief, against the Government, and in the Rebellion.

The Laird of *Grant* 1000 Men, all, with their Chief, for the Government. . . .

The Laird of *Appin* [Stuart] 300 Men, all, with their Chief, against the Government, and in the Rebellion. These Men did not behave so well as was expected.

The Laird of *Mac-Leod* 1000 Men, most, with their Chief, who is a Minor and Neutral.

The Laird of *Mac-Kenning* [Mackinnon] 200 Men, all, with their Chief, against the Government, and in the Rebellion.

The Laird of *Glenco* 100 Men, all with their Chief, against the Government, and in the Rebellion.

The Laird of *Glenmoriston* 100 Men, all, with their Chief, against the Government, and in the Rebellion.

Mac-Neil of *Barra* 120 Men.

Chrisolme of *Straglass* 100 Men, with their Chief, in the Rebellion.

Appendix Two

The Loch Lomond Expedition*

The Clan-Gregiour is a race of men so utterly infamous for thieving, depredation, and murder, that after many acts of the councel of Scotland against them, at length, in the reign of King Charles I., the Parliament made a strict Act suppressing the very name. Upon the Restauration, viz. in the year 1661, when the reins were given to all licentiousness, and loyalty, as it was then call'd, was thought sufficient to compound for all wickedness, that act was rescinded. But upon the late happy Revolution, when the nation began to recover her senses, some horrid barbarities having been committed by that execrable crew, under the leading of one Robert Roy Mc gregiour, yet living, and at this present in arms against His Majesty K. George, The Parliament under K. William and Q. Mary annulled the said Act rescissory, and revived the former penal Act against them.

This Act is still continuing in force; but upon hopes given them, as 'tis said, by the E. of Mar, of having that brand of infamy taken of 'em, and getting their name restor'd on condition they would appear for the Pretender, about the end of September last [1715] they broke out into open rebellion under the conduct of Gregor Mc

*From *The Loch Lomond Expedition*, *MDCCXV*. See Bibliography.

gregiour of Glengyle, nephew to the above mention'd Rob. Roy Mcgregiour, and in a considerable body made an excursion upon their neighbours, especially in Buchanan and about the Heads of Monteith, and coming upon them unawares, disarmed them.

Afterwards, upon Michaelmas Day [September 29], having made themselves masters of the boats on the water of Enrick and Loch-Lomond, about seventy men of 'em possess'd themselves of Inchmurrin, a large isle in the said loch, whence, about midnight, they came a shore on the parish of Bonhill, three miles above Dumbarton. But the country taking the alarm by the ringing of the bells of the several parish churches about, and being frighted by the discharge of two great guns from the castle of Dumbarton to warn the country, they thought fit to scamper off in great haste to their boats, and return'd to the isle, where, not contenting themselves with beef, which they might have had, ther being several cows on the isle, they made havock of a great many deer belonging to His Grace the Duke of Montrose, whose property the isle is, and row'd off with them towards the head of the loch, taking along with them all the boats they cou'd find, and drew them up upon the land at Innersnaat, about eighteen miles up from the mouth of the loch, and in a little time after, went off in a body with their fellows towards Mar's Camp. Upon what consideration it is not yet commonly known, but so it is, that in the end of the last week, they returned to their former habitations on Craigroyston and the parts adjacent on the north-east side of the abovemention'd Loch-Lomond, and upon Monday last, being October 10th, they mustered their forces.

This their return and rendezvouzing brought the country about under some frightful apprehensions. The Jacobits were at a great deal of pains to perswade people that there was no harm to be feared from them; that supposing they shou'd come doun upon the Lowlands, yet

they wou'd spoil them of nothing but their arms; that it
wou'd be their wisdom peaceably to part with these, because if they shou'd make any resistance, and shed the
blood of so much as one Mc gregiour, they wou'd set no
bounds to their fury, but burn and slay without mercy.
But the people considered that this was false reasoning;
that the quitting of their arms wou'd be just as wise conduct as when the sheep in the fable, at the desire of the
wolves, parted with their dogs; wherefore they resolved
to do their best to defend themselves against those mis-
creants who neither fear God nor regard man.

For this purpose, and in order to bridle these rebels in
their excursions, a strong guard of one hundred and
twenty volunteers from Paslay, having been sometime
before posted at Dumbarton, and about four hundred
voluntiers, partly of the Right Honourable the E. of
Kilmarnock's men, partly of the people of Air, Kilwin-
ing, Stevenson, etc., having garrison'd the houses of
Drumakill, Cardross, and Gartartan, it was resolved to
retake, if possible, the boats from them, by which they
kept the countrey round in a terrour. . . .

For effecting this, on Teusday October 11th, about six
a'clock at night, there came to the Key of Dumbarton,
from the men of war that are lying in the Firth of Clyde,
four pinnaces and three long boats, with four pateraroes, and about one hundred seamen, well hearted and
well armed, under the command of Captain Charlton,
Captain Field, and Captain Parker, with four lieutenants
and two gunners. About two or three hours after, there
came up to them a large boat from Newport-Glasgow,
with two large screw guns, under the command of Captain Clark. All these being join'd by three large boats of
Dumbarton, upon the morrow about nine in the morning they all put off from the Key, and by the strength
of horses were drawn the space of three miles up the
river Levin, which next to Spey is reckon'd the most
rapid river in Scotland.

When they were got to the mouth of the loch, the Paslay men, and as many more as the boats cou'd conveniently stow, went on board; and at the same time, the Dumbarton men, the men of Easter and Wester Kilpatrick, of Rosneith, Rew, and Cardross, marched up on foot along the north-west side of the loch, and after them, on horse back, the Honourable Master John Campble of Mammore, unckle to His Grace the Duke of Argyle, attended by a fine train of the gentlemen of the shire, viz. Archbald Mc aulay of Ardncaple, Aulay Mc aulay, his eldest son, George Naper of Kilmahew, Walter Graham of Kilmardinny, John Colquhoun of Craigtoun, John Stirling of Law, James Hamilton of Barns, with many others, all richly mounted and well armed.

When the pinnaces and boats, being once got in within the mouth of the loch, had spread their sails, and the men on the shore had rang'd themselves in order, marching along the side of the loch for scouring the coast, they made all together so very fine an appearance as had never been seen in that place before. and might have gratified even a curious person. The men on the shore marched with the greatest ardour and alacrity. The pinnaces on the water discharging their Pateraroes, and the men their small arms, made so very dreadful a noise thro' the multiply'd rebounding echoes of the vast mountains on both sides the loch, that perhaps there was never a more lively resemblance of thunder.

Against evening they got to Luss, where they came ashore, and were met and join'd by Sir Humphrey Colquhoun of Luss, Baronet, and chief of the name, and James Grant of Pluscarden, his son in law and brother german to Brigadier Grant, follow'd by fourty or fifty stately fellows in their short hose and belted plaids, arm'd each of 'em with a well fix'd gun on his shoulder, a strong handsome target, with a sharp pointed steel of above half an ell in length screw'd into the navel of it, on his left arm, a sturdy claymore by his side, and a pistol

or two with a durk and knife in his belt. Here the whole
company rested all night. In the mean time, many reports were brought to them, contrived or at least magnified by the Jacobites in order to discourage them from
the attempt; such as, that Mc Donald of Glengarry, who
was indeed lying with his men about Strafillan, sixteen
miles from the head of the loch, had reinforced the Mc
gregiours, so that they amounted at least to fifteen hundred men, whereas ther were not full four hundred on
the expedition against them; That the loch being narrow
at Innersnaat, where the rebels were lying, they might
pepper the boats with their shot from the shore without
any danger to themselves, being shaded by the rocks
and woods. In a word, that it was a desperate project,
and would be a throwing away of their lives.

But all this could not dishearten these brave men.
They knew that the Mc gregiours and the Devil are to be
dealt with after the same manner, and that if they be
resisted they will flee. Wherefore on the morrow morning, being Thursday the 13th, they went on in their expedition, and about noon came to Innersnaat, the place
of danger. In order to rouse those thieves from their
dens, Captain Clark loos'd one of his great guns, and
drove a ball thro' the roof of a house on the face of the
mountain, whereupon an old wife or two came crawling
out and scrambled up the hill, but otherwise ther was no
appearance of any body of men on the mountains, only
some few, standing out of reach on the craggy rocks
looking at them.

Whereupon, the Paslay men under the command of
Captain Finlason, assisted by Captain Scot, a half pay
officer, of late a Lieutenant in Collonell Kerr's Regiment
of Dragoons, who is indeed an officer wise, stout, and
honest; the Dumbarton men, under the command of
David Colquhoun and James Duncanson of Garshaik,
Magistrates of the Burgh, with severals of the other
Companies, to the number of an hundred men in all, with

the greatest intrepidity leapt on shore, got up to the top of the mountain, and drew up in order, and stood about an hour, their drums beating all the while, but no enemie appearing, they thereupon went in quest of the boats which the rebels had seiz'd, and having casually lighted on some ropes, anchors, and oars, hid among the shrubs, at length they found the boats drawn up a good way on the land, which they hurled doun to the loch; such of 'em as were not dammaged they carried off with them, and such as were they sunk or hew'd in pieces. And that same night they return'd to Luss, and thence, next day, without the loss or hurt of so much as one man, to Dumbarton, whence they had first set out altogether, bringing along with them the whole boats they found in their way on either side the loch and in the creeks of the isles, and moor'd them under the cannon of the castle. And thus in a short time, and with little expense, the Mc greigours were cow'd, and a way pointed out how the government may easily keep them in awe.

There are two or three things may be remarked on this expedition.

First, that tho' the Mc greigours deserved extremities, and our men were in a sufficient capacity to have destroy'd and burnt their whole goods and housing, yet they did not take from them to the value of a shoe latchet, save one fork which might have been used as a weapon.

Secondly, The Providence of God was very observable, in that tho' for three days before it had blown a prodigious storm, yet in the morning, when our men were to go on board from Dumbarton, it calm'd, and they got a fair wind in their poop the whole way up the loch. When they had done their business it kindly veer'd about and brought them safely and speedily down the loch, immediately after which, on the Friday's evening, it began to blow boisterously as before.

Thirdly, The cheerfulness of the men who went on

this expedition deserves to be notic'd and applauded. They were not forced to it, as the clans are by their masters and chiefs, who hack and butcher such as refuse to go along with them: witness Duncan Mc farland in Rowardennin. But they offer'd themselves voluntarly to it. No wonder, for men begin now to be convinced that all is at stake.

Bibliography

Accounts of the Burning of the Villages of Auchterarder, etc. Edinburgh 1843

ALLARDYCE, COL. J. (ed.) *Historical Papers relating to the Jacobite Period 1699–1750.* 2 vols. Aberdeen, 1895

BAYNES, J. *The Jacobite Rising of 1715.* London, 1970

BEVAN, B. *King James III.* London, 1967

BLOMFIELD, SIR R. *A History of French Architecture.* London, 1911

BROWN, P. HUME. *History of Scotland,* Vol. III (1689–1843). Cambridge, 1909

BULLOCH, J. M. *The Gay Gordons.* London, 1908

BURTON, J. HALL. *History of Scotland, from the Revolution to the Extinction of the Last Jacobite Insurrection (1689–1748).* 2 vols. London, 1853

CAMPANA DE CAVELLI, MARCHESA. *Les Derniers Stuarts à Saint-Germain-en-Laye.* 2 vols. Paris, Geneva, 1871

CAMPBELL, R. *The Life of the Most Illustrious Prince John, Duke of Argyle and Greenwich.* London, 1745

Carte MSS. Bodleian Library, Oxford

CHAMBERS, R. *History of the Rebellions in Scotland,* etc. Edinburgh, 1829

Collection of Original Letters and Authentick Papers relating to the Rebellion of 1715. Edinburgh, 1730

Collection of Original Papers about the Scots Plot. London, 1704

Complete Collection of State Trials. London, 1809–28

DANGEAU, MARQUIS DE. *Journal,* Vol. VIII (1701–2). Paris, 1854–60

DENNISTOUN, J. (ed.) *The Loch Lomond Expedition, MDCCXV.* Glasgow, 1834

DORAN, J. *London in the Jacobite Times.* 2 vols. London, 1877

DU BOSCQ DE BEAUMONT, G., and BERNOS, M. *La Cour des Stuarts à Saint-Germain-en-Laye, 1689–1718,* Paris, 1912

DULON, J. *Jacques II Stuart*. Paris. 1897

FORBIN, COMTE DE. *Mémoires*. Amsterdam, 1730

FOX, H. M. *André Le Nôtre, Garden Architect to Kings*. London, 1963

FRASER, J. *Major Fraser's Manuscript: His Adventures in Scotland and England*, etc. Edited by A. Fergusson. 2 vols. Edinburgh, 1889

FRASER, S. *Memoirs of the Life of Lord Lovat*. London, 1746

GREW, E. and M. SHARPE. *The English Court in Exile*. London, 1911

HAILE, M. *James Francis Edward, The Old Pretender*. London, 1907

HAMILTON, E. *The Backstairs Dragon: a Life of Robert Harley, Earl of Oxford*. London, 1969

HARTMANN, C. H. *The Quest Forlorn*. London, 1952

HEARNE, T. *Reliquiae Hearnianae*. Oxford, 1857

HISTORICAL MANUSCRIPTS COMMISSION *Stuart Papers at Windsor* (ed. A. and H. Tayler) London, 1939

The Historical Register

HOGG, J *The Jacobite Relics of Scotland* 2 vols. Paisley, 1874

HOOKE, N. *The Secret History of Colonel Hoocke's Negotiations in Scotland in 1707*, etc. Edinburgh, 1760

HOUDARD, G. *Les Châteaux Royaux de Saint-Germain-en-Laye, 1174–1789*. 2 vols. Paris, 1909, 1911

INSH, G. P. *The Scottish Jacobite Movement*. Edinburgh, 1952

JESSE, J. H. *Memoirs of the Pretenders and Their Adherents*. London, 1860

KEITH, J. *A Fragment of a Memoir of Field-Marshal James Keith, Written by Himself, 1714–1734*. Edinburgh, 1843

LA FAYETTE, MARIE MOTIER, COMTESSE DE. *Mémoires de la Cour de France, 1688–9*. Paris, 1890

Letter from Mr. Lesly to a Member of Parliament in London. London, 1714

Letters which passed between Count Gyllenborg, etc. London, 1717

LOCKHART OF CARNWATH, G. *The Lockhart Papers*. 2 vols. London, 1817

Memoirs concerning the affairs of Scotland from Queen Anne's Accession to May 1707. London, 1714

MACAULAY, T. B. *History of England from the Accession of James II*. 5 vols. London, 1849–61

MACKINNON, J. *The Union of England and Scotland: a Study of International History*. London, 1896

MACKY, J. *Memoirs of the Secret Services*. London, 1733

MAHON, LORD. *History of England from the Peace of Utrecht to the Peace of Aix-la-Chapelle*. London, 1836

MAR, JOHN, EARL OF. *Legacies to Scotland* (Vol. XXVI of the Publications of the Scottish Historical Society). Edinburgh, 1896

MELVILLE, L. *The First George in Hanover and England*. London, 1908

MIDDLETON, D. *The Life of Charles second Earl of Middleton (1650–1719)*. London, 1957

OLIPHANT, T. L. K. *Jacobite Lairds of Gask*. London, 1870

OMAN, C. *Mary of Modena*. London, 1962

ORMONDE, JAMES, DUKE OF. *The Jacobite Attempt of 1719*. Letters of James Butler, second Duke of Ormonde, relating to Cardinal Alberoni's project for the invasion of Great Britain on behalf of the Stuarts, and to the landing of a Spanish expedition in Scotland (ed. W. K. Dickson). Edinburgh, 1895

PATTEN, R. *History of the Rebellion in the year 1715*. London, 1745

PETRIE, SIR C. *The Jacobite Movement*. Revised edition, London, 1959

The Marshal Duke of Berwick. London, 1953

Political State of Great Britain, The. London, 1715

PREBBLE, J. *The Darien Disaster*. London, 1968

RAE, P. *The History of the late Rebellion rais'd against His Majesty King George by the Friends of the Popish Pretender*. Dumfries, 1718

SAINT-SIMON, DUC DE. *Historical Memoirs* (ed. L. Norton). 3 vols. London, 1967–71

SÉVIGNÉ, MME DE. *Letters* (ed. V. Hammersley). London, 1955

SHIELD, A. and LANG, A. *The King over the Water*. London, 1907

SIMPSON, W. D. *The Earldom of Mar*. Aberdeen, 1949

SINCLAIR, JOHN, MASTER OF. *Memoirs of the Insurrection in Scotland in 1715* (annotated by Sir Walter Scott). Edinburgh, 1858

SKELTON, C. O. and BULLOCH, J. M. *The House of Gordon*. 3 vols. Aberdeen, 1903–12

Stuart Papers belonging to His Majesty the King preserved at Windsor Castle, Calendar of (ed. F. H. Blackburne Daniell). London, 1902

TAYLER, A. and H. *1715: The Story of the Rising*. London, 1936

The Old Chevalier, James Francis Stuart. London, 1934

TAYLOR, J. *The Pennyless Pilgrimage*. London, 1618

TAYLOR, J. *A Journey to Edenborough*. London, 1705

TERRY, C. S. *The Chevalier de St George and the Jacobite Movements in His Favour 1701–1720*. London, 1901

THACKERAY, W. M. *The Four Georges*. London, 1866

THORNTON, P. M. *The Brunswick Accession*. London, 1887

TRANTER, N. *The Fortified House in Scotland*, Vol. IV. Edinburgh 1966

TREVELYAN, G. M. *England under Queen Anne*. 3 vols. London, 1930–34

True Account of the Proceedings at Perth etc. Written by a Rebel, A. London, 1716

TULLIBARDINE, MARCHIONESS OF. *A Military History of Perthshire, 1660–1902*. 2 vols. Perth, 1908

TURNER, F. C. *James II*. London, 1948

WATT, W. *A. History of Aberdeen and Banff*. Edinburgh, 1900

WYNESS, F. *Royal Valley: The Story of the Aberdeenshire Dee*. Aberdeen, 1968

Index

Other Panthers For Your Enjoyment

Not Only for Students . . .

☐ Chaucer (in modern prose by **THE CANTERBURY**
David Wright) **TALES** 40p
The best version available. 'In Mr. Wright's modern English the
tales become pure story-telling without losing the flavour of the
oldest of English writers' – *The Bookman*. And *Tribune* adds: 'Mr.
Wright can be as coarse as Chaucer'.

☐ (translated by David Wright) **BEOWULF** 25p
Our only epic poem, and perhaps the earliest considerable poem in
any modern language; it brings the doom-laden society of 6th
century Anglo-Saxondom to glowing life. Wright's translation
surpasses even William Morris's.

☐ Frederick Engels **THE CONDITION OF**
THE WORKING CLASS
IN ENGLAND 40p
The modern world in all its facets was born 150 years ago in
England. This is the classic account of that harsh birth.

☐ D. E. Jones **INTRODUCTION TO**
PSYCHOLOGY 50p
'This is the best introductory text I have read – simple terms and
simple sentence construction, supported by examples from
everyday life. If you are new to the field, here is your first book' –
Housecraft

☐ J. W. B. Douglas **THE HOME AND**
THE SCHOOL 40p
Dr. Douglas's famous study of 5,000 boys and girls through their
primary school years is essential reading for teachers and parents
and all who are concerned with education. The conclusion begins to
emerge that the success of a child's school career is much more
connected with his home background, his social background, than
it is with his original brightness.

☐ J. W. B. Douglas and others **ALL OUR FUTURE** 40p
This important sequel to THE HOME AND THE SCHOOL takes
the study of the 5,000 boys and girls from their eleventh to their
fifteenth years, and the earlier book's suggestion – that not so much
intelligence but social background ensures academic success – is
reinforced. Both books have been recommended as basic reading by
Unesco's *Bulletin of the International Bureau of Education*

History

☐ **K. R. Andrews** **DRAKE'S VOYAGES** **40p**

Mr. Andrews is one of today's historians – he has no time for myths. And so: Drake's drum – out! Playing bowls on Plymouth Hoe – out! But Drake as not much more than a pirate – in. And Drake as the greatest navigator of his day – very much in. Altogether an epic narrative.

☐ **Christopher Hill** **PURITANISM AND REVOLUTION** **52p**

The standard background book to the English Civil War by the Master of Balliol, Oxford – *the* specialist on the period. This is scholarship which is a delight to read. And if you want the tone of the book. *History Today*'s review sums it up: 'Hill's attitude is a simple and rare one – it is the underdog who matters'.

☐ **Joyce Marlow** **THE PETERLOO MASSACRE** **60p**

An account of a shameful day in England's history when armed soldiery attacked a peaceful demonstration of poverty-stricken Lancashire workers, wounding and killing them almost at random. 'A dramatic story of politics, economics, misery, hate and fear. It's always in human terms' – *Daily Mirror*

☐ **Harold Perkin** **THE AGE OF THE RAILWAY** **50p**

In a matter of a few years the laying down of thousands of miles of railway track liberated the great part of the British population from the 'idiocy of rural life'. It was the decisive moment of the Industrial Revolution, and its effects are still with us. Professor Perkin's account covers the whole epic period, and although only just published is already a bestseller.

☐ **A. J. P. Taylor** **THE TROUBLE MAKERS** **35p**

The political loners 'agin' the policy of the government of the day have played an important part in the forging of many of the freer aspects of today's society. Britain's most famous historian investigates the activities of such 'eccentrics' from Charles Fox at the end of the 18th century to the uncompromising opponents of Munich in the 1930's. 'A serious historical investigation and one of the most entertaining books for a long while' – *Financial Times*

☐ **Angus Calder** **THE PEOPLE'S WAR** **90p**

Fully lives up to its subtitle – *Britain 1939–45*. Rationing, interminable queuing, day and night blitzes, V1's and 2's, and as ever the inevitable jumped-up bureaucrats. 'Supersedes any other attempt at painting the whole picture' – *Evening News*. 'The cumulative effect is overwhelming' – *Time* Magazine.

Great Lives

☐ Antonia Fraser   **MARY QUEEN OF**   90p
                                             SCOTS

The most acclaimed biography in years, and an international
bestseller. 700 pages, 16 pages of illustrations. 'Full of romance,
violence, intrigue' – *Newsweek*. 'This biography has long been
needed' – *The Scotsman*. 'Antonia Fraser has a high feeling for the
central tragedy' – *Sunday Times*

☐ Elizabeth Longford   **WELLINGTON:**
                                   The Years of the Sword   75p

'Lady Longford has aimed to use every document, military,
political and personal, which illuminates Wellington the man. She
certainly did and to excellent effect. We can see Wellington in every
setting and can understand him better than before. A fine
achievement, giving as it does a rounded and profound portrait' –
Times Literary Supplement

☐ John B. Wolf   **LOUIS XIV**   75p
Glittering portrait of Louis, the Sun King, known as an absolute
ruler of France, and as profligate in his private life. 'A fair and
balanced portrait' – *The Observer*. 'The comprehensive picture of a
perpetual pageant of ceremonies, bonfires, fireworks, Te Deums,
revelry and what-have-you devised by one of the greatest showmen
who ever lived' – *Michael Foot, Evening Standard*

☐ translated and introduced by   **THE MEMOIRS OF**
     David Cairns   **OF BERLIOZ**   £1
By the composer of *Symphonie Fantastique* and *The Damnation of
Faust* – the towering account of France's stormy Romantic
movement and of his own triumphs and defeats. A must for
musicians, historians and, perhaps above all, anyone looking for a
great and passionate life story.

☐ Alfred Einstein   **SCHUBERT**   75p
Popularly known as the 'lilac time' (whatever *that* means) composer,
Dr. Einstein quickly disposes of such nonsense and restores this
greatest of all lyrical composers to his real stature. 'A tribute to
Schubert magnificent indeed' – *Music & Letters*

☐ Alfred Einstein   **MOZART**   75p
The world-famous Salzburg Festival commemorates Mozart's
sublime music, but it has nothing to say about his impoverished
life and burial in a pauper's grave. Dr. Einstein's authoritative work
gives us the man – and his genius – whole. 'Dr. Einstein's
MOZART is unique' – *The Guardian*